CLANDESTINO
IN SEARCH OF
MANU CHAO

'Correr es mi destino'

Manu Chao, "Clandestino"

GW00777103

To Dad and Michelle

and kudos to Andy Morgan

PUBLISHING DETAILS

Clandestino: In Search of Manu Chao © 2013 by Peter Culshaw

First published in 2013 by
  Serpent's Tail, 3A Exmouth House
  Pine Street, Exmouth Market
  London, EC1R OJH
  www.serpentstail.com

10 9 8 7 6 5 4 3 2 1

Printed and bound in the UK by Clays, Bungay, Suffolk.

Typeset in Lino Letter and Sun Light to a design by Henry Iles.

352pp
A CIP catalogue record for this book is available from the British Library.
ISBN 978-1846681875

FSC
www.fsc.org
MIX
Paper from
responsible sources
FSC® C018072

The paper this book is printed on is certified by the © 1996 Forest Stewardship Council A.C. (FSC). It is ancient-forest friendly. The printer holds FSC chain of custody SGS-COC-2061

CLANDESTINO
IN SEARCH OF
MANU CHAO

by

Peter Culshaw

CONTENTS

INTRO: CASA BABYLON

*'When they look for me I'm not there,
When they find me I'm elsewhere'*

From 'Desaparecido'

The Casa Babylon in Córdoba could actually be the perfect venue to catch Manu Chao. I've come here with the band, on a twelve-hour bus ride across the pampas from Buenos Aires to a *boliche* – a club that has a cartoonish ambience somewhere between a large village hall and a bar from the Wild West, complete with buxom bar-girls and security guys frisking for guns. The sun's going down but it's still over 100 degrees and sweat is pouring from the crowd. *'¡Que Calor!'* is the first thing anyone says to you.

Manu is performing with a street band called Roots Radio, whom he first played with three days ago in Buenos Aires. 'I like the challenge of putting a new band together fast,' he says in the tiny furnace of a dressing room. Roots Radio's members include a percussionist called Kichi, who Manu met busking in Barcelona. Kichi was an economic refugee from the Argentine economic collapse of 2001 but he has now returned to his homeland and is living in the *barrio* of San Telmo.

The show has only been announced earlier in the day, but it's rammed with a thousand or more fans. It's so hot that the guitars drift out of tune mid-number. Manu shouts, 'Apocalyptic!' The music whirs again and one of the bar-girls with particularly vertiginous curves and a low-cut T-shirt dances on the bar, rivalling the action onstage.

Everyone knows the words to the old numbers like "Clandestino" and "Welcome To Tijuana". What's surprising is that everyone knows the newer numbers, too. Manu's latest album *La Radiolina* is only just out, but the audience sing along to "Me Llaman Calle", about the prostitutes in Madrid who'll rent out their bodies even if their hearts aren't for sale, and "La Vida Tómbola", a song about the damaged Argentine demigod Diego Maradona.

Manu is properly famous in Argentina. He can't walk a block without being stopped, although he says his fame is nothing compared to Maradona. But even in the case of Manu, who could have filled a stadium tonight, there's a certain craziness in the way people react when they meet him. Manu's last-minute, improvised gigs, like this benefit, are one way to keep things scaled down and real. 'It's normal when you are … ' Manu tries to explain, struggling for the word, ' ... famous ... You're maybe too much like a god, or maybe too much like an asshole.'

Here in Córdoba, as far as the lottery of life is concerned – the 'tombola' of Manu's song – many of the local kids seem to have drawn the short straw, born and raised in tough neighbourhoods, the *villa miserias* or shanty towns where there are few jobs and little welfare. But plenty of them get in free tonight thanks to La Luciérnaga ('The Firefly'), a street kids' charity. The rest of the audience pay 15 pesos (about $5) with all the proceeds of the concert going to La Luciérnaga.

Many of the crowd are hard-core Manuistas. Even the name of the club, Casa Babylon, is derived from the title of Manu's last album with Mano Negra, his previous band, who became legendary in these parts after a TV host asked them the meaning of anarchy and they proceeded to trash the studio, live on air. Mano Negra's logo of a black hand over a red star is tattooed on a few shoulders and arms. I make a new friend of a huge security guy, nearly seven feet tall and built like a walk-in fridge. He's covered in tattoos and introduces a sweet, delicate, petite girl as his *novia*.

The audience are ecstatic that their hero has beamed down for a night. The moment Manu steps out to face the audience, the reaction is so intense it's like standing next to a jet as it's taking off. Later, when local street rapper Negro Chetto ('Black Snob') leaps onstage and improvises over a Manu track, the place goes delirious.

We'd met Negro Chetto earlier, over lunch at the headquarters of La Luciérnaga. The association was set-up by a man called Oscar Arias, who explains that when he started his project, around sixty percent of the under-20s in Córdoba were living in poverty, many of them selling things like candies and flowers in the street, washing car windows at traffic lights, or drifting in and out of crime or prostitution. The organisation is funded like the UK's *Big Issue*, from sales of a magazine, so Manu gives it an interview, ignoring all the other local media requests. Why help La Luciérnaga rather than anyone else? 'I don't really choose the projects, they choose me,' Manu answers. 'We met them touring in 2000 and the idea of the newspaper was good. You look into someone like Oscar's eyes and you think you can trust him. Sometimes you are wrong. But now we have a strong relation.'

Negro Chetto was a squeegee merchant at traffic lights for years before coming into contact with Oscar and his organisation. At the time they were setting up a company called Luci Vid, who now have contracts to wash windows at places like Córdoba's business park. As well as holding down a job, Negro Chetto has been recording an album. He doesn't have enough money to press up any CDs, but Pocho, Manu's record company guy in Argentina, says he'll try and sort something out for him. 'Music and Jesus saved me,' sighs Chetto, crossing himself.

Tonight at Casa Babylon, everything is chaotic, last-minute and under the mainstream media radar. 'We raised some money, but the best thing was the energy,' Manu says after the show, sopping with sweat and elation. 'Regenerating

energy! The kids went back out of there with strong energy –
and so did I.' He mentions the guy who was following us on
his motorbike from La Luciérnaga earlier. 'That was Pedro;
he was a street kid in 2000, now he's a father.'

I sleep like a baby on the tour bus that night, full of music
and alcohol, and wake up to find that we're already half way
back to Buenos Aires. 'The bus rocks you like your mother,'
Manu says. A metal cup with straw full of the pungent local
herb tea known as maté is being passed around, as the white
light of the sun bleaches the landscape and the bus speeds
along the flat plains.

What happened in Córdoba was a Manu Chao moment; an
unscripted happening, a spontaneous fiesta that somehow
managed to change someone's life. It was 2007 and I'd met
Manu a few times before, starting with an interview on the
release of his second solo album *Próxima Estación: Esperanza*
in 2001. But some time after that trip to Córdoba I resolved to
find out more about him, to attempt to answer the question
'Who the hell was this guy?' ... to write this book.

Manu kindly agreed – or at least tolerated the idea – and
allowed me to follow him through four continents over
the next few years. But this was no rockstar-authorised
biography. Manu was often reluctant to talk about himself.
His story only slowly came into focus as he lived up to his
own lyrical self-portrait as *el desaparecido*, 'the disappearing
one'. What he did want to do, though – and this, I realised,
was the root of his involvement – was to broadcast the causes
and people he associates himself with: water rights in Bolivia,
indigenous revolution in Mexico, mental patients in Buenos
Aires, prostitutes' rights in Spain, refugees in the Western
Sahara. He was the guy siding with the dispossessed of this
world, Don Quixote tilting at all the mad windmills. I was to
be his Sancho Panza, getting to see the realities firsthand, in
the slipstream of Manu and his band, Radio Bemba.

When I first set out to meet Manu Chao in 2001 I had been told the man I was looking for had a small *pied à terre* in Barcelona with no outside space, because the 'street is my courtyard'. He could, when in town, be found busking in his local bar. He owned bees but no mobile phone or watch. He was always on the move, addicted to travel, never able to spend more than a few weeks in the same place, never planning more than three months ahead. He was – as the line goes in "Desaparecido" – 'the disappearing one ... hurry[ing] down the lost highway ... When they look for me I'm not there, When they find me, I'm elsewhere.'

I couldn't complain I hadn't been warned. But nor could I resist the impulse. Like so many others, I had sensed on *Clandestino*, Manu's first solo album, a passion and directness in those pared-down tunes that I hadn't come across since Bob Marley. Sometimes, music makes you rethink the world. *Clandestino* seemed to look both backwards to a time when songs meant something, when people thought music could change the world, and forwards to a new globalised pop. At the cross-fade of the millennium, it sounded perfect – a creation that united, irresistibly, a European and South American perspective, a radical pop masterpiece that just happened to sell millions.

If I'd been more up to speed on French rock music, I would have been less surprised. Manu Chao's previous outfit, Mano Negra, had been the biggest band in the history of French rock, with legions of followers in Europe and in South America, where they still have a mythic status. Plenty of people agree with their manager Bernard Batzen when he claims that, had the band actually promoted their albums properly, instead of going off on quixotic missions like a four-month boat trip around Latin America, or a rail trip through the guerrilla chaos of Colombia, had they not broken up before their bestselling album, *Casa Babylon*, was released, they would have been as big as U2 or Coldplay. But if they had, would Manu Chao's story have been so compelling?

Manu's reputation was one of fierce honesty and integrity. The word was that, unlike most other activist rock stars with their jet-set compassion and five-star lives, he actually walked his talk, lived with scarcely any possessions, a musical nomad. But surely no one could have that kind of purity his fans ascribed to him?

His musical style – a mix of punk, latin, ska and reggae – was an inventive global cross-pollination and the more he found his own voice, the more his audience grew. For legions of misfits who don't accept the world as it is, and for the marginalised he supports, Manu represents a beacon of hope. Beyond that lay a string of barely tenable contradictions: a self-confessed 'shy guy' who sung to crowds of 100,000 in places like Mexico City, a worldwide star who fights against globalisation, a man-of-the-people backpacker who has made millions, a propagandist who turns down most interviews. Even his name and his origins – French? Spanish? Basque? – seemed peculiarly opaque.

The lives of Manu Chao, from his teenage years as a Parisian rock'n'roller, through assorted underground French bands, to explosive global success, followed by some kind of mental breakdown and then rebirth with *Clandestino*, seemed a story worth telling. So here, five years on from that memorable hot night in Casa Babylon in Córdoba, is the result. It's a book in two parts, which begins with the Manu Chao story – the early years in Paris, the rise and fall of Mano Negra, and his spectacular reinvention with a string of multi-million-selling albums. And then I meet Manu in Barcelona and we're off on the road for Part Two, blazing a trail through New York, Buenos Aires, Western Sahara, Mexico, Paris, Barcelona, Brixton and Brazil ...

PART ONE

LA VIDA TOMBOLA

The lives of Manu

CHAPTER 1:
A DOUBLE LIFE

'He was a pain in the neck aged four –
and he still is!'

———

Gabriel García Márquez

José-**Manuel Thomas Arthur Chao** was born in Paris on 21 June 1961. He attributes his love of the sun to this midsummer's day arrival. His birthday also coincides with the annual *Fête de la Musique*, the day on which the whole of France surrenders itself to music in all its miraculous forms. So, the Manu Chao story begins with sun and music.

Manu's parents were both Spaniards – and first generation Parisians. His mother Felisa's family was from Bilbao in the Basque country, his father Ramón's from Vilalba, in the northwest province of Galicia. Both places are on the edges of Spain. The Basque character is supposedly stubborn, proud and fundamentally self-respecting, while Spaniards regard Galicians as melancholic and inscrutable. Or, as Ramón tells it, 'They say that if you meet us Galicians on the stairs, you never know if we're going up or down. We are quite subtle in our movements.'

Felisa's father, Tomás Ortega, was a champion at pelota – one of the Basques' odd, insular sports – and became a communications expert for the Repúblicans in the civil war against Franco. His speciality was blowing up the telephone systems of towns that were about to fall to Franco's forces. One day, not long into the civil war, Tomás happened to hear a radio broadcast from Seville in which a leading Françoist general vowed to kill him. Choosing life and exile over death and homeland, he fled on the last boat out of Valencia to Algeria, where the authorities sent him to an internment camp.

The Spanish refugee camps in Algeria were often situated in the arid fringes of the Sahara desert and, after the Vichy government took over, they were essentially forced labour camps. Inmates regularly died of thirst, disease, overwork and torture. Tomás came from tough Basque stock, the kind that sailed wooden tubs across the Atlantic to fish for cod off the Grand Banks before Columbus was even born. He survived. Meanwhile, his wife, daughter Felisa and her sister were sent to a camp for refugees in the Roussillon region of southern France. The family were eventually reunited in Algeria, before settling, a decade later, in Paris.

Tomás was an important figure for Manu: 'When I was young my grandfather use to tell me all about his adventures

Baby Manu with his Basque-exile grandparents, Tomás and Felisa.

in great detail: the civil war, his exile from Spain, Algeria. He never wanted to go back to Spain, even after Franco died. I was greatly influenced by him, the fighter against injustice who defended his ideals to the end of his days. He was a great person, very rude but very honest.'

Manu's paternal grandfather, José, ran the Gran Hotel Chao in Vilalba, a small Galician town set in the fertile valleys of the province of Lugo, with a medieval tower and a rich tradition of independent newspapers. Galicia is full of people with the Chao family name, and their ancestral seat is in the town of Ribadavia, about 170 km south of Vilalba. José came back to his motherland from Cuba, the country of his birth, at the age of twenty. He had six children. One, José Chao Rego, became a well-known author and theologian. Another, Ramón, became an internationally renowned journalist – and the father of Manu Chao.

Journalism, however, was not part of the map that José, a patriarch of the old school, had drawn out for Ramón. Back in Cuba, José had developed a passion for the opera and when his young son began to demonstrate sparkling musical gifts, José indulged the idea that his offspring could be a Galician Chopin. Ramón excelled at the piano from an early age, and used to perform on demand for the Hotel Chao's many distinguished guests, including the artist Fernando Álvarez de Sotomayor, who gave the boy an original drawing dedicated 'to the precocious artist'. At the age of ten, Ramón gave his first public concert at the Circulo de Bellas Artes in Lugo and, shortly afterward, the mayor of Vilalba awarded him a bursary to study piano, harmony and composition in Madrid. There he managed to win a prestigious national music prize but also spent much of his time playing truant and bunking off to the National Library or the Prado to follow other passions.

In 1956, at the age of twenty-one, Ramón was favoured by a fellow native of Vilalba, the eminent Spanish politician Manuel Fraga Iribarne, who persuaded the Françoist Commissariat of Popular Education to send this rising star of Spanish classical music to study in Paris. It's an irony that Ramón, who holds stalwart left-wing views, has often reflected upon; how he arrived in the French capital thanks to a man who became Franco's last, heavy-handed interior minister.

The scholarship was an opportunity for advancement but also, in the end, a chance for Ramón to escape the mental manacles of his overbearing father. He studied hard for four years, under two of the most famous music teachers in France at the time, Lazare Lévy and Magda Tagliaferro, putting in ten-hour days of practice, and it seemed that a bright future in the classical concert halls of the world was beckoning. But Ramón grew steadily disillusioned with the path that his father had chosen for him. Living in Paris, which in the 1950s was a great Byzantium of ideas and radicalism with Jean-Paul Sartre, Simone de Beauvoir and Juliette Gréco holding court, Ramón would hang out in existentialist cafés with Spanish-speaking students, many of them with communist affiliations. He felt ashamed that his musical career was being propped by Spain's fascist government and in 1960 he found the courage to give

it up, answering a newspaper advert seeking 'someone who knows music, Spanish and Portuguese'. He didn't touch a piano for the next sixteen years. Instead, he swapped his piano for a typewriter and started a long career in the Latin American service of RFI, the French equivalent of the BBC World Service. A few months after Ramón rejected his own musical destiny, Manu Chao was born.

In his book *The Train Of Fire and Ice,* about Mano Negra's mad, epic train journey across Colombia, Ramón claims that

Ramón Chao, aged ten, around the time of his first public concert.

Manu's connection with Latin America is genetic. His own grandmother, Dolores, left Galicia for Cuba, fleeing her drunken, quarrelsome husband. There, through the network of Galician émigrés, she managed to find work as a maid in the house of Mario García Kohly, a minister in Cuba's first independent government, and a part-time poet. Ramón believes that Kohly's poem "Tu", which became a famous *habanera* set to music by the composer Sánchez de Fuentes, was about Dolores: *'adorable brunette, of all the flowers, the queen is you.'*

Furthermore, Ramón is convinced that his father was Kohly's son. José was conceived after Dolores left Spain, and when the cuckolded husband followed her to Havana he was found murdered in a backstreet the day after he had found her. Ramón believes José had a strong resemblance to Kohly. All of which 'leaves my detective thesis in no doubt': Manu Chao is the great-grandson of a great Cuban poet.

The tale elicits a wry raise from Manu's eyebrows. 'Only half of what my father says is true. But it's always beautiful. He is a writer and a musician, so you cannot expect him to be precise with reality. I have heard so many stories about Cuba from my father. It's the same for all the Galician families who emigrated to Cuba. Nobody knows what happened there, whether it's all legend. But if I have Cuban blood I am very proud.'

The DNA of Manu's creative and yearning spirit could be traced back to the tragic hope, desperate courage and lethal adventures of his immediate forebears. That stubborn streak of uncompromising rebelliousness was present in the rude and sincere life of his grandfather, Tomás Ortega. A sharp and precisely enquiring mind is the gift of his mother Felisa, a scientific researcher with an impressively abstruse list of publications to her name (one such is 'The successive action of oxidations and electrochemical reductions on the superficial structure of electrodes of polycrystalline gold'). To his father, Manu owes a gift for music and words. But that's not all. Ramón's decision to break free from both his ambitious father and his backward homeland betrays stubborn courage and a refusal to succumb to clan pressure.

Manu has a good relationship with his parents: 'They are my friends. The most important education I got from them was about honesty. They're honest people and they never tried to fool others about money or things like that. It's not very easy to be honest in this world, because if you are honest you are always fucked. But I prefer to be fucked than have a bad conscience.'

Boulogne-Billancourt, the Parisian suburb to which the Chaos moved in the early 1960s, was less than 10km southwest of the Eiffel Tower but a world apart. The gilded life of Paris's west end, with its luxury apartments and starched brasseries, petered out just beyond Porte St Cloud and the orbital *péripherique* motorway. Whilst the avenues and squares of the northern part of the Boulogne-Billancourt are full of elegant art deco urban architecture, to its south is a sump of heavy industry where, on the Île Seguin, Louis Renault built his huge automobile plant, on the mass-production lines of his American rival Henry Ford, turning this backwater into a smoking, clanking, industrial city. The factory was a perennial focus of serious unrest, with a major strike in 1936 bringing down the government and another in May 1968 almost repeating history. It closed in 1992 and is today a wasteland in the midst of the Seine.

Thanks to its cheap rents, proximity to central Paris and a mix of cultured bourgeois and raw working-class culture, Boulogne-Billancourt became a favoured bolthole of artists, writers and filmmakers. The French film industry was based there until the 1990s and artists like Marc Chagall and Juan Gris found the bohemian atmosphere congenial. It was this milieu that attracted a left-leaning intellectual family like the Chaos to Boulogne-Billancourt and later to its neighbour, Sèvres, just across the Seine, where Manu Chao spent most of his childhood and adolescence.

The blend of working-class culture and intellectual bourgeois idealism that characterised Sèvres in the 1960s

Manu (left) and cousin Santi, around 1972.

was to provide both the physical and mental landscape in which Manu Chao's adolescent battles were fought. It's hard to imagine how marginal the French provinces and suburbs were in the postwar decades, before the DIY punk scene and Mitterrand's reforms came to the rescue and spread cultural activity beyond the Paris *péripherique* and the centres of a few other major French cities. In the 1970s, places like Sèvres were bombshells of boredom waiting to explode.

Inside the cosy Chao apartment, however, Manu and his younger brother Antoine could bathe in the love, cultured passions and intellectual curiosity of their parents. There were mountains of books and a steady flow of great music pouring from the record player. Manu's young ears unfurled to the sounds of the Latin world: *son, rumba, cha cha cha, boleros, flamenco, sevillanas, cante jondo* and, when Chile plunged into political darkness in the early 1970s, the protest music of Victor Jara and Cuban *nueva trova* singers like Silvio Rodríguez and Pablo Milanés. The gay black Cuban *bolero* singer Bola de Nieve ('Snowball') was one of Ramón's favourites and Manu still listens to him with pleasure. Despite the traumas of his own musical journey, Ramón also remained devoted to classical music. Felisa and Ramón loved listening to Mozart's Italian operas, like *The Marriage of Figaro* and *Don Giovanni*, and the piano music of Bach, Beethoven and Chopin. The first guitar piece Manu learned was by Cuban composer Leo Brouwer.

The Chao household was also a focus of Franco-Hispanic intellectual life. In his role as a reporter for RFI's Latin American section and roving Spanish freelance journalist, Ramón came into contact with many of the leading writers and thinkers in contemporary France, and exiles from revolutions and dictatorships in Chile, Uruguay, Argentina and other Latin American political hot spots would drop by the apartment in Sèvres for company and stimulation. Manu might return from school to find the Uruguayan author and Nobel Laureate Juan Carlos Onetti, who had been imprisoned in a mental asylum in Montevideo, lounging on the sitting-room sofa shooting the breeze; or another, even more famous Nobel prize-winning author, the Colombian Gabriel García Márquez, having tea with his parents.

Years later, Manu would refer to passages in Márquez's *One Hundred Years of Solitude* when he was planning Mano Negra's fabled train trip across Colombia. The train carried a gigantic ice sculpture which was inspired by the opening sequence of Márquez's classic, in which José Arcadio Buendía takes his children to a tent at a fair, guarded by a giant with a hairy torso and a copper ring in his nose, and touches ice for the first time. The band's train tour finally disintegrated in the coastal town of Aracataca, Márquez's ancestral home and the inspiration for the Buendías' hometown of Macondo in the novel.

Another regular at casa Chao was the Cuban novelist and philosopher of music Alejo Carpentier. It was he who minted the phrase '*lo real maravilloso*' – 'magical realism' – which was to become the name of an entire literary universe. Carpentier also wrote the definitive work on Cuban music, *La Música en Cuba,* as well as a novel called *Lost Steps,* which features a New York musicologist who travels to the jungle of Orinoco looking for lost instruments only to find the origins of music instead. Ramón and Carpentier became very good friends and Ramón later published a book of conversations with the great Cuban writer. When Manu was four years old, Carpentier gave him a pair of maracas, a simple gesture with more than a fair share of symbolic resonance.

Ramón also makes a startling claim that it was that Roland Barthes, a philosopher who achieved the kind of fashionable intellectual superstardom only possible in France, who was responsible for the existence of Mano Negra. One afternoon, Ramón went to interview him for *El Triunfo* magazine and, after discussing their hobbyhorses of semiotics and politics, Barthes began to play his piano and Ramón joined in. As the great philosopher and the delighted journalist coursed like wood sprites through a four-handed *étude* by Schubert, Barthes was astonished by Ramón's extraordinary virtuosity and insisted that he should buy a piano, reminding Ramón that all 'men of the mind' should have a pastime to release the mental pressure. On his way home, Ramón went into an instrument shop and ordered a mini-grand.

The children were apparently unaware that their father was a highly accomplished pianist, and their reaction of wonder when the piano arrived a week later and their father revealed his closet talent, remains one of Ramón's most precious memories of their childhood. 'Their mouths were open in amazement,' he recalls. 'It was one of the most beautiful moments of my life.'

After his startling revelation, Ramón attempted to drum some knowledge of musical notation and scales into Manu and Antoine, until, about a year later, Felisa took him to one side and said 'Be careful, because you are turning into your father, who was a dictator.' So Ramón desisted with good

grace but on the proviso that the boys go to the Conservatoire and carry on learning the instrument of their choice.
For Manu it was guitar, and for Antoine, the drums.

Manu calls Ramón 'my professor of craziness.' He was an
unorthodox, nurturing dad, congenial and sociable, a free
and independent thinker, a motorbike fiend and a highly
rated creative artist in his own right. Ramón's body is covered with tattoos – one for each of the books he has written. One of them, *A Secret Guide to Paris*, published in 1974,
featured 'everything forbidden by the fascists in Spain':
brothels, swingers clubs, radical cafés, anarchist bookshops,
publishers and communist meeting points. Another, a novel
called *Le Lac de Côme* (Lake Como) is a thinly veiled autobiographical account of Ramón's childhood in Vilalba, with
its menagerie of strange characters. The book was banned
by the local library in Vilalba and Ramón was told that, if he
ever were to entertain thoughts of returning to the place of
his birth for any length of time, not to bother.

The milestones of history came and went. France exploded
with revolutionary fervour in May 1968 and Manu remembers his father waiting at the front door, wearing his journalist's armband whilst his mother stood there crying and
pleading with him not to go and cover the riots in the centre of Paris. In 1969, Manu and Antoine were woken up in
the middle of the night to watch Neil Armstrong landing on
the moon on a fuzzy old black and white TV. Later, in 1975,
champagne corks were popped when Franco died.

By the age of fourteen, Manu was fed up with the dull con-
formity of his music lessons at the Conservatoire de Chaville.
He told his father he wanted to stop. He was already tinkering around the notion of forming a band with his brother
Antoine and his cousin Santiago 'Santi' Casariego. Manu
and Santi were the same age, and soulmates, with a fascination for rock'n'roll. Manu spent many hours round at the
Casariego house listening to his uncle Adrian singing Cuban
and Spanish songs with his Spanish guitar, and joining in the
choruses with Santi and his sister Marina.

Despite the intellectual riches foisted on the young boy by his unorthodox parents, despite the boyish conversations with giants of modern literature, the feeling began to grow deep inside Manu that he had to find something else – let's call it a passion – that wasn't Ramón's or Felisa's, but his and only his. That passion had to be instinctive, not intellectual, something conjured up by the danger that rode on the opening riffs of songs by Chuck Berry or Little Richard, that lurked in the streets outside the warm and welcoming family flat, in the grey boredom of the squares, parks and avenues of Sèvres and Boulogne-Billancourt, in the grating argot of the local roughnecks and rude boys, in the butt-strewn bars and caged football pitches of the neighbourhood, in the tawdry shopping centres and amusement parks under the cold dull skies of suburban Paris.

He began to lead a double life. At home, at school and in the staid corridors of the Conservatoire, Manu was close to a perfect student – obedient and shy. After the school bell had rung, Manu would hit the pavements and his world would change. Out there it was all football, girls, spliff and rock'n'roll. 'Sèvres was not a dangerous place but it had its delinquents,' Ramón remembers. 'At home Manu was very sweet and loving, and would meet intellectuals. But the minute he would walk out the door, he would hang out with a lot of low life.'

As a young teenager, Manu began to frequent a famous squat in the nearby rue des Caves, where the old hippies taught him and his gang a thing or two about life and ways to live it differently, often getting little thanks and some petty destruction in return. 'There were devils amongst us,' Manu confesses. Hippy activists from rue des Caves once invaded Manu's school and imprisoned his teacher in a cupboard. Manu even went on a few big demos. He joined the Sèvres branch of the Communist Youth League, though he claims that was only 'for love, not for the love of communism, but for the love of a beautiful blonde' who was branch secretary.

At fifteen, Manu's musical dabblings began to solidify into the idea of actually forming a band. Santi and Antoine were obvious bandmates – fellow travellers, bedroom buddies and intimates – and Manu bought himself a transparent bass and stuck an advert up for other band members in his local green-grocers. 'I came into their world as a bassist,' Manu recalls. 'That's how my life changed completely.' Through that advert he met a teenage guitarist called Fredo – and, through him, en-countered for the first time the appeal of the street, or *caillera*.

La caillera was Manu's name for his local street posse of working-class French, Spanish, Portuguese, Armenian and North African kids, whose dads often worked in the Renault factory. The more benign and legal pastimes of these sub-urban gangs were playing football, chasing girls, flipping pinball or table footie at the Café de la Mairie, their local HQ. Then there was dope smoking, shoplifting and maybe robbing a petrol station or a bit of night-time breaking and entering. The diminutive Manu was adopted as the gang mascot: 'They wanted me around. I think they thought I was lucky for them. I never got involved in their violent stuff, but I was I there.' Although he was scared at times, Manu sur-veyed all this delicious delinquency with a kind of 'morbid curiosity'. And it meant he was protected in the *barrio*. 'They never broke into my parents' house.'

For Manu, this street life just outside the front door of his apartment block was his passport to freedom, both physically and mentally. All those Spanish and Cuban songs, that French crooning, those classical arias, arpeggios and glissandos were all well and good, but Manu was a white boy who needed a riot of his own. It was a bid for freedom and it wasn't without risks. By all accounts Manu was a conscientious, hard-working student at school, and one of his teachers was moved to declare to his parents that he could become anything he wanted to. The future for other members of the Sèvres massive was less rosy, especially when heroin and cocaine arrived on the scene. 'Of all my friends, I was the lucky one. I won the lotto,' Manu told me. 'I've made a living from my passion for music. The moment I began to make music, I was never bored again.'

Fredo's parents were a lovely couple who ran a launderette, and Manu, Santi and Fredo would rehearse in the kitchen of their flat in lower Sèvres, standing in plastic bowls to avoid the very real chance of electrocution. The trio pumped out rude and crude versions of the classics: "Blue Suede Shoes", "Louie Louie", "Tutti Frutti", "Roll Over Beethoven" and "Memphis Tennessee". To begin with they didn't have a singer, and a favourite ruse was to invite singers to come and audition so that the trio could laugh at them. One of them was a punk, the first that Manu had ever seen. The louder the trio played, the louder this punk would sing. So he was invited back two or three times to see just how dark a shade of purple his face could become when he reached inhuman decibel levels. 'We were stupid,' admits Manu.

There were little gigs about the neighbourhood. Sometimes *la caillera* would come along and wreck the place. That made finding more gigs harder. After a while the trio got themselves a name, Joint de Culasse, which means 'head gasket' in French. It was suggested by Antoine. Manu remembers that his brother had a passion for all things mechanical and would spend hours mending old motorbikes, especially English models like Norton or Triumph. It was, in any case, a suitable name for a band formed in the shadow of the Renault factory. But 'Joint de Culasse' also zings with jokey puns. 'Joint' makes an obvious reference to the beloved weed. 'Culasse' could be interpreted as a fragrant blend of the French words for 'arse' (*cul*) and 'tart' (*pétasse*). Whatever the meaning, the mission was clear: loud, fast, raw no-nonsense rock'n'roll powerful enough to blow both your head-gasket and your mind.

In the pre-punk France of the 1970s, you were either a sad conformist lover of French *chanson* and *variété,* or you were a rocker. To rock'n'roll purists like Manu and Joint de Culasse, nothing good ever came out of France, musically at least. When rock'n'roll appeared with the arrival of Bill Haley and Elvis in the 1950s, it was packaged by the French music business as Music hall des jeunes. Rock'n'roll numbers were translated and the backing tracks watered down to suit French tastes, often to the great frustration of the artists themselves. Consequently, as far as the purists were concerned, French rock idols like Johnny Hallyday were a pathetic joke, as were popular groups like Les Chats Sauvages and Les Chaussettes Noires. A bare handful of figures – Serge Gainsbourg, Jacques Dutronc, Françoise Hardy, Alain Bashung – had any real sense of rock spirit.

In the early 1970s, there were a few French bands – Gong, Magma, Heldon – who tried to do something original and interesting. But the dreadful and all-pervasive feeling that no great rock music could be sung in any language other than English put a severe dragnet on the creative potential of the local French music scene. Magma actually went as far as inventing their own language, which they called Kobaïan. 'French just didn't sound suitable for our music,' said Magma's leader, Christian Vander. When punk arrived, there were a couple of French hits, by Telephone and Plastic Bertrand (who was actually from Belgium), but they were treated as novelties rather than anything else. "God Save The Queen" or "Ça Plane Pour Moi", anybody?

'Singing rock in French seemed like singing Flamenco in German! It just didn't make sense,' quips Jean-Yves Prieur ,aka Kid Bravo or Kid Loco, founder of the seminal French alternative label Bondage. 'It wasn't visceral and rock is by nature visceral and dangerous. Take Chuck Berry, or the Sex Pistols or the Rolling Stones ... they trailed real revolution in their wake. Telephone was kids' music. They weren't a threat to anyone. In the late 1970s our eyes were riveted on what was happening in London.'

For Manu and *la caillera*, salvation came from over the channel, across the Atlantic, or nowhere at all. 'I think the first globalisation that happened on this planet was English music,' Manu says. 'The Stones and the Beatles conquered the world. We were French kids and we didn't have the opportunity to listen to anything except English music. The only music which could reach young people was in English, not French, not Spanish, nothing else.'

The required playlist of the suburban *rockeur* usually depended on skin colour and background. Manu and his white mates shared their tastes with hundreds and thousands of leather-jacketed wannabe rock'n'roll rebels across the land: Elvis before the draft, Chuck Berry, Little Richard, Jerry Lee Lewis, Eddie Cochran, Gene Vincent, The Rolling Stones, The Who and Otis Redding. The Arab kids in the neighbourhood preferred Earth, Wind and Fire or Maze, a tribal distinction that led to plenty of arguments. It was only Bob Marley and James Brown that offered common ground.

Rock'n'roll gave Manu a licence to think for himself. 'I thank music for being my school,' he says with gratitude. Was he a rebel? 'Personally I never had any rebellion with my parents,' Manu asserts. 'I've been lucky with them.' Nonetheless, conflict loomed, both internally, and with his family.

At the age of sixteen Manu underwent a crisis, almost a breakdown. 'I would think of death all the time and get this strange feeling like vertigo,' he remembers. 'I'd be completely paralysed.' As a student, Manu said he was quiet, to the point of being almost mute. 'All year I only spoke two words.' That summer, Manu went on holiday in Greece with some friends, but this failed to shake him from his taciturn terror. 'I didn't talk for one month. It wasn't their fault.'

Ramón and Felisa were already well aware of Manu and Antoine's musical ambitions, and they went to see Joint de Culasse play a few times. Ramón was fairly relaxed about it all, insisting only that both his boys finish their baccalaureate exams. But Felisa wasn't so sure. 'I can understand why,' says Manu. 'She came from nowhere. Her grandfather was imprisoned and the family was left with nothing. So for my mother, studying was essential.'

As the baccalaureate loomed, Manu became more and more withdrawn at school. There was only one person who could pierce his gloom and engage his mind, and that was a young philosophy teacher by the name of Henri Peña-Ruiz. Manu felt that Peña-Ruiz respected him and his talent. Thirty years later, France's *Philosophie* magazine organised a reunion between them. The young philosophy teacher had become a renowned thinker, writer and authoritative defender of secularism in education and public life. 'I remember philosophy classes,' Manu says in the interview. 'They were a breath of fresh air for me, and I swallowed them like pink milk. But, in truth, at that time, it was as if I was no longer at school. I'd met other people, who weren't in education, and I hung out with them at night. I was also half autistic. I had no friends in my class and I spoke very little, maybe a few words the whole year. That's why those philosophy classes were a real discovery for me. They showed me that it could be interesting to talk and that words could have meaning.'

Henri Peña-Ruiz remembered a shy student with shining eyes and all the talent necessary to pursue a career in philosophy or teaching. He enrolled Manu into the *Hypokâghne*, a two-year preparatory course for entry into one of *les grandes écoles*, France's elite higher learning institutions. But Manu was already elsewhere in mind and spirit. His baccalaureate results were terrible. His instinct was calling him to music.

Manu's mother was horrified by his career choice. She went to the school to talk to Peña-Ruiz, who, true to his vocation, had taken a philosophical view of the crisis. 'He wants to make music? But that's great,' he reassured Felisa. 'Your son is an artist. You must on no account contradict his vocation.' Felisa remained unconvinced.

As the end of school approached, the turmoil created by Manu's choice only grew deeper, and more emotional. But he stuck to his guns with a stubborn conviction that was to re-emerge at almost every pivotal moment of his life. 'The choice was hard,' he told *Philosophie* magazine. 'And my mother suffered because of it for the next ten years. But when you have a passion, you can't share it with anything else. I love philosophy and it wouldn't have bothered me to devote myself to it. On the other hand, my street mates were also a wonderful and fascinating education for me. So I threw myself into a career as a singer.'

The decision felt right, and that was the most important thing about it. Patient, diligent study in order to achieve betterment and intellectual peers had lost out to risk, uncertainty, the street and rock'n'roll. 'One thing you don't learn at school is to trust your instincts,' says Manu. 'In class we must be rational and think with our heads and not our guts. For me, when I mentally map out my plans, things always go wrong. But when I trust my instinct, I score much better.' And his instinct was music, nothing else.

Manu made one concession to his distraught mother. He promised her that if he wasn't earning a decent living from music by the age of twenty-five, then he would give it all up and live a 'normal' life. 'When you're eighteen, twenty-five seems old,' he says. 'But twenty-five arrived and I had nothing … not a dime.'

CHAPTER 2:
THE ROCK'N'ROLL FLAME

'Some people had Mecca;
we had Canvey island!'

Manu Chao

Aged eighteen, living with his parents on the margins of Paris, musical success was for Manu a dream and a decade away. He was still a quiffed-up rocker and Joint de Culasse true keepers of the rock'n'roll flame. Every rehearsal, every gig, was a ritual offering to the gods of shake, rattle'n'roll. Manu and his pals were so in thrall to Chuck Berry and others in the rock'n'roll pantheon that they saw no need to write their own songs. There were so many classics to cover. Cousin Santi, the drummer, puts another more prosaic spin on their music repertoire; 'We would have quite liked to play like Santana as well, but we weren't good enough.' According to Manu, Joint de Culasse would occasionally throw in a couple of Stooges numbers, but they never went down too well.

Sèvres was rocker territory. Punks who floated into the suburb were either given the rockabilly psycho stare or welcomed with the blunt fist of some sauced-up member of *la caillera*. Inter-tribal music warfare had recently been imported to Paris from London, along with other more constructive aspects of the punk revolution. The punks, *les keupons* in Parisian slang, went about their business in fear not only of *les rockeurs* but, even worse, *les skins*. Manu Chao spent most of the late 1970s and early-1980s in the relatively safe confines of Sèvres, hanging out with his rocker crew. But he wasn't always just the innocent mascot of the gang. He well remembers being in the audience when a punk band called Cain and Abel came to play in nearby Issy-les-Moulineaux and got thumped for their pains. Years later, when he started busking in the Metro with Daniel Jamet, Cain and Abel's guitarist, who eventually joined Mano Negra, Manu had a little explaining to do. Jamet remembers being genuinely frightened for his life.

But Manu Chao would never remain happy banging out cover versions of "Blues Suede Shoes" and "Brown-Eyed Handsome Man" for the rest of his life. He had the kind of curiosity that needed to explore the musical zeitgeist. Punk was one strand, though he was on his own. 'The gang in Sèvres listened to rockabilly and some black music,' he remembers. 'James Brown was acceptable. But nothing after 1962, really. All the guys were tough rockabillies, a lot of them immigrants from Portugal and Spain. They were kind of rebels who weren't rebels. Punk started and the big guys sent us to fight the punks. When I bought the first punk album to the neighbourhood, I was risking my life. It was *Inflammable Material*, the first album by Stiff Little Fingers. But Dr Feelgood was OK for us, because they were still a little rock'n'roll.'

Manu's love of the English rhythm'n'blues scene, which emerged in the mid-1970s in Canvey Island and Southend, was intense. 'Dr Feelgood is the only band I've ever really been a fan of, because I fell in love with them when I was a teenager.' Wilko Johnson was Dr Feelgood's guitarist, whose criminal fraternity suits, jerky duck walk and plugged-into-the-mains guitar style made him look like he was on speed on day release from an asylum; 'He was a Martian, totally a Martian – I saw hundreds of shows of him.' (Wilko, incidentally, was not the Canvey Island hard-drinking macho guy as you might imagine from songs like "Roxette". He is a complex character – a medieval literature graduate, able to read Icelandic sagas in the original, and a keen astronomer, who installed a giant, possibly illegal telescope for star gazing on the roof of his house in Canvey Island.)

When Manu was still in thrall to Dr Feelgood, Joint de Culasse was looking for a bassist. 'So like stupids we went to Canvey Island to try and find one. We went to all the pubs asking if anybody knew of a bass player, and everybody said, "OK, little guys, go home." We slept outside, on buses, in the subway. It was like a *pèlerinage* – a pilgrimage – for us to go to Canvey Island. Some people have Mecca; we had Canvey Island.'

But Manu's greatest hero of them all was Lew Lewis, an obscure but brilliant figure in the Essex r'n'b scene: 'A crazy guy who played harmonica *librio*, crazy, crazy! I read in the papers that he'd made an assault of the post office opposite the place where he was living. He went to jail. When I got to know Lee Brilleaux of Dr Feelgood, I asked him about Lew and he just said, "Oh my God!" and crossed himself looking up to heaven. He said that he was the best of all of them.' Lew Lewis was the wild man of Southend who played harmonica with Eddie and the Hot Rods. Although they had a few minor hits like

Big in Sèvres. The sound of 1970s Essex: Dr Feelgood (Wilko Johnson second right) and Lew Lewis of Eddie and the Hot Rods.

"Teenage Depression", their records never really translated the energy of the band live, and they didn't quite have the right attitude, haircut or trousers to surf the punk wave. Their timing was unlucky, too, hitting the headlines at five minutes before midnight on the eve of punk's Year Zero.

If r'n'b from the Essex delta, east of London, was acceptable fare in Sèvres, other punk bands weren't. Joint de Culasse virtually ignored the embryonic French punk movement that hit Paris in 1977 with bands like Métal Urbain, Stinky Toys and Guilty Razors. Nonetheless, Manu and his band's gigs in and around Sèvres began to attract a greater and greater number of local rockers, who often left a trail of destruction in their wake. 'We weren't presentable,' Manu recalls. 'Everywhere we went, it was mayhem.' In Sèvres there was a sizable Armenian community and it was often the Armenians who 'protected' Manu and his mates, controlling the bad business between the various gangs. And the protection went two ways: 'When an Armenian was hurt,' Manu remembers, 'we'd fill an entire carriage on the metro.'

In 1980, Manu met Marc Winandy for the first time. 'He was the most anarchist guy I ever knew in my life,' Manu asserts. Winandy had suffered a battered childhood in Belgium and had been sexually abused. He got embroiled in the cigarette smuggling racket and made large sums of money before being beaten blue by a Greek Mafioso. He'd also become a part-time porn star who claimed to have 'the biggest dick in the business'.

In the early 1980s, Winandy took it on himself to help all the little suburban bands in the southwest of Paris who had nowhere to play and, if they did find somewhere, were harassed mercilessly by the police. He programmed music at the Maison des Jeunes et de la Culture (MJC) in Boulogne-Billancourt. There was a network of MJCs, youth clubs with performance spaces, all over the country and, especially in *la ceinture rouge*, the belt of communist- or socialist-run suburbs that girdled the centre of Paris. Often they were the only places where local rock bands could perform in public.

Winandy also organised 'suicidal' gigs and tours for bands like Joint de Culasse wherever and whenever possible. His motto: a gig that doesn't end in the local police commissariat isn't worth the effort.

Winandy became Joint de Culasse's first manager and part-time drummer. Using his underworld sex contacts, he would find the band gigs at orgies, where they would have to warm up the revellers before the mass ensemble erotic action. 'Because we were romantics, we didn't care about that business,' Manu claims. 'We just went to play and after the show someone would say, "Here's your money. Now, do you want to shag my wife?" And we'd say, "No thank you," take the money and leave.'

Winandy himself possessed an appendage of legendary proportions, more than 20cm in length according to local lore. At the conclusion of Joint de Culasse gigs his favourite party piece was to bang out a jungle rhythm on the bass drum with his astonishing member. After a while, word got out and people came from miles around to see the show. 'His story is incredible,' says Manu. 'He was my professor, a very important guy in my life. He was always in jail. Everybody thought he was my father. Sometimes a police officer would call me and say, "Please Manu, get your dad out of here." He was totally crazy.'

With the Stiff Little Fingers album *Inflammable Material* already tucked away on rotation in the closet, Manu began to seek out new musical kicks. His horizons were ready to expand and 1981 was to prove a pivotal year. On 4 May, he went to see his first real punk gig, The Clash at the Palais des Sports, not far away in the 15th arrondissement of Paris. Billed on the tickets as a *concert metal hurlant* (heavy metal concert), the band opened with "London Calling", followed by "Safe European Home" and "The Leader". A while later came "White Man in Hammersmith Palais" and "Guns of Brixton".

The effect of this encounter on Manu was decisive. The sight of all the punks pogoing and moshing down at the front, the mad energy, the guerrilla chic onstage, the barely apprehended words of no compromise spitting from Joe

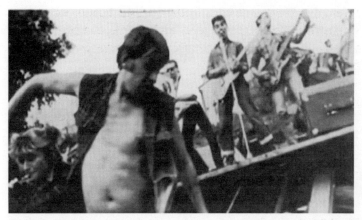

Marc Winandy struts his stuff in front of Manu's first band, Joint de Culasse.

Strummer's mouth, the echoes of ska, reggae, r'n'b, hip hop and jazz, and the notion that all these styles could all be mixed up into one big musical blast, it all jammed Manu's ears and eyes wide open. 'When I began to write songs, The Clash were my model,' he told the French music magazine *Les Inrockuptibles* many years later. 'I'd never seen a gig like that. The place was like a sea with huge waves rippling through.'

1981 was a year of profound change in France. The country had been subject to the same petrol-shocks as the rest of western Europe in the early 1970s. Huge swathes of manufacturing industry had perished or been moved to countries where labour was cheaper. Working-class Paris was becoming a ghost of its former self. The radical generation of students, trade unionists and left-wing activists who had almost managed to pull off the second French Revolution in May 1968 were hungry for real power and an opportunity to reverse the policies of right-wing presidents Georges Pompidou and Valéry Giscard d'Estaing, who had ruled France in the 1970s. The election of President François Mitterrand on 10 May 10 1981 brought a socialist incumbent to the Elysée Palace for the first time in twenty-three years. It felt like a new dawn for the French Left.

At first, Mitterrand's programme seemed a socialist's dream come true: nationalisation, an increase in the minimum wage, the thirty-nine-hour week, abolition of the death penalty, a wealth tax, and the mutation of pirate radio stations into independent 'free' broadcasters. Anyone involved in the arts seemed to have their prayers answered by the appointment of the charismatic Jack Lang as Minister of Culture. Lang vowed to succour and champion creativity, both highbrow and popular, with the aim of making France a powerhouse of pluralist creative expression.

But a familiar and depressing tale unfolded as the left-wing intellectuals and leaders of 1968 began to enjoy power and justify its endless compromises. In 1983, the socialists lost municipal elections and the right-wing Jacques Chirac became mayor of Paris. Three years later, Chirac became prime minster, in 'cohabitation' with the left-wing presidency, and the dreams of 1981 were diluted even further.

Although the mainstream left were wholeheartedly behind Mitterrand in 1981, a radical fringe of anarchists, Marxist-Leninists, Trotskyites and nonaligned free thinkers dismissed Mitterrand as irredeemably tainted by his association with Vichy France during the Second World War and his dubious role as Minister of the Interior during the Algerian War of Independence. These ultras were known collectively as *Les Autonomes* (The Autonomous Ones), or *Les Totos* for short, and it was they who supplied the philosophical direction for the alternative squat culture that was about to shake the French music scene to the core.

In the early 1980s, Paris was a dilapidated, divided and sometimes dangerous place. The old central working-class districts of Ménilmontant, Belleville, Barbès, Montparnasse, Stalingrad and Nation were strewn with crumbling substandard housing stock and deserted factories and workshops. This situation was a tragedy for the working-class people who had lived in these areas for generations and who were about to be swept away by the brutal redevelopment and urban cleansing of their beloved neighbourhoods. But it was also an opportunity for Les Totos and their younger and rather less ideological punk allies.

A young Manu with his Gretsch semi-acoustic.

The time had come for direct action. As in England, an alliance of young rudderless punks and older ideological hippies and activists began to construct their own alternative network of squats, bars, free festivals, cultural spaces, labels and record shops. The most famous early squats were in the rue Vilin and rue des Cascades in Belleville, but soon tottering old apartment blocks and factories had been converted into experiments in open rebellion, all over the capital and in most major French cities, too. A whole new generation of bands were born of the learn-three-chords-then-form-a-band philosophy of punk. Their names were soon grafittied all over the shabbiest walls of the French capital: Guernica, Les Wampas, Parabellum, Orchestre Rouge and the darkest, loudest, most brilliantly radical of them all, Bérurier Noir, known as 'Les Bérus'.

These bands found a sympathetic creative home in squats that matured into alternative rehearsal and performance spaces, notably Art-Cloche in Montparnasse, Usine Pali-Kao and La Miroiterie in Ménilmontant, Electron Libre on the rue de Rivoli, and l'Hôpital Ephemère near Place de Clichy. The almost complete disinterest shown by mainstream record labels in this spiky youth movement was overcome by a flood of self-produced releases, usually consisting of a grubby cassette in a plastic bag accompanied with a dense Xeroxed booklet screaming dire images of injustice, morbid cartoons and southpaw slogans.

The closed doors and ears of the mainstream media, including such venerable organs of French rock as *Rock'n'Folk*, were circumvented by a samizdat flood of alternative fanzines. These combustible cultural artefacts were available mainly at gigs but also in a small but dedicated network of independent record shops. Pre-eminent among these hubs of underground culture was New Rose on the Left Bank and Open Market near Les Halles.

Although Manu Chao was still living with his parents in Sèvres, his eventual seduction by the prevailing post-punk zeitgeist was inevitable. Together with his brother Tonio, his cousin Santi and a bunch of mates, Manu squatted an old rubber factory in Sèvres and rechristened it Issue de Secours (Emergency Exit). The aim was to create a space where the youth of the suburb could get together, play music as loud as possible, smoke spliff, mend bikes, drink liquor and be themselves. The Chao brothers and their friends dedicated hours to redecorating and soundproofing the old place, installing a bar and a little sound system.

Issue de Secours soon became extremely popular. Joint de Culasse and many other bands would rehearse and there were gigs every Saturday night. Of course, the battles with the forces of law and order began almost immediately. For them, Issue de Secours was little more than a den of depravity, illegal drugs and drinking, and noise pollution.

At the time, the *Mairie* (town hall) of Sèvres was ruled by the Communist Party and although the anarchist DIY credo of punk never sat comfortably with the communists, the Issue de Secours crew did manage to come to an acceptable accommodation with the mayor. For a while at least, the squat survived and even thrived. But all that changed with the election of the right-wing Mayor Caillonneau in 1983. Caillonneau's primary cultural ambition seemed to be the elimination of Issue de Secours, though, thanks to the fighting spirit of *la caillera,* it took him several years to get his way. First, the electricity and water were cut off. Then a mass eviction involving several vanloads of police took place.

Marc Winandy organised a protest gig. 'It was like a commando operation,' recalls Tom Darnal, whose band GPS played alongside Joint de Culasse. 'We had twenty minutes to bring the equipment and start to play. We were sure the police would try to stop the event. They charged in – I climbed on the wall of a warehouse and jumped from roof to roof and ended up, having dropped some pills, at Marc's place.'

Finally the building was bricked up and razed to the ground. This wasn't an isolated incident. The forces of reaction had gained control of the capital and many of the city's original art squats were closed down, often brutally.

The demise of Issue de Secours was a rare failure on the Chao CV, although a valuable political lesson in direct action. Throughout this best and worst of times, Manu kept playing, kept listening, and kept searching for his musical voice. After Joint de Culasse recorded and released their first and only album, *Super Boum Rock'n'Roll,* on the Force label in 1982, his apprenticeship of the rock'n'roll masters was complete. The album was a straightforward delivery of the promise in its title; fourteen tracks of high-energy covers including "Great Balls Of Fire", "Louie Louie", "Roll Over Beethoven" and "Oh! Carol". There were four Chuck Berry numbers in all. It was recorded in the tiny Studio Darniens in Boulogne-

Billancourt where sound engineer Xavier Escabasse captured a dynamic, live sound. The band, however, hated the cover, depicting a sheeny photo of a couple of jiving chicks and a black-drainpiped rocker, and spray-painted it when they sold it at their gigs.

Super Boum Rock'n'Roll didn't sell and wasn't noticed. Serviceable and energetic as it was, it represented a superior kind of rock'n'roll karaoke, loved by a small coterie of suburban rockers. Manu had to broaden his horizons if he was going to contribute anything new, or make a living at his chosen profession. The next steps in Manu's musical journey were suitably chaotic. It was as if his priority was to play with as many different musicians as possible in as many formations as possible. The boundaries between these various groups, both in terms of membership and time scale were often blurred and indistinct. While Joint de Culasse were still rocking down in Sèvres, Manu put a band called Les Flappers together, with the ever-present cousin Santi on drums, and two other mates called Pépé and Yann. There was also another band called Parachute, in which Manu played with Pascal Borne on guitar.

There was a further project, too, that became the clear evolutionary link between Manu the textbook rock'n'roller and Manu the pied piper of globalised Latino punk. It began in the basement of the Chao home in Sèvres, and matured in the rehearsal rooms of Issue de Secours. It featured Manu on guitar and vocals, Pascal Borne on guitar, Jean-Marc Despiegnes on bass, and, of course, cousin Santi on drums. The band chose to call themselves after the title of a James Brown song, "Hot Pants". It was, perhaps, a name that sounded hipper and more evocative to French ears back then than it does to Anglophone ones now, but it served well enough.

The year was 1983, Manu Chao had just hit the age of twenty-two. There were three years to go before he had to honour that promise he had made to his mother.

CHAPTER 3:
HOT PANTS

'If Hot Pants were a car it would be a 1950s Buick parked at the corner of a Chicano bar'

Nancy Jazz Pulsations

The Hot Pants sound was evolutionary rather than revolutionary. At its core there was still a rock'n'roll heart, with a wired and raucous Dr Feelgood edge, but there was more variety and melodic invention than before, with echoes of Otis Redding soul and The Clash were becoming distinct. However, Hot Pants' groundbreaking innovation didn't come from across the English Channel or the North Atlantic but from Spain. In truth, Manu had never completely lost touch with his Spanish heritage. Those old Spanish and Cuban songs that he had learned from his father, grandfather and uncles were still coursing through his veins, and every summer, in August, the Chao family would holiday in Spain, often in AndaLucía.

There, for some years, the old *flamenco* of southern Spain had been reinventing itself, mixing with rock and jazz elements, and forging a new hybrid that came to be known as *nuevo flamenco*. Its torch-bearers were Lole y Manuel, Tomatito, Juan Carmona and Miguel Poveda, but above all the guitarist Paco de Lucía and the doomed romantic singer Camarón de la Isla, who died of a heroin overdose in 1992.

But it wasn't so much the dazzling guitar work of the new flamenco maestros, or the vertiginous heart-rending wail of the best singers that captivated Manu. It was the fact that *nuevo flamenco* reflected a new attitude, a new daring, a new sharpness in dress and look, a rebellion of the soul in a new post-Franco Spain.

Carlos Saura vividly captures the essence of this rebellion in his film *Deprisa, Deprisa* (Hurry, Hurry), which came out in 1981. Its story follows the adventures of two young car thieves called Pablo and Meca who put together a gang and terrorise the suburbs of Madrid before being gunned down after a botched bank robbery. The film encapsulates the spirit of a country emerging from the cultural and social straitjacket of fascism and into a new dawn of liberal democracy, with its sweet and sometimes dangerous freedoms.

Deprisa Deprisa and other Spanish films, like Buñuel's *Los Olvidados*, made Manu realise that Spanish kids – or French kids, or even Latin American kids – could be punks in their own way; that they could also be cool and dangerous without denying their own culture. The music that serenaded the libertine adventures of Pablo and Meca in Saura's film was a mix of *nuevo flamenco* and the heavier more rhythmic *flamenco rumba* of new Spanish groups like Los Chichos, Los Chinguitos and Los Marismeños. 'The soundtrack of *Deprisa, Deprisa* was a bible for us,' Manu remembers. 'It was the rock'n'roll of Spain, listened to by the bad guys of the neighbourhood. And these guys hadn't even listened to rock'n'roll.' Manu still wears a tattoo of the words 'Deprisa Deprisa' on his arm and he would reference the film many years later when he recorded his first solo album.

Connecting with their Hispanic roots was a way out of the derivative rock'n'roll cul-de-sac which Manu, Tonio and Santi had backed into with Joint de Culasse. Manu rearranged all his current obsessions into a new evolutionary formula: rockabilly, Canvey Island, The Clash, *nuevo flamenco*, gypsy *rumba*, a touch of James Brown and Otis Redding. A critic writing in *Nancy Jazz Pulsations* described this mix in

Photocopier days – a Hot Pants band shot, with aliases already in place. They are credited, from left, as: Jean-Marc 'El Tiloul' (bass), Santiago 'Ignacio de Loyola' Casariejo González (drums), Pascal Borne (guitar) and Manuel Chao (guitar, vocals).

automotive terms: 'If Hot Pants were a car it would be a 50s Buick parked at the corner of a Chicano bar.'

The few surviving videos and clips of Hot Pants show a small, wiry, baby-faced Manu dwarfed by his enormous Gretsch semi-acoustic guitar, mixing vocal passion with pogo leaps and duck walks, whilst bassist Jean-Marc Despeignes and drummer Santi pump out a steady backbeat and Pascal Borne looks blank and mean on the guitar.

Hot Pants were the first Sèvres band to break out of the neighbourhood and their early life was spent playing gigs for a few francs in squats, bars and clubs, not only in Paris but further afield in Normandy, Brittany, the south and west of France. The band usually earned just enough for petrol and food. Manu was living hand to mouth and supporting himself with odd jobs as a bicycle courier, or pumping gas at a local petrol station, or as an assistant at RFI, the radio station where Ramón worked. He had the solace of a very close-knit and inspiring circle of friends, which included his brother and cousin, but also his first girlfriend, Anouk Khelifa, and a fellow local music fanatic called Tom Darnal.

Anouk had an Algerian father and an Armenian mother and her dark sensitive looks captivated Manu when he met her at a concert. After a shaky beginning, their relationship gradually deepened and Manu fell in love. Anouk's creativity, intelligence, tender attentiveness and beauty were a kind of refuge for his own ever-restless personality. Manu would spend many hours in the warm friendly embrace of the Khelifa family home, eating, talking, sleeping and getting away from it all. Anouk had dreams of becoming a singer herself and Manu opened up doors for her into the arcane world of music.

Tom Darnal was a sharp, good-looking music nut, who had befriended Manu and Santi at the conservatoire in Sèvres. His record collection was massive and varied, corralling many styles that Manu hadn't given much consideration to in the past, such as funk, electronica and early hip hop. Darnal was a founder member of Garage Psychiatrique Suburbain, or GPS for short, a hard-core psychedelic punk outfit, who became the sworn rivals of Joint de Culasse in the Sèvres and southwestern suburban music scene. Manu and Darnal became firm friends and avid fellow travellers in their lust for music and life.

Even when some recognition began to creep up on him, Manu never felt comfortable with the implicit membership of any hip Parisian scene. When he went to trendy discos in Paris, full of rock glitterati and intelligentsia, he felt like a peasant. 'We weren't part of that,' he claims. 'We didn't like it and we weren't welcome.' This was an early manifestation of Manu's aversion to musical aristocracy and the fawning cliques that surround them. Despite his relentless ambition, despite his desire to be the best and his reputation as a *bosseur* or hard grafter, the slightest whiff of exclusivity or one-upmanship made Manu uneasy. Paris is a very elitist town, where the most powerful and influential showbiz execs and producers broker the biggest deals and air-kiss the stars of stage, studio and screen. Manu preferred, if it was humanly possible, to bypass that whole modern showbiz court of Versailles and find success in his own way and on his own terms.

Among his most precious memories of that era were his long summer holidays on the coast. Every July and

Tom Darnal in Garage Psychiatrique Suburbain (GPS)

August, Manu and friends would migrate to Brittany, particularly the old walled port city of St Malo, for sea, sand, busking and girls. 'It was wonderful,' he remembers with fondness. 'One of the best times of my life. You had your food and drink and lots of English girls, very pretty girls, looking at the nice musicians and inviting them to their boats. There wasn't much money in your pocket, but the parties were nice.'

One summer, when Manu was busking in the cobbled streets of St Malo with Schultz, a musician friend from Parabellum, one of the leading alternative bands in Paris, the pair had a run-in with the local street mafia. There was an accordionist busker who, according to Manu, was faking blindness and playing traditional songs for middle-aged English ladies, who just lapped up the cliché like crème fraiche. The accordionist was making a fortune, maybe 3,000 francs (450 Euro) a day. But according to Manu, he was also working with the police, who let him hog his street pitch in return for information about the goings-on in the neighbourhood. Manu and Schultz set-up nearby and, despite only playing for a few hours a day, broke the informant's business.

Unsurprisingly, the accordionist wasn't happy. He went to the Boxing Club of St-Malo and hired three heavies to pick a fight with Manu and Schultz in a bar, to scare them into leaving town. Most members of the boxing club were black but Manu and Schultz also had a black friend from the neighbourhood in their busking team. The next day, this friend was hanging out in St-Malo chatting up a girl when he met the three black guys from the gym, who said, 'Why don't you come with us? We need to scare these upstarts.' So they went to the bar where Manu and Schultz were having a drink – but as soon as their friend saw them, he told the three heavies that he was on their team. So nothing happened. The next day the faux-blind accordionist was playing to a circle of admirers when the hard guy on Manu and Schultz's team burst in and broke his glasses, much to the shock of the tourists. Happy days.

Not long after Hot Pants came out of the basement, Manu Chao started to write his own songs. 'For years and years I only played covers,' Manu explains. 'And when people told me I should write a song I said, "What for? There are so many wonderful songs already. I don't have enough time in my life to sing all the songs already recorded that I want to sing." Before doing your own stuff, I think it's important to go to school, and for that you need professors. Chuck Berry was my professor, Lou Reed was my professor, The Clash were my professors, and much later Jacques Brel and Edith Piaf were my professors in French.' Later, to that roll call of professors, Manu added Bob Marley.

When Manu did start writing songs in 1984, he conjured up a winner on what he claims is his very first attempt: "Mala Vida". It later became Mano Negra's debut single, their first video clip, and one of their greatest successes. It's still in Manu Chao's set over twenty-five years later: *'Tu me estas dando mala vida / yo pronto me voy a escapar / gitana mia por favor / ve y dejame respirar'* (You gave me such a bad life / I'm going to escape soon / Please my gypsy girl / let me breathe).

The opening lines of the song evoke Manu's perennial obsession with the notion of being trapped and his desire for escape. The song was demoed on a cassette with a couple of others and ended up on a compilation of French alternative rock called *Romance 85*. Its cover featured a demure girl in stockings, suspenders and high heels and, as well as Hot Pants, the record featured tracks by Bijou, a girl trio from Dijon singing 'Tous Les Soirs" (Every Night), another track released by Manu under the Parachute name. Other songs by Hot Pants found their way on to two other compilations the very same year; *Les Héros Du Peuple Sont Immortels* and *Hot Chicas*. The latter also featured tracks by Manu's brother Antoine Chao's new band, Chihuahuas.

Romance 85 caught the attention of Rico Maldorer, who had set-up a label called Gougnaf Mouvement. It was the home of French punk acts like Les Rats, Manu's friend Schultz's band Parabellum, and Les Thugs from the western city of Angers. In accordance with the spirit of the times, there were endless discussions about equality between all the acts. Each artist had to have the same amount of time in the studio and an equal level of label support. 'If there is a hierarchy, it is among the public, not with us,' declared Maldorer.

The French rock scene was still dogged by its old inferiority complexes and a depressing sense that no one outside the country would ever take them seriously. 'If Les Thugs were American, everybody would be on their knees before them,' complained Maldorer. (Les Thugs were later to forge a reasonably successful international career and sign to Sub Pop, the Seattle label who launched Nirvana.) The numbers were still small. Gougnaf Mouvement's top band Parabellum sold around 6,000. But *Romance 85* was a step up for Manu.

Hot Pants' first single was released on Gougnaf in 1985, and it featured a Manu Chao original, "So Many Nites", on the A-side and another, "Lover Alone", on the flip side. It sold about 3,500, nothing earth-shattering, but enough, along with their raucous live show,

Manu's first song to be released: the "So Many Nites" single on Gougnaf

to establish Hot Pants as contenders on the Paris scene, which was then entering a rollercoaster phase of intense alternative creativity.

There was another reason why Manu began writing his own material. The particular blend of rock'n'roll, soul, punk and gypsy *rumba* that was bubbling up in his imagination just didn't exist. It needed to be created from scratch. But, in rising to that particular challenge, Manu was starting to ride the zeitgeist. Paris was fast becoming the capital of what was then called *La Sono Mondiale*, and later came to be known internationally as 'world music'.

The immigrants who came to France in the 1970s to man the country's declining industrial base had, at first, kept a low cultural profile, quietly earning their pay and going back home every summer to be with their families. In the early 1980s, however, a new generation of kids born of North and

West African parents began to consider France their home and assert their cultural identity. Arabic, Berber and African music styles emerged to play their part in the Paris mix, and a whole new generation of media outlets was created on the back of these changes, including the polyglot Radio Nova, whose founder Jean-François Bizot also ran the magazine *Actuel*, the unofficial bible of the new Paris. With this growing trend of breaking free from overarching Anglo-Saxon models and prospecting for new sounds and rhythms far from rock's mainstream, it was perhaps inevitable that the French would also begin to rediscover their own oft-maligned musical past.

A key and physically imposing figure in this process was François Hadji-Lazaro, also known as 'Gros François' (Fat Frank), who, once he had shaved off his hippy locks at the end of the 1970s, looked like the French brother of Buster Bloodvessel from the British ska outfit Bad Manners. Hadji-Lazaro grew up in a working-class Parisian family and discovered Bob Dylan and folk music in the early 1970s. He taught himself guitar and a whole gamut of other folk instruments, like the accordion, bagpipes, banjo, violin, ukulele and jew's harp. After giving up his job as a teacher, he began to busk in the metro, and earn a few spare francs as a bouncer and sound engineer at early squat gigs. Eventually he founded the group Pigalle, named after the seedy red light district of Paris at the foothills of Montmartre. His next band, Les Garçons Bouchers (The Butcher Boys), came close to being stars in a scene that was suspicious of the very idea of stardom.

What Hadji-Lazaro pioneered was a roughneck revival of *chanson réaliste* and *musette*, the proudly Parisian working-class musical styles of the 1920s and 1930s, which were forged in the riotous sleaze of the Moulin Rouge and the cabarets of Montmartre, the *bals musettes* of the Val de Marne and the brothels of the rue de Lappe. With their absinthe-soaked melodies, impenetrable slang and switchblade balladry, the old *chanson réaliste* songs drew inspiration from the lives of the pimps, prostitutes, hard men and orphans who called the slums of Montmartre and Belleville home. It was a style popularised in the 1930s by singers like Fréhel, Edith Piaf and Yvonne George.

Hadji-Lazaro, though, was never one to wallow in mournful nostalgia. He mixed *musette* and *chanson réaliste* with ska, punk and rockabilly to create a riotous burlesque hymn to the dirty Parisian streets of the mid-1980s, full of immortal lines like *'La bière ça me rends amoureux, la bière ça me reveille la queue'* (Beer makes me randy, beer wakes up my dick) or *'Avec mémé au supermarché / dans le rayon fromages / Et je l'ai baisée dans la chambre froide / aux crocs de boucher'* (With my chick in the supermarket / at the cheese counter / And I screwed her in the cold store / amongst the meat snacks). It was a very localised breed of urban 'folk' that painted Paris in stark, yet affectionate, satirical colours, just as the songs of Madness and Ian Dury did for London. Hadji-Lazaro almost single-handedly made the accordion hip in punk rock circles.

The harder-core members of the alternative Parisian scene, like Jean-Yves Prieur, manager of the Bondage label, which was home to dark and radical bands like the uncompromising Bérurier Noir, dismissed Pigalle and Les Garçons Bouchers as backward, cliché-driven *gavroche rock* – *'gavroche'* meaning an impish Parisian street urchin. But one man's insult is another man's compliment, and Hadji-Lazaro knew that his music had one enormous advantage over that of bands like Les Satellites, Les Dogs, Dirty District, Guernica, OTH, and Parabellum, in that it couldn't have been concocted anywhere else in the world except Paris.

Hadji-Lazaro had managed to pull off a feat that had seemed almost impossible just a few years before; the creation of a modern style of rock that was unmistakably and unrepentantly French. Thanks to him, musicians started weaving accordions into pile-driving beats and trying to look like Jean Gabin in a black and white 1930s cop thriller; all berets or trilbies, grimy scruffy suits, Doc Martens and braces, with rakish neckerchiefs and tabs behind the ear.

Pigalle and Les Garçons Bouchers, however, could never be accused of peddling some kind of disconnected sepia-tinted fantasy of life in modern France. After all, Fat Frank was a skinhead, albeit a left-wing and progressive one, and in the mid 1980s skinheads were boot boys on the front lines of French social conflict. The majority of them had drifted towards the racist philosophies of Le Pen and his Front National, a party that was inexorably gaining ground in national and local elections at the time. A minority became 'red skins', a sub-species who still loved the music and believed in the brute urban cool of the skinhead identity but had no truck with any racist or neo-fascist philosophy. Some of these red skins formed vigilante forces like the Red Warriors.

Bérurier Noir, with their rallying cry of *'la jeunesse en-merde Le Front National!'* (The youth shits on the National Front!) would often use the Red Warriors as their security detail. As it did in England, the fight against neo-Nazism and the Front National in France galvanised the alternative music scene. 'Everything started mixing because the problem became the skinheads, the racists and the fascists,' remembers Manu Chao. 'So the community started to join together to fight them. The reggae guys, the punk guys, the rockabilly guys came together to be in a majority and fight the fascists. That was the start of the alternative music scene in Paris, when the community started mixing together.'

Paris had, of course, been under the control of the Nazis less than forty years earlier and Manu's grandparents had had to flee the fascists in Spain, where Franco had been in power until his death in 1975. With such a background, the fight against fascism wasn't a politically fashionable pose, as it sometimes appeared to be in England, but something utterly serious, a clear and present danger.

Manu Chao met Hadji-Lazaro in 1984, and soon found he had plenty in common with the charismatic musical innovator. They started jamming together in the bars of the Paris Barrocks association, an influential network of sympathetic local venues founded by Pascal 'Rascal' Suquet, Ronan Omnès and their friends at the bar Chez Jimmy in Ménilmontant. The association was formed to fight against old laws dating to Vichy times that forbade a musical performance after a ten o'clock curfew, which made it almost impossible for a rock group to play legitimately in a small bar or club in Paris. Paris Barrocks offered a place for bands like Les Wampas, Parabellum, Hot Pants, Chihuahua and, later, the whole so-called punkabilly wave of Les Météors, Les Cannibals and Les Stingrays, to play their first 'official' gigs in public.

One night at Chez Jimmy, Manu and his mate Schultz from Parabellum were asked to give an impromptu performance of their busking repertoire to fill a gap in the programme left by a support act that had failed to show up. It went down well, and so they were asked to come back, and slowly the act evolved into a band called Los Carayos. The name was a bastardised fusion of the Spanish expletive *carajo*, as in *'Ay carajo!'* which means something like 'Oh fuck!' or 'What the hell!', and *carallo*, which is Galician slang for 'penis' and an affectionate insult for guys in Galicia.

As their name suggests, the main priority at the beginning was just having a laugh and keeping things simple. It was a chance for Manu, Schultz and Manu's brother Antoine to throw all kinds of musical curiosities into the blender, from country, bluegrass and western swing, via rockabilly, punk and ska to *espagnolades* and *cajuneries*, and see what kind of joyous mess might result. Los Carayos were augmented by Alain Wampas from Les Wampas on double bass and François Hadji-Lazaro on violin and braces. A highlight of their shows was their performance of "Rawhide", which was pumped out with high-octane cowboy flair whilst Hadji-Lazaro plucked away on his mandolin and Manu Chao indulged his love of the Link Wray twang. The predominant vibe was one of sweaty rockabilly, with some dumb-ass yo-deling thrown in. Nonetheless, the band ended up recording three albums. The first was a live album called *Ils Ont Osé* (They Dared), recorded at Le Cithéa and mixed in a couple of days. It was followed by *Persistent et Signent* (the French equivalent of the saying 'They stuck to their guns') in 1987.

These two albums were released on Hadji-Lazaro's brand-new label, Boucherie Productions, which, alongside Bondage,

Los Carayos, 1987, featuring 'Fat Frank' Hadji-Lazaro (in the dungaree shorts);
Manu is far left in the polka-dot shirt.

became the definitive imprint of the alternative Paris scene
of the 1980s, responsible for albums by Hot Pants, Happy
Drivers, Les Garçons Bouchers and Mano Negra amongst
others. Necessity drove Hadji-Lazaro to invention, but it's
doubtful that anyone with fewer broad and varied talents,
who lacked the respect and faith shown to Hadji-Lazaro,
could have pulled off such a multi-tasking minor miracle.

Persistent et Signent featured a song by Manu Chao called
"Oscar Tramor", a mangling of another song title, "Busca Otra
Amor" (Looking for Another Love), by the Mexican singer Irma
Serrano, which appeared on the soundtrack of a kitsch and
sexy film called *Noches de Cabaret* in 1978. Manu rearranged
the original into a story about an alcoholic toreador who
prayed to God for protection from the bull's gouging horns

every night before going to sleep. 'Oscar Tramor' eventually became Manu's pseudonym and alter ego. On Mano Negra's debut album *Patchanka*, you can see a faked police picture of Manu above the name 'Oscar Tramor', which led numerous journalists to suppose that this was his real name.

Songs by Los Carayos appeared on couple of compilations; *Hot Chicas*, which also featured Hot Pants and Chihuahua, and *Mon Grand Frère Est Un Rocker* (My Elder Brother Is A Rocker), an overview of the combustible French underground scene, which was then fast reaching its apotheosis. A final album *Au Prix Ou Sont Les Courges*, (a surrealist title which means something like "The price of marrows being what it is"), came out in 1990, by which time Mano Negra was taking up all of Manu's time.

Everybody in Los Carayos was playing with at least two bands, and months were often divided equally, fifteen days with one and fifteen days with the other. It was a loose arrangement that suited everyone for a time. But in the end, when Manu Chao's next band Mano Negra began to devour all his available time, he announced that enough was enough. 'We wondered if we could carry on without Manu,' Alain Wampas remembers. 'We thought about it for two seconds before deciding that Los Carayos was the five of us.' 'Los Carayos were popular with everyone,' according to Manu. 'With the punks, with my neighbours, with the elderly.' They were referred to, ironically, in the Anglophone tradition of bands like Blind Faith (a quartet of already famous stars), as the 'supergroup' of the Paris alternative scene.

Meanwhile, Hot Pants had accelerated out of the squats and bistros, and the band was even getting the odd mention in the mainstream media. In February 1985, *La Dépêche du Midi* wrote that they were an *'ensemble immanquablement joussif'* (an unmissably joyful group) and in April 1986 *L'Express* noted the band's assurance and a standing ovation that followed a memorable show in front of 1,500 people at the prestigious annual Printemps de Bourges, a festival with a reputation for breaking new talent. The other band on the bill that night

were the Kingsnakes, a group whose story was to be inter-
twined with that of Manu Chao and Hot Pants over the next
few years.

Actor, TV star and journalist Jackie Berroyer 'discovered'
Hot Pants at Bourges, his antennae alerted by Manu's stage
presence and his 'measured, determined charisma.' At the
time, the two media worlds of mainstream and alternative
were so distinct that it was seen as a bold move for Berroyer
to interview Manu for *Rapido*, the fashionable TV show
fronted by Antoine de Caunes. 'So you like these unknown,
under-the-radar artists?' asked de Caunes on air. 'Especially
talented ones. You will be hearing a lot more from this guy,'
answered Berroyer. 'Is that a threat?' countered de Caunes.
'It's a prophecy,' replied Berroyer.

Berroyer still has the unedited rushes of what was
Manu's first TV interview buried under books, records and
mementoes in his flat in Paris. It took place in Manu's room
at his family's home in Sèvres. During the interview, Manu
talked about his love for both *flamenco* and the songs of
Hank Williams, how the new *flamenco* guys rock like Johnny
Thunders of The New York Dolls, and declared that if he
was Spanish that was the style he would play. What he plays
instead is a bastard version, a '*flamenco bâtarde*'. Manu said
he was learning English so he could write songs, mainly
from the novels of Chester Himes, a black thriller writer
from Brooklyn who lived in Paris. 'He was unusually focused,
and determined,' recalls Berroyer, who became friends with
the young *flamenco* fan. 'He had a bright-eyed goodness,
intelligence and sharpness that was very appealing.'

In their own propaganda, Hot Pants declared that they were
against *megalos*, or megalomaniac supergroups, against the
blasé et morose public and against crooked show promoters.
Each concert, they promised, would be like a bullfight. That
Hispanic blood was boiling up again. Their album *Loco
Mosquito* ended up on another independent label with the
punk musketeer name of All Or Nothing. It was recorded in
May 1986 at Studio Do in Bordeaux and produced by Didier
Pasquier. At 29 minutes, it was a short and sharp evocation

of Hot Pants' scorching live set. The final track was "Ma Dear", by the supreme master Chuck Berry. The Clash can be heard in the raw melody of "African Witch", the spirit of Dr Feelgood with a Hispanic undertow is evident in "Rosamaria", a punked-up version of the song "¡Ay! Que Dolor" by Los Chinguitos. "Ya Llego" is a Manu Chao original with lyrics in Spanish and English. "Junky Beat" is a nod to the beat writer William Burroughs.

Manu called the album 'rockabilly with soul' and now claims that *Loco Mosquito* is his production that has best stood the test of time. The band was invited to perform abroad and did some fiery and memorable gigs in Granada and Barcelona. A few times they nearly made it to London, but didn't get there in the end. 'We'd never played there before and London was a mecca.'

Loco Mosquito only sold in the low thousands. If the Joint de Culasse was 1957 revisited, the Hot Pants album was really only a leap forward to 1977, an album worthy of influences like The Clash and Dr Feelgood, but still not really ahead of the curve, despite the innovative Hispanic elements.

On 21 June 1986, Manu celebrated his twenty-fifth birthday, although 'celebrated' might not be the most appropriate word, given the anxious context of the moment. All those years ago, aged eighteen, he'd promised that he would give up music if nothing happened when he got to this age. 'I had nothing,' he recalls. 'Not a dime. It was interesting, but economically zero. My mother was worried, although my father not so much.' Tom Darnal remembers that Manu kept his anxiety about his mother and the promise he had made to her very quiet. 'After all, that's not a very rock'n'roll thing to be concerned about,' says Darnal.

Manu carried on. It was all he could do. One potential break, which he saw as a major opportunity, was an offer to become part of the Kingsnakes. The band had a mythical aura in France, having been dubbed 'the greatest rock band in the world' by the French magazine *Rock'n'Folk*. The group was formed in 1980 by guitarist Daniel Jeanrenaud, the proverbial son of a

Hot Pants, pictured on the sleeve of *Loco Mosquito*. From left: Manu, Jean-Marc Despeignes, Pascal Borne and Santi.

preacher man, who was born in Marseilles and moved to the States. He teamed up with a couple of members of the flamboyant Flamin' Groovies, the oblique heroes of the early punk scene who had an enormous reputation in the late 1970s. Even more talismanic, from Manu's point of view, was the fact that Jeanrenaud's guitar, a 1951 Gibson ES-300, had been baptised 'Nadine', ever since Chuck Berry himself borrowed it one night at Bill Graham's club in downtown San Francisco.

In 1986, Jeanrenaud was back in France and living in Paris. 'The guy was like Bob Marley to us,' Manu recalls. 'A professor of the blues. He was having problems with his band, especially his guitar player, who was the worst musician of the lot, and one day he told me that he was doing an international tour with the Kingsnakes, starting in fifteen days and due to visit Belgium, California and maybe London. 'We want you to be the guitar player,' he said to me. 'I almost called my mum then and there and told her she didn't have to worry now because I was in a big band.' Manu was invited to a rehearsal for a tryout.

'I would have given my life to be in that band,' Manu continues. 'I was dressed my best, carrying my favourite guitar and I went to the bass player's house, who was a Portuguese guy called José Moita, an incredible player. Like most Portuguese, he died driving his car. I arrived and José asked me to wait while they had a couple of beers. We waited an hour and then they stopped off to buy a bottle of strong Portuguese spirit on the way to the rehearsal. By the time we got there, we were drunk, and José says to me "Son, the rehearsal is finished. You can go home now." I didn't play a note. Two days before the tour, Daniel came to me and said I wasn't going to go. It was the first really big disappointment in my career.'

This rejection triggered another Manu crisis. How many big opportunities does one musician get in his career? How many chances does anyone get? Manu felt that the Kingsnakes were his big break and he'd blown it. Jeanrenaud was the closest he would get to a Wilko Johnson figure, a Gallic Chuck Berry. Perhaps it wasn't too late to study after all, become a journalist like his father, or even go into medicine. To make matters worse, Santi had also auditioned for the Kingsnakes as drummer and had been accepted for the South American tour. Manu's cousin had been the backbone of Hot Pants as well as all Manu's other bands. He seemed more determined and ambitious than Manu, and perhaps more realistic. With his departure, Manu felt in danger of losing his musical backbone and his closest creative ally.

'In the end,' says Manu, 'the whole episode made me strong. I was sorry, but it made me more determined.' Indeed, far from calling curtains on his musical career, the setback was one of the catalysts for the creation of Mano Negra. Manu decided that his next band would be utterly free of compromise. It would be world-beating, all or nothing, a band as good as The Clash, or any other of his musical heroes. Its kernel would be comprised of his brother Antoine and his cousin Santi –

in other words, the family 'firm' that gave Manu much of his self-assurance and mental stability.

Antoine had been exploring Latin and jazz music with his band Chihuahua, and Manu felt that these genres should be essential elements in his grand new scheme. In fact, at the very core of this new dream pulsed the idea that all of Manu's favourite styles could be mashed up to make something entirely new; rock, Latin, punk, ska, r'n'b, reggae – a kaleidoscope of different sounds and rhythms. It would be an integrated and yet hybrid sound that faithfully reflected his own musical and cultural heritage, with a political edge that drew fire and purpose not only from his personal and family history, but also the increasingly polarised world of Paris in the 1980s. Manu spoke to Santi about his idea and tried to dissuade him from leaving for South America, but his cousin was determined to go.

As it turned out, Jeanrenaud had multiple problems to deal with in the ranks of the Kingsnakes, including bassist José Moita's penchant for strong spirits and then his death behind the wheel just after the group's return from the South American tour. Santi persuaded Jeanrenaud to hire Manu and then Pascal Borne and Jean-Marc Despeignes from the Hot Pants, effectively engineering a reverse takeover of the Kingsnakes by Hot Pants.

'Eventually, I won my battle,' says Manu, but just as he was installing himself in the Kingsnakes, his new vision took complete control and consumed him entirely. 'We became the "super" backing band of this guy, but I already knew what I wanted to do. I wanted to mix everything and the Kingsnakes didn't want to mix anything. So I got out and formed Mano Negra.' Out of the new Kingsnakes/Hot Pants union, only Santi followed Manu, although he later played drums on a self-titled Kingsnakes album, which came out in 1988.

Manu was now on a Blues Brothers-style mission from God to round up his dream team of musicians. He had already come up with a perfect name for the band, which he had discovered in an ancient, underground comic book by the artist Dominique Rousseau. Mano Negra (The Black Hand), a secretive group of anarchists who operated in AndaLucía in the 1880s, was also the name, as Manu later discovered, of a group of Hispanic New Mexicans who were fighting for land and water rights in the 1960s and 1970s. (Only much later did Manu learn that a right-wing paramilitary group of vigilantes in Colombia were also known as La Mano Negra.) There's also a Spanish expression *'Aquí hubo mano negra'* (There was a black hand in this), which means that something has been made illegally or lacks moral integrity.

The imprint of the Black Hand had an aura of clandestine radicalism that made it a perfect band logo. Manu stencilled it at home, adding a red star to make sure that people understood that the allegiances of this particular Black Hand were firmly to the left of the political spectrum.

The name was a statement in itself, implying a political subversion absent from either Los Carayos or Hot Pants. Manu had been on first-name terms with left-wing writers and intellectuals since childhood, and had been brought up in a politically active family. He'd actively rejected this part of his background in his music up until now, but it was an accommodation with this heritage, combined with the polarising atmosphere of rebellion and anti-fascism in Paris, that made Manu determined to imbue his new group with uncompromising and politically rebellious energy.

In 1987, Manu happened upon a trio of musicians – 'Jo' Dahan, Daniel Jamet and Philippe Teboul – busking down in the metro. They were collectively known as Les Casse Pieds (something equivalent to 'The Pain in the Necks') and he already knew them vaguely. Not only was Daniel Jamet that luckless guitarist from Cain and Abel that Manu had welcomed so ungraciously to his suburban southwestern stomping grounds back in the early 1980s, but Les Casse Pieds were also regulars at the Studio Campus rehearsal studios in rue Bréguet Sabin, where Hot Pants and Los Carayos also rehearsed. But seeing them down in the dingy and malodorous confines of the metro was a revelation.

Not long afterwards, Bernard Batzen, a leading French concert agent who was soon to become Mano Negra's first manager, remembers Manu Chao blurting: 'I've just seen the best band in the world, and they were playing down in the metro!' With indecent speed, Manu became a guest member of the band and for six months or so they spent their days playing underground, moving from carriage to carriage to avoid the beefy-looking TDP (Transports de Paris) security guys with their muzzled Alsatian dogs, banging out songs designed to last a single stop and leave time for one of the team to walk round the carriage with a plastic cup collecting the francs and centimes.

'The metro was the best school,' Manu recalls. 'When you play in a venue, people have paid to see you and the battle is already won. If you don't do a shitty thing, it's OK. If you play on the subway, the reaction of your audience is usually, "Oh, hell, here's someone else coming for money." So you don't have an hour, you only have three minutes to change their minds and make them happy to give you some money.'

'If a wagon was full of French, we'd have a special songs for them,' Manu remembers. 'If it was more North African, we would just play "Sidi H'Bibi" straight off.' This song was eventually released as a Mano Negra single, sung in Algerian Arabic. It was adapted from a wedding song traditionally sung at both Jewish and Muslim weddings in Algeria, like an ancestral bridge between two communities, and it still features in Manu's live repertoire.

A bizarre episode from these metro busking days gave Manu and his friends from Les Casse Pieds their first major magazine coverage. Another band member, singer and pianist Manu Layotte, who, according to Manu Chao, was a brilliant liar, concocted a fable about an Australian filmmaker by the name of Philip Maudson who intended to make a Hollywood film about a band who busked in the metro, starring Tom Waits and Willy DeVille.

The band took this story round to several magazines, all of whom rejected it as the fantasy it clearly was. Eventually, however, *Elle* magazine ran a small piece with a tiny picture, calling the story a modern fairy tale. The day after *Elle* appeared, all the newspapers picked it up. *Elle*'s credibility had turned it into an irresistible story that, in true tabloid tradition, was too good to check. A spread in the prestigious *Nouvel Observateur*, France's equivalent to *Newsweek*,

Les Casse Pieds down in the metro, left to right: Daniel Jarnet, Philippe Teboul, Jo Dahan, Laurent (Lolo) and Tomás.

followed and then various Japanese magazines and French TV stations picked it up on it, too.

The writer Keith Barrett confirms the veracity of this far-fetched tale in his book *Truth Jihadi*, in which he relates that he was approached by 'four ragamuffins who looked like an early version of the Ramónes', asking him to act the part of a fictional Australian film director and come to a café near the Bastille. Barrett thinks that it was Manu Chao who approached him, but it was more likely Manu Layotte, the 'brilliant liar' whom he describes as hyper, skinny and nervous.

Since he looked similar, Layotte and crew asked Barrett if he would pretend to be the fictional Philip Maudson. Barrett went along with the ruse, giving interviews to assorted French media and telling them 'in a bogus Australian accent' how he was a friend of Francis Ford Coppola, how he had screen-tested the band in a chateau in the French countryside and how the film *Le Paris d'Amérique*, whose fictitious title he actually forgot in the heat of a very awkward moment, was due out in June.

Another filmmaker called Yves Boisset got involved in the hoax and filmed a clip of Barrett pretending to be the Australian film director directing Les Casse Pieds on the metro, which was then broadcast continuously on TV monitors throughout the metro system. Barrett was very amused by the people who were moved to compliment the producers of the film on the skill and attention to detail with which they had recreated the Paris metro in a Hollywood studio lot. Several weeks later, just as the story was about to be exposed as a hoax, the band went to the left-wing media and declared that the aim of the whole stunt was to show how easily the media could be fooled and manipulated.

Keith Barrett later converted to Islam and became one of the world's leading 9/11 conspiracy theorists. In his book, he wrote that the Casse Pieds hoax 'aroused my metaphysical curiosity of what was real and what is fake.' For him, the Paris metro episode was a formative demonstration that you can't believe what you read in the papers. Equally, for Manu, it confirmed what he had always thought: that the media is distorted and unreliable, and that journalists are easily manipulated and seldom to be trusted.

Hoax or no hoax, what is certain is that the most success-ful alternative 'underground' band in the history of French rock was born literally down under the ground, on the metro. There's no doubt in Manu's mind: 'The tunes of Mano Negra started in the subways.'

CHAPTER 4:
THE RISE OF THE BLACK HAND

'It was half improvised ... sometimes it was a real mess – a bordel.'

Philippe 'Garbancito' Teboul

T he opening riff of "Mano Negra", the first track on the first Mano Negra album, *Patchanka*, has an apocalyptic, cowboy swagger. It leads into a one-minute-forty-four-second fanfare of intent, turbo-charged by Antoine Chao's trumpet and mixed, cheekily, over what sounds like a stadium full of 50,000 fans wildly cheering their heroes. Considering the fact that, when it was recorded, Mano Negra had only played to minuscule gatherings in the greater Paris area, this demonstrated not only chutzpah but also a kind of magical thinking. In just a few years, the band did indeed summon up those crowds, roaring for real.

What was the source of this magic that launched music from a garage in the outskirts of Paris into the hearts of millions across the world and inspired a new generation of bands halfway across the planet in South America? Occultists, from Paracelsus onwards, tell us that magic, or the realisation of the apparently impossible, can be achieved by the correct combination of will and imagination. Manu certainly had a rich imagination and an unusually focused will. The blend of these two essential ingredients created the alchemy that propelled Mano Negra to the four corners of the globe. As their manager Bernard Batzen said, 'Manu had a really developed intuition, and he was really sharp. He worked hard. The band was a hard-working band.'

The magic also stemmed partly from Manu's genius at cooking up different elements of Latin, punk, reggae and rock in a new, palatable way. It also lay in the band's strong inter-locking personalities, assembled by Manu. 'A great band isn't about wonderful musicians,' he asserts. 'The Clash weren't that good as musicians. But as a band they were great. It was the people, the attitude, the energy.' And one final, indeed crucial, element was that Manu had caught the mercurial spirit of the time – the late 1980s. His bands had always been defiantly retro but now, at last, he was surfing the newest waves. Within a couple of years, Mano Negra would become the biggest rock band in France, much of Europe and most of South America. Even the Japanese went nuts for them, and there were strong outposts of fanatics from Russia to the UK.

Back in 1987, all that success was nothing more than a wild dream. But as Manu started to rehearse the band intensively at the garage in Sèvres, and play gigs supporting better-known groups like Les Satellites, he became more and more convinced of his new vision. An initial stumbling block was that of commitment – it would be almost impossible to create a world-beating outfit with part-timers, and in the alternative scene it was *de rigueur* to be in several bands at once.

The initial idea was to gather musicians around the core trio of the two Chao brothers, Manu and Antoine, and cousin Santi, who would be the trusted foundation of a molten, fluid band. Collaborators would then be roped in as and when necessary. Initially at least, Manu always expected bands like Los Carayos and Les Casse Pieds to run in tandem with Mano Negra. 'All the groups mixed together at the time,' remembers Antoine. 'It was part of the movement, but also a desire and a survival instinct. You had to play in several groups to get by. If there was a problem, we'd all play on the same bill. It was music as combat sport.'

'I was also playing in three or four bands,' confirms Manu. 'One band you like for one thing, another for something else.' This ability to jump around happened to fit both the habit of the alternative scene of the day and Manu's *loco mosquito* character. Being unswervingly faithful to a band full-time would be a leap into the unknown for a commitment-phobe (or lover of freedom) like Manu.

But, with Mano Negra, Manu finally found the faith to take that leap. Manu talks about it in terms of a guy who's been playing the field for years and then suddenly thinks of getting married. 'One day you find a band and musically that's what you want to be doing. What's more, everyone in it is a friend and you want to be with them all day. You're going to stop looking elsewhere, aren't you?'

That commitment, however, took about a year from the formation of the band. To begin with there was just a single, "Takin' It Up", released, naturally, through Francis Hadji-Lazaro's Boucherie Productions. It was little different from the rockabilly-meets-Clash sound of the Hot Pants and wasn't a hit, though it did get Mano Negro their first TV slot. The core trio were augmented on the single and on the TV show by a band called Dirty District, a local Sèvres crew and fellow travellers of the Chaos, who shared Manu's love of reggae, Stiff Little Fingers and singing in English.

When Mano Negra and Dirty District appeared on TV to perform the single, the announcer was confused. 'So there are two bands together here?' 'Right.' 'And are you on the way to be being famous?' 'Nah, we're just filler,' said Manu, to the accompanying sniggers of his fellow musicians.

The first gig this combination performed under the name of Mano Negra, as far as anyone can remember, was at a bar called Fahrenheit, though they had done other, sporadic, experimental live shows with shifting personnel at various underground dens, including a party on a barge called *La Péniche de Santa* (Santa's Barge) which was moored alongside the Quai d'Ivry, where they billed themselves as *Les Boules de King Kong* (King Kong's Balls).

This intermittent street-level activity managed to stoke up enough interest to persuade Boucherie to sign up Mano Negra for an album. Rehearsals took place in the garage of the Chaos in Sèvres. Felisa and Ramón get a prominent thankyou on the album credits, which, considering the sound of half-formed Latino punkabilly that ricocheted around the house and no doubt wrecked their tranquillity during those formative months, they no doubt richly deserved.

On several tracks, the trio were joined by Dirty District: K'shoo and Gilles on guitar, Geo on keyboards and Fred on bass. Others featured the trio and Les Casse Pieds, notably on a metro favourite called "Darling Darling", or by Jean-Marc, the bass player from Hot Pants, Mamek from the Chihuahuas and Alain from The Wampas. The rushed result, after four days and four nights of intense work, has the raw urgency of a heat-seeking missile.

The album's title 'Patchanka' was a punked-up version of the word *pachanga*, a Cuban dance music pioneered by Los Papuines in the mid-1950s. It's a happy-go-lucky style that mixes violin-based *charanga* and the trumpet-led sound of the Cuban *conjuntos*. But, as Santi explained, 'the title also meant "patchwork", both of music and musicians.' It was also a call to arms, a catchy brand name for a new sound that Manu hoped might fly as a kind of manifesto. 'Patchanka is a wild sound for proud souls and lonely hounds', sings Manu on "Indios De Barcelona", one of the album's highlights, which became an electrifying mainstay of Mano Negra's live show.

FAHRENHEIT 100°

PRODUCTION MJC ISSY

MARDI 4 OCTOBRE 88
ZENITH PARIS de 19 h à 0 h 30
(ouverture des portes 18 heures)

WAMPAS - ROAD RUNNERS - KINGSNAKES - CHIHUAHUA - THE DELTONES
LES SATELLITES - LA MANO NEGRA - WASHINGTON DEAD CATS
LOS CARAYOS - OTH - PARABELLUM

N° 110142

INVITATION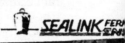

Possibly the first Mano Negra gig, in a line-up that also included Les Wampas, Kingsnakes, Los Carayos and Parabellum.

The album itself is a ragged, multicoloured quilt of disparate styles and flavours, including the passionate *flamenco* soul of "Salga La Luna", a nod to Aerosmith and Run DMC on "Killin' Rats", a borrowing from Iggy Pop's "Lust For Life" on "Ronde De Nuit", the wacky ska track "Lonesome Bop" and dashes of rockabilly, salsa and punk scattered liberally here and there. The whole thing kicked off with that killer cowboy punk-salsa fanfare.

This established the template for all Manu Chao's future albums: short, sharp songs in different languages with eclectic styles that make their point and don't hang around. Only one number, the last, makes it beyond the three-minute mark. The lyrics are in French, Spanish and English and are non-specific in their anti-establishment attitude, although Hitler gets mentioned as a 'rat'. Elsewhere there are songs of doomed love and dreams of escape. The languages are mashed together with little regard for grammar. The result is a globalised lingo, a backpacker's argot, used the world over by travellers who don't have English as a first language.

Patchanka also marks the first use of distinctive semi-comic sound effects, like the speeded-up, chipmunk-style backing vocals on "La Ventura" or the cartoon fairground organ played on a cheap Casio keyboard that bring the curtains down at the end of the album. These were scraps of silliness that were lobbed into the mix perhaps as a kind of inoculation against that *rockeur* desire to be cool at all costs. Humour was mixed in with the politics and angst.

Even if the hotchpotch of influences behind *Patchanka* are only partially digested, the whole was something new. More important was the sheer attitude and sharpness on display, anchored by Santi's rock-solid, muscular drumming. As well as studying for a business degree, he'd also been doing karate lessons and was ninja fit.

Jean Labbé, the lanky, long-haired sound engineer at Mix'It studios, who has the pallor of a lifetime spent in basements twiddling knobs, felt he'd struck gold. He remembered there was a 'magical quality that doesn't happen very often' about the sessions. 'On one track that wasn't working, Manu took a Spanish guitar and, boom, he got it. It was explosive. Then we put the vocals on and mixed it in two hours and mastered it that morning. I wasn't sure they'd keep the track, but it sounded incredible to me.'

One of the first people to hear the tapes was Manu's old friend from Sèvres, Tom Darnal. He was a keyboard player and a graphic artist, who designed *Patchanka's* front cover, with its patchwork of visual scraps from the Chao universe. Driving in Tom's car one day, Manu slipped a cassette into the machine. He recalled what blared from the car's tinny speakers as an amazing, almost shocking, leap forward: 'Immediately I thought that here finally was a French band who were making music that crossed borders and could go global.' Tom was the man who had lent Manu early hip-hop and electro discs by artists like Grandmaster Flash and Run-DMC, and he was determinedly modernist in his listening habits. 'Manu's other bands had been old-style,' he says. 'To me, even the Kingsnakes, good as they were, were four or five years too late. But with this new band, the way the music combined French elements, Spanish music and punk was really clever.'

Darnal also began to feel that Manu had the potential to become some kind of cult hero. 'And I was happy to be part of the creation of such a legend,' he says. He put a passport picture of Manu on the album cover, with his *nom-de-rock* Oscar Tramor and the byline, in English: 'Wanted by the CIA – for subversive lyrics, corrupting songs, outrageous guitar-playing & sexually explicit voice committed in this album.'

'Hot Pants and Los Carayos were imitating, but you have to go through that,' Manu reminisced, sitting in a Colombian café in Brixton, London, twenty years later. 'It's like, before you make modern art, you should have some technical skill and learn how to draw like Picasso did before he invented his own method. I had already been through the school of rock'n'roll. For the first time the songs were mature and, little by little, we invented our own style.' At the time, his own description of *Patchanka* was 'modern musette supported by Apache lyrics and a "chorizo" mentality.'

Tom Darnal started angling for a place in the band. At Saint-Germain-en-Laye, where Mano Negra were booked to support Les Satellites, Manu finally agreed with Tom that the band was sounding great but the keyboard parts on the album, played by Geo from Dirty District, were missing. Tom arrived at the Sèvres garage with 'a shitty little keyboard'. 'We were a bunch of friends, technically not so great,' he says with unforced modesty. 'I slept in the garage for a least a month.'

Manu realised that the album was hot and going places. But it needed promotion and it would take some time to fashion the band from Manu Chao's rag-tag army of friends and get it up to speed. With Dirty District touring, Manu talked three members of Les Casse Pieds into joining the team permanently. That's how drummer Philippe Teboul and guitarists Daniel Jamet and Jo Dahan joined Manu, Antoine and Santi to form the first immovable line-up of Mano Negra.

At last Manu had found the right personalities, but he still wasn't satisfied with the instruments that each of them played. Like a football manager constructing his perfect team, Manu went about the task of assigning positions to his players. 'We couldn't have three guitarists, so Jo switched to bass. Philippe, who was nicknamed "Garbancito", wanted

Tom Darnal's cover design for the *Patchanka* album – a patchwork of Mano Negra icons and miscellanea.

to play drums, but we already had Santi, so I suggested he try percussion. He liked it and it worked. Tomásin wanted to play bass, but I told him he was gonna be the sound man. He became a great sound engineer.'

Initially, Philippe wasn't keen on his shift from drums to percussion. 'I had no idea what *timbales* were at the time and there was no way I wanted to be a tambourine player in a rock band. I'd look like an ass. I just didn't get it.' According to Manu, Philippe eventually realised that freedom from the drummer's seat enabled him to develop as a musician. 'The fact that he couldn't play his favourite instrument made him more interested in the form of the songs,' Manu says. As it turned out, Philippe's Latin-style percussion was one of the key musical elements in the band's sound.

'Mano Negra started like a good Ford Mustang but came out as a Ferrari, perfectly chromed, the whole bit,' Philippe recalls. 'The Casse Pieds had the gift of improvisation, so the work plus the improv gradually created that particular Mano sound. It was half improvised, but it was beautiful! Santi, though, wasn't too happy about it. Sometimes it was a real mess – a *bordel.*'

Unlike most of the others, Santi, with his drive and a degree in business studies, had alternatives to life as a rock'n'roll hopeful. Well-paid jobs were open to him. And at the time, the Kingsnakes, his other band, were better known and technically more advanced than Mano Negra. So Manu was aware that Mano Negra would have to amount to something fairly rapidly to avoid losing him. Tom Darnal recalls a few late-night conversations with a concerned Manu about whether Santi or Les Casse Pieds would stick around. In the end, with the momentum building, everyone stayed on board.

Like some kind of provisional revolutionary government, some of the band were given 'portfolios'. Tom became the Minister of Propaganda, in charge of image, Santi became the Minister of Finance (of course) and Philippe became Minister of Jams. He had to organise jam sessions – everywhere and anywhere – something that kept the group energy focused when they weren't onstage.

One of the first people outside of the band's circle to hear the album was Bernard Batzen, who was to become Mano Negra's manager. He was booking acts for the Printemps de Bourges, a hugely influential French music festival with a reputation for spotting hot new talent. Hot Pants had played the festival a few years before. For the April 1988 edition, Batzen contacted Manu and secured an agreement for Mano Negra to play. The band were due to share the bill with the likes of Barry White, Frank Zappa and Serge Gainsbourg. At the last minute, Manu told Batzen that the band 'wasn't ready' but turned up anyway and played a busker's set with Les Casse Pieds.

Not long afterwards, however, Manu decided it was time to unleash the new Mano Negra line-up on the world. Charles

Guilleaux, a promoter who had known Manu for years, had opened a club called the Demi Lune and was putting on the cream of the alternative scene there – bands like Parabellum, OTH and the Rats. Guilleaux booked the new-look Mano Negra for two nights and the bar was packed to overflowing on both. The pharmacist opposite woke next morning to find two punks from the town of Lorient sleeping in his BMW.

The word on *Patchanka* was out. With the release of the single "Mala Vida", a song that had previously been released by Hot Pants, there was a feeling that things were about to explode. It was the first record by Manu to actually hit the charts in France, although admittedly only the lower reaches of the top 50. But the burgeoning alternative network of radio stations that had been encouraged by Mitterrand's culture minister Jack Lang at the beginning of the decade picked up on the song and played it into the ground. Francis Bergeron filmed a video clip to accompany the single, a piece of speeded-up slapstick in the spirt of Buster Keaton spiked with alternative Parisian squat culture humour.

Everyone loved the video – everyone except for Manu, who felt that the treatment was too burlesque for his agonised love song. He'd argued that the punky "Ronde De Nuit" should be released instead. Its chorus of *'Paris va crever d'ennui'* ('Paris will die of boredom') was pure gallic Clash and its lament that 'all the Apaches are in jail', its subversion of the Marseillaise – *'Allons enfants de la patrie / contre nous de la tyrannie'* (Come on, children of the fatherland / Tyranny is against us') aimed at 'the clown' in City Hall, in other words the conservative mayor Jacques Chirac, who was floundering in multiple corruption scandals at the time – all appealed to Manu's desire to make a radical impact.

With the three Casse Pieds on board, and Tom on keyboards, the band was almost fully formed. Then, at a concert of the emerging *nouvelle chanson* rockers Les Têtes Raides, Manu was captivated by the manic antics of trombonist Pierre Gauthé. He thought that his technique and stage presence would be perfect for Mano Negra, doubling up with Antoine on trumpet to form a brass section with power and balls. After all the musical chairs, the group lined up, ready for liftoff, as follows (with nicknames in brackets):

Manu Chao (Oscar Tramor) – lead vocals, guitar
Antoine Chao (Tonio Del Borño) – trumpets, vocals
Santiago Casariego (Santi El Águila) – drums, vocals
Philippe Teboul (Garbancito) – percussion, vocals
Daniel Jamet (Roger Cageot) – lead guitar, vocals
Joséph Dahan (Jo) – bass, vocals
Thomas Darnal (Helmut Krumar) – keyboards, vocals
Pierre Gauthé (Krøpöl) – trombone, vocals
Tomás Arroyos (Tomásin) – sound man

Mano Negra's first key gig was promoted by Bernard Batzen at the New Morning in October 1988. The venue was a celebrated proving ground for new French talent. 'It was clear something was really happening,' remembers Batzen. 'The band was happy with how I had organised the gig. A few days later Manu came to see me and asked if I wanted to manage the band.' Batzen, who had just started a new booking agency called Azimuth, had been totally bowled over by the band's performance and accepted Manu's proposal gladly.

His first job as manager was to help the band to set-up their own company, Patchanka SARL. Soon afterwards he opened a dialogue with Fabrice Natal at Virgin France. 'I saw a video tape they had done of "Mala Vida", live, out in the suburbs somewhere,' says Natal. 'I thought it was incredible. The energy was amazing. It was a real joy. I told them I'd love to work with them. I asked Manu and Thomas if they had a demo of new material and they said, "We don't do demos." Instead they suggested we come to see them at Les Trans Musicales in Rennes in December 88.' Like The New Morning, Les Rencontres Trans Musicales de Rennes, or just Les Trans for short, is still considered an essential rite of passage for any aspiring French rock band. Natal adored the live show and offered Mano Negra a contract.

For a band born in the Parisian squat scene of the early 1980s and steeped in the radical philosophy of the French alternative rock scene, the very idea of signing a contract with a major record label was seen as a sell-out by the purists, a turncoat betrayal of the worst order.

Patchanka SARL had been set-up as a collective with strict majority voting. It was understood that Manu had the lead on artistic matters, but on other questions, like where and when to play or how to deal with finance and business, the group would function as a democracy and would meet regularly to thrash out major decisions. It was also understood that Santi, fresh from business college, was the best person to take charge of the band's finances. In a spirit of equality, not just the eight members of the band, but Frank the lighting guy, Thomas the sound man and Jako the roadie would also get a vote and participate in meetings. It was a set-up that would cause Manu plenty of grief in the coming years.

There was a considerable amount of agonising among the members of Mano Negra about the Virgin contract. Batzen recalls spending one night at the Chao flat in Sèvres as the debate raged on for hours and Felisa cooked spaghetti for everyone in the kitchen. Despite the band's affection for Fat Frank, there was a growing sense that Boucherie Productions really didn't have the clout, the organisation or a distribution network powerful enough to cope with the success that now seemed, at last, within reach. Neither the new single nor the

Mano Negra take on their classic line-up, from left: Santi Casariego, Philippe Teboul, Jo Dahan, Manu Chao, Tom Darnal, Pierre Gauthé (sitting up), Daniel Jamet, Antoine Chao.

album were being pressed fast enough to keep up with demand. Mano Negra needed the infrastructure of a major, if they had dreams of succeeding internationally.

Santi's appraisal of the whole dilemma is blunt and honest: 'We had been outside the system because the system didn't want us. Once they did, we wanted to be part of it.' At the time, Santi and Manu were most keen to sign with Virgin. Jo and Antoine were most opposed. In the end, the vote was carried in favour of signing by a margin of just one.

Reflecting on this crucial if painful episode over twenty years later, Tom Darnal reckons that the intense atmosphere of heart-searching was exaggerated, in part at least, to make a good impression with the band's alternative fans. All the members of the band had been struggling for years and La Mano looked like being the best chance that they were ever going to get. What swung the debate in the end was the extent to which Virgin were willing to compromise in order to secure the contract: total artistic freedom, and autonomy for Tom and the band to design their own covers and control their own image.

The band were also perfectly aware that the Sex Pistols and the The Clash, their most influential punk predecessors, had also emerged from an alternative scene and had signed to major labels – Virgin and CBS respectively. Of the three French bands with global potential who emerged out of the alternative squat scene, Les Négresses Vertes also signed to a publishing deal with Virgin Music within a week of Mano Negra. The third, Bérurier Noir ('Les Bérus'), whose album covers featured mock police uniforms, pigs' heads and clowns, took the hard line and decided that self-immolation was preferable to selling out.

'If La Mano and Les Satellites [who were on the Bondage label and also signed to Virgin] had gone on being independent for another year,' Loran, the singer of Bérurier Noir, later declared, 'the indie movement could have brought the majors to their knees. But we realised it was impossible to wage a cultural revolution in France. So we got the hell out of it all.' A Les Bérus video of a clown being enticed away from the circus with drink was seen by many, including Manu, as a parable for Mano Negra's perceived treachery.

Fat Francis Hadji-Lazaro's band Pigalle did a song called "Chez Rascal and Ronan", a romantic elegy to the glory days of the alternative scene, which featured the lyric *'Comment donc ils fait pour vous convertir / Vous qui étiez si incorruptibles?'* ('So how do they convert you? / You who seemed so incorruptible?') In the end, Fat Frank, who stood to lose more than most from Mano Negra's momentous decision, did manage to secure a cut of the action in return for ceding control of Mano Negra's master tapes, which floated his label for another couple of years.

'The alt scene was a whole period of our lives,' Manu Chao later commented. 'All those bands had been hanging out together for a long time. They were strugglers who more often than not got a sandwich and a kick up the arse after three hours onstage in some bar. It was one hell of a movement; spontaneous, marvellous. But everything was spoiled in the end by petty little fucked-up arguments. The alternatives have only themselves to blame for the end of the alternative movement. We just had to get out of there, because everyone began mistaking their friends for their enemies, whereas the real enemies were elsewhere entirely.'

The Bondage label and their stable of purist punks were intensifying their war of words against what they saw as the quaint *gavroche* nonsense of the bands on Fat Frank's Boucherie Productions, including Hot Pants and Los Carayos. Bands were forbidden to appear onstage with acts from the rival label.

Manu's attitude to these internecine spats was unequivocal. As he later told French rock magazine *Les Inrockuptibles*: 'Both Les Bérus and Gros François were pretty much responsible for this sense of strife and panic. They lost so much energy fighting against each other, and trying to prove who was the godfather of the scene and who wasn't. I was completely wary of these different factions. The alternative movement had become like a uniform, not in the provinces, but here in Paris. It was like, "We're genuine and they're not." I don't like that kind of discourse.' The atmosphere was becoming suffocating and unbearable. Manu Chao was being upbraided for his arrogance and control-freak tendencies. It was time to bow out, to move on up.

Manu himself got on reasonably well with Les Bérus, and when they told him they weren't receiving royalties because they didn't believe in copyrights, he pragmatically suggested to them that they should collect them and then give them away. As it turned out, several years later, Les Bérus did try to claim their royalties, but Bondage no longer had the money, and a resulting court case ended up, as Manu predicted, with 'the worst solution'. The lawyers benefited more than either the band or any deserving causes.

Most people in the know agree that the intense era of blood, sweat, tears and inspiring music that was the alternative

French rock scene of the 1980s came to a climactic end on 11 November 1989, three days after the fall of the Berlin Wall. That night, Bérurier Noir, the undisputed Pied Pipers of the hard-core tendency, took to the stage of the famous Olympia music hall in Paris for the third in a series of three savage and incendiary concerts. They had never sounded better, and when they launched into the song "Porcherie", and brought all the young punks to a feverish boil with the cry 'We are white, we are black, we are yellow … WE ARE DYNAMITE!!' it really seemed as if the Bastille was about to be stormed all over again. Then at the end of the show Les Bérus announced that this was to be their last ever gig. That was it. The end of an era …

CHAPTER 5:
GOING SOUTH

'I understand the song ... you're describing
our shitty lives.'

A Mano Negra fan from Lima, Peru

Mano Negra were in Peru when Les Bérus performed their act of self-immolation at the
Olympia. It was Bernard Batzen who had the
inspired idea of sending the band to South
America. He, like others, was convinced that Mano Negra
had the potential to cross borders and become huge all over
the world, and he was not alone in his ambition. International success was an obsession for many ambitious managers
and execs working in the French music industry at the time.
They were fed up with having to narrow their ambitions for
world domination to France, Belgium, Switzerland, Quebec
and a few French-speaking islands lost in the Caribbean and
the Pacific Ocean.

So Batzen lost no time in putting his conviction to the test.
He started to work his contacts at the Alliance Française, a
state organisation whose aim is to promote French culture
in every corner of the globe. The band were becoming hotter and more together, and it was important to keep them
on the road and performing. After laying down some new
songs back at Studio Mix-It for their Virgin debut, the group
headed off for a life-changing trip to Peru and Ecuador.

The journey had an immediate and profound effect, particularly on Manu and Antoine. They had been brought up listening to the dissidents and poets of South America and now at last they were experiencing the oppressed and the benighted condition of the continent, as well as its dazzling beauty, at first hand. 'We arrived in Lima, which seemed a ravaged place,' recalled Antoine. 'We were really seeing the "open veins" of South America.' (The reference is to Eduardo Galeano's celebrated book, *Open Veins of Latin America: Five Centuries of the Pillage of a Continent*, which Venezuelan president Hugo Chavez gave to President Obama as a gift

The only tourists in Peru – Mano Negra arrive in Machu Picchu, from the Mano Negra scrapbook compiled by Tom Darnal and the band.

in 2009.) 'The place seemed to be foundering like a sinking ship, with poor folk bailing out the wreckage.' Jako, the roadie, remembered that the band were 'overwhelmed by the slums'.

They certainly weren't in Kansas any more … or Paris, with its well run venues and experienced technicians. The South American gigs were often shambolic and occasionally dangerous. One in Cuzco almost ended in tragedy. 'It was the first gig ever put on by foreigners there,' Santi remembers. 'They hadn't even seen bands form Ecuador or Argentina. It was 3,700 feet up and there was a lack of oxygen. We were eating coca leaves to keep ourselves on our feet.' The stage itself was a rickety structure, two stages in one, and the sound system consisted of rows of tiny amps and speakers which local technicians had somehow wired together. 'I have absolutely no idea how it held,' Santi says. Manu remembers negotiating all afternoon with the army about security.

When the band finally made it onstage, Philippe collapsed during the second song. The organisers had thoughtfully provided oxygen cylinders and he sat by the side of the stage with an oxygen mask on. There was a police cordon about three metres from the stage, but a horde of local kids forced their way past it. Three quarters of the way through, the stage collapsed. Even the normally unflappable Santi was freaked. 'Two Peruvian guys got hit by amps, Philippe had collapsed and I saw Tom under the stage, Manu fell and I thought this is the end, the ultimate. We were in serious shit.'

The reaction of the fans in South America changed Mano Negra's outlook. One of them came backstage after the show Lima and told them that "Mala Vida" was a description of his life, and that of most people he knew. To the band it had never been much more than a love song with a mildly bitter twist. 'He said, "I understand the song. You're describing our shitty lives." So something intense was getting across. Suddenly I saw it as a responsibility,' Antoine remembers. Both Tom and Manu recall the incident as a tipping point in the band's perspective.

This was a genuinely dangerous time to be in Peru, with much of the country under the sway of the brutal Sendero

Luminoso (Shining Path) guerrillas, a Maoist revolutionary movement with a personality cult around its leader Abimael Guzmán. They were infamous for their killings of those they saw as enemies of the struggle – and two foreign tourists were beheaded during the band's stay. Their activities meant that even in the tourist areas like Cuzco, Mano Negra were practically the only foreigners.

Despite, or perhaps because of, its dangers, the trip expanded the band's political horizons significantly, but Mano Negra was also a hedonistic rock'n'roll band on its first ever serious outing. Initially, Manu resisted the easy drugs. Jackie Berroyer, who had been invited along to South America partly to say thanks for his *Rapido* TV clip and the impact it had had on Manu's career, recalls seeing Manu in a bar that was 'like some cartoon South America – guys with hats, guitars and vagabond drug-dealers with guns' and Manu saying, 'I don't need drugs – I feel I'm already on Mars.' The boss of the hotel in Lima where Mano Negra stayed asked Tom Darnal if he was looking for anything and produced a large bag of weed out of his jacket pocket. When Darnal hesitated, the hotel-manager produced a large bag of cocaine out of his other pocket. 'I'll take both,' Tom said.

Even the *bosseur*, hard-working Manu, ended up having a cocaine binge. 'I was given half a kilo,' he says. 'It lasted one week. In Europe cocaine was the drug of the elite, but in the suburbs where we came from it was hashish or heroin. In Paris you could only get coke in the kind of clubs that would never allow us in.' Manu ended up with an aching jaw and an over-cranked nervous system. 'For me, this kind of shit didn't help. It's a stupid drug. There is nothing more boring than going to a party when everyone is on it.' Years later, he found other more conducive drugs like peyote in South America.

When the band paid a visit to a TV station in Lima, things became surreal. 'The TV station was surrounded by the army, who controlled it,' Manu recalls. 'Outside there were fans and mothers with their children shouting out, "Marry my daughter!" We were appearing on a variety show aimed at poor people, and everyone on it was very smart. We were wearing second-hand Brixton-style gear from the 1960s and the presenter asked us where we were from before announcing, "They've come from Paris to show us the latest style." When he asked me if I was married and I answered "No", a girl suddenly jumped out and kissed me. The whole of Peru was watching. Then the presenter said, "Dance!" and I heard this slow, strange music coming on over the speakers. It was "Mala Vida", except they were playing it at the wrong speed, at 33rpm. The announcer eventually realised there was a mistake.'

Another TV show featured hundreds of dancing girls and rabbits. For the band, it was like being in *Alice in Wonderland* whilst off their heads on drugs.

Tom Darnal remembers Manu being more disciplined than most of the rest of the band. A nickname, 'The Jesuit', began to stick to Manu. It wasn't entirely friendly and Tom thinks that it was a little unfair: 'He wasn't a puritan by nature, but he could be a bit moralistic. He didn't like the band to exploit young girls. And as far as I know, he was always faithful to Anouk.' Anouk, who was still Manu's long-term girlfriend, became an honorary member of the band, helping out on PR and videos. She was even beginning to have some musical ambitions of her own. Some of the other guys, on their first foreign tour, living dangerously, sky high on adulation and coke, were less circumspect with the willing Latinas.

Whatever anxieties they had harboured in the past about their ability to please foreign audiences and make it overseas were now banished. The band performed more of their Spanish songs, like "Patchanka", and beefed up the salsa-flavoured elements in their repertoire. The newest band member, Pierre Gauthé, proved his mettle in the testing fire of the tour. 'Antoine wasn't a *salsero* and neither was I,' he remembers. 'The refrain in "Patchanka" is a pseudo-salsa chorus which was maybe a bit mechanised, but Antoine had a gift, he had amazing energy. I had to learn to play like my ass was on fire. We combined knowledge and expertise.' Antoine was the more visceral player, Pierre the more musically trained. Together they packed an astonishing punch.

Mano Negra at their peak, back in France in 1990. Manu is grabbing a hank of Daniel Jamet; Philippe Teboul looks on from the percussion.

Although none of the band were Latino musicians, the audiences in South America loved the sheer vigour of the brass and the way in which it combined with the rock and punk energy. Mano Negra went out to South America almost as musical tourists but learned a lot there, building up a new cohesion and confidence. They came back a changed band. Photos and film clips of the tour found their way back to France and boosted the band's already strong mystique. The promotion of their next album, *Puta's Fever*, used plenty of South American footage (up there on YouTube for the curious). Manu called the continent *rambotico*, from the Spanish word *estrambotico*, meaning 'outlandish' or 'freaky'. 'It's a new word I invented,' he says. 'I felt I had come home.'

Back in France, their brains still swarming with South American impressions, Mano Negra set about trying to finish their debut album for Virgin at the plush Studio Marcadet in the 16th arrondissement near the Bois de Boulogne. Whereas *Patchanka* had been the work of an ad hoc 'patchwork' of friends, this time round a permanent and well-drilled Mano Negra were producing their first coherent band album.

Some of the old tracks, such as the longer version of "Patchanka" which had surfaced in South America, were revisited and reworked, something that became a pattern with Manu. The album opened with another version of the surf-punk workout "Mano Negra" before segueing into "Rock'n'Roll Band", a rollercoaster ride which would win no prizes for its original rhyming: 'If you wanna dance / Take a chance'. But Mano Negra weren't aiming to win the Prix Goncourt or become members of the Academie Française, so no one cared.

Several tracks on *Puta's Fever* became live staples, including the wacky "Magic Dice", with its drunk fairground organ. The song was the first sighting of Manu's obsession with chance and was inspired by reading Luke Rhinehart's book *The Dice Man*, in which the main character rolls a dice to take his decisions, a habit the band adopted. If the right road to take seemed unclear, the dice and the gods of randomness were called upon to decide.

Another highlight was a laid-back, latin-reggae track called "Guayaquil City", written by Tom and Manu after their trip to Guayaquil in Ecuador – a tale of murder, strikes, Colombian drug barons and Chinese gangsters. 'The city will explode / So hot it can't endure' went the lyric.

The *Puta's Fever* sessions also produced a bewitching trio of singles. First came the bouncy rock-rap "King Kong Five" – Mano Negra's fantasy name – which could be played live in different tempos and styles. Then there was "Pas Assez De Toi" (Not Enough Of You), a perverse love song whose lyrics translate as: 'I feel like turning up the gas / Like blowing my brains out / Like explaining to you how / Your indifference doesn't affect me / I can very well go on without you.'

Sell-out? The band own up to all charges on *Puta's Fever*, aligning with the sex workers of Pigalle.

The third single, "Sidi H'Bibi", was the old metro busking favourite that showcased Daniel's fluid, accomplished guitar playing. Absurdly, for what is only a celebratory wedding song, it was banned by mainstream radio in France, who judged it too comforting to the enemy because it was sung in Arabic and released during the first Gulf War. Despite, or even because of, the ban, it was a top 20 hit in France.

The band returned from South America to face a fully loaded concert schedule. That had been their instruction to Batzen: book as many gigs as possible. 'From that point on we never really went home,' says Tom. The tour dates just came rolling in – Amiens, Nantes, Bordeaux, Barcelona, Roskilde, Rotterdam, Geneva, Rotterdam and their first date in London.

Journalist Andy Morgan remembers Mano Negra's visit to London's legendary Marquee Club, where there was a real sense of anticipation. John Lydon, previously of the Sex Pistols, milled amongst the hipster crowd. In a review for the British folk and world music magazine *Folk Roots* (now *fRoots*), Morgan enthused about 'a welter of original songs in English, Spanish, Arabic and French. Full throttle ska merged into lilting Latino via thrash metal, dub reggae and … believe me … most points in between. Guitarist Daniel Jamet drove his Les Paul to the absolute threshold of feedback and noise and then with equal ease broke into a jazzy doodle that old Les himself might well have been proud of.'

A second London gig at the Town & Country club ended in a fight between the local security crew and the band. 'They came after us with sticks,' recalls Frank Mahaut, Mano Negra's lighting guy. The band's friends from Archaos, the French punk circus, also happened to be in town. An all-night session of mutual drinking and dope smoking was needed to calm everyone down. But the gig was a stand-out. A few weeks before he died in 2010, the revered English DJ Charlie Gillett recalled it as one of the most exciting he'd ever seen: 'Manu did the crowd surfing thing and the band generally instilled delirium in everybody who saw them.'

The band's work rate was ramping up. To illustrate their commitment to hard graft, Batzen mentions that he was offered a show in Lausanne on Christmas Eve 1989 and thought the band might turn it down. But in the end, not only did they perform the show, 'they also jammed for hours afterwards in different combinations playing great punk, salsa and soul music'. Christmas Day was spent recuperating.

The Iveco van Mano Negra travelled in was jammed with the nine band members and crew, plus boxes of T-shirts, posters and records. 'It was more crowded than a Tokyo capsule hotel,' said Jacques the indefatigable roadie. 'Like stuffing nine people into a one-man apartment. But that van carried us everywhere we needed to go, so hats off to it.'

Often they played two shows in one day and usually sold out both. Jo says that the adulation was great to experience, but adds that it was hard not to change with success. 'Everyone starts looking up to you and laughing at your jokes. Which is stupid. But every night we ruled. We really thought we were the best band in the world.'

Virgin were delivering on their promises to promote the band to the hilt and *Puta's Fever* was given high-priority marketing status. A TV clip of the time shows Manu saying, 'We played in London, we're number three in Holland, number two in Italy and we've never even set foot there. I don't know what's going on.' He looks quizzical and slightly taken aback by the vertiginous ascent of the band.

The biggest venues in Paris beckoned, too, but instead, in March 1990, Mano Negra and Batzen hit on the wonderful notion of doing a tour of Pigalle, the old red-light district below Montmartre. From a business point of view, this was crazy. The band could have easily sold out the Zenith arena or some other big Parisian club for fifteen times the money they would earn in the bars and theatres of Pigalle. But the band reckoned that some of the old Pigalle sleaze joints that usually programmed strip shows would make ideal venues. 'We'd seen these clubs like the Folies Bergères and L'Erotica, beautiful rooms that we thought would be amazing to play some rock in,' Manu said at the time. 'We did it because it was wild idea,' says Santi. 'It was a media coup, a great example of alternative, creative marketing.'

The band reacted to the accusations of sell-out by calling their new album *Puta's Fever*, deflecting all that earnest criticism by referring to themselves as *putas* (whores). The album title and Pigalle tour were perfectly in tune with Tom's deliciously erotic retro album cover. It was a titillating story for the media, who duly lapped it up. The whole campaign was also Manu and the band's way of showing solidarity with marginalised workers in the sex industry and the frequently exploited hookers whose clients were, as often as not, hypocritical moralisers.

At the time, the record industry was in a panic thanks to the widespread practice of making cassette copies of new albums, which, it claimed, was seriously damaging sales. Record companies had launched a Europe-wide campaign with the slogan 'Home taping is killing music!' Mano Negra's take on the issue, pithily expressed in a slogan on the album artwork, was 'Home fucking is killing prostitution.'

The live shows in Pigalle were wild and the band often carried on playing outside on the street to fans who couldn't get into place Pigalle. Some of them ended up dancing gleefully on top of cars. All this mayhem was the cue for 'major problems with insurance companies and car owners', Bernard Batzen recalls. But it was all good footage. François Bergeron made an atmospheric film of the Pigalle tour, capturing the band's shows as well as *putas* of indeterminate sex and other denizens of the night like the preserved-in-aspic *chansonnier* Pierre Carré, who had been singing on most nights in a bar called Noctambules on place Pigalle for over forty years. In other scenes, Manu drives a motorbike, with Pierre and his trombone perched precariously on the back seat, while Daniel, who was the group's most accomplished comic, sings a raucous hung-over version of the song "Roger Cageot", half-submerged in a morning-after pile of cardboard boxes and apocalyptic debris.

As the film demonstrates, too, the 'Mustang-turned-Ferrari' Mano Negra were now inducing pogo hysteria on a regular basis. Manu had become an accomplished showman, a passionate, charismatic frontman who timed his crowd surfing to perfection, diving into the seething mob right at the start of the sixteen-bar instrumental breaks in tracks like "Magic Dice" and climbing back onstage just in time to resume singing at the start of the next verse.

Mano Negra seemed unstoppable. Their debut gig in New York carved out what appeared to be promising foothold in North America. Another blazing gig took place at the industry showcase South by Southwest in Austin, Texas. The organiser, Brent Grulze, told Batzen in 2010 that it was perhaps the best of the many thousands of performan that he had witnessed there.

After that initial show in New York, Virgin were keen to test Mano Negra's impact in the United States. The band had reservations, muttering about the cultural imperialism of the Great Satan, but then again The Clash had sung "I'm so Bored of the USA" all those years ago and ended up playing stadiums there. So when the offer came of a tour supporting Iggy Pop, who had been a longstanding hero of Manu's, and the inspiration behind his stage diving antics, it seemed the perfect way in.

In fact, the experience left the band hugely disillusioned. In contrast to the habitually friendly chaos of their shows, Mano Negra were exposed to the well-oiled machine of the American music industry, with its semi-industrial methods and rigid chains of command. 'Things were different than they were in France,' Manu commented. 'There was a terrible hierarchy between the technicians, the musicians, the star singer and his manager. It was the mentality of an army. Iggy had been important to me for fifteen years. I was looking forward to meeting the guy who did *Raw Power*. Instead, I met a sergeant-major.'

Mano Negra felt they were subjected to all the dirty little tricks that a headliner can use to undermine their support band. They weren't allowed to change the lights or the sound set-up onstage. The overall PA volume was lowered while they were performing, to reduce their impact. Their fans weren't allowed to dance onstage. Mano Negra's habit of treating sound, lighting guys and roadies as equals was utterly alien. When the band wanted to do an Iggy cover, they were forbidden to do so. Iggy himself turned up just before each gig and disappeared immediately afterwards, without making the slightest effort to socialise.

Once, Tom did a stage dive into the audience and Iggy's tour manager threatened to confiscate his backstage pass if he repeated the offence. Tom threw it at him, and the rest of the band went backstage and threw their passes at him too,

Mano Negra take on the streets of New York for the first time, from left: Jo Dahan, Pierre Gauthé, Santi, Tom Darnal, Philippe Teboul, Manu Chao, Antoine Chao, Jako (stage manager) and Daniel Jamet.

in solidarity. Manu wasn't sure whether to blame Iggy for all of the things that had gone wrong. 'But, on the other hand, it was his tour,' he adds. 'He should take responsibility for it.' Since then, Manu says he has avoided meeting his heroes.

Thanks to the incredible reaction they had received in South America, even if things were more chaotic and dangerous there, Mano Negra were more attracted to the southern half of the Americas. They never went back to the States. 'We just played the wrong venues,' thinks Tom Darnal. 'If we had played places where there was a more mixed audience, especially of Hispanics, many of whom had already discovered us, places like Brooklyn, the tour would have gone a lot better.'

Frank Mahaut, the lighting manager, added, 'To really crack it in the States you had to put in an enormous amount of time. After that experience, we found it easier to make the choice between North and South America. We knew which one we identified with.' Their belief that they were the best live band in the world at the time wasn't so far-fetched and, when they decided to boycott the States, Manu just said it was 'their loss'. The Anglo-Saxon world would have to live without them.

For Bernard Batzen, the whole episode and the decision that was taken by the band on their return to France remains a disappointment. 'By then I'd been booking bands for years, and have done ever since then. There has never been any other band to touch Mano Negra. If they had persevered in the States, I really believe they would have been as big as U2. Imagine that – a French band! But it wasn't to be.'

At least Manu could tell his mother that he'd finally made it, admittedly a few years after his self-imposed deadline. The rest of the world, or mainland Europe, South America and Japan at the very least, had taken the band to their hearts. The next year things would get even more intense and the first cracks in this tight-knit group of friends began to appear. A slow-burning fuse had been lit and it was fizzling slowly towards a spectacular implosion.

But all of that happened after two of the most extraordinary tours in rock history: the first round the ports of South America in a cargo boat, and the second by train across the badlands of Colombia, through territories controlled by guerrillas and *narco-traficantes*.

CHAPTER 6:
THE FALL OF THE BLACK HAND

'Tomorrow you are going to be the breakfast of my dog.'

Security guard, Nîmes, to Manu Chao

T he Mano Negra bandwagon was burning up the mileposts with well over a hundred official concerts in 1990. But for each one of those, there were nearly as many spontaneous improvised shows. 'We'd meet a guy at a gig', Jo recalls, 'who owned a bar, a club or came from a squat and we'd end up playing another show there later.' Like in the old black and white movies, the banner headlines were spinning into view as the road signs zoomed by and the pages of the calendar were torn off one by one in quick succession: Finland, Italy, Belgium, France, Spain, Germany, Australia, Japan ... the pace was dizzying and relentless.

The trusty Iveco van was put out to grass in favour of sleeker, air-conditioned tour buses, large enough to host jam sessions from which new ideas would emerge. Manu has a rule that every idea should be recorded or jotted down before it disappears. As the Chinese say, if you don't write an idea down, you write it on water.

Some nights were more memorable than others. The Olympia in Paris was a milestone for Manu. The venue, which

The black hand takes Olympia – the gig that convinced Manu's father, Ramón.

had been opened in the 1930s by the renowned impresario Bruno Coquatrix, was another pillar of the Parisian music scene, where everyone from the Beatles to the Stones and Bob Dylan to James Brown had given unforgettable performances. 'There was a giant black hand on the hoarding outside,' Manu remembers. 'It was the band's symbol and logo, which I'd stencilled back in Sèvres, using my own hand as a model. My most far-fetched dreams had come true.' It was at the Olympia that Ramón finally understood that his son was really something, 'When I'd met Ramón at the time of Hot Pants, I told him I thought Manu was a great talent,' Batzen remembers. 'He replied that he only knew about classical music and so was no judge. But after the Olympia concert, he came up to me, shouting, "You were right! You were right!"'

In November 1990, Mano Negra travelled to Japan for the first time. 'We'd heard the Japanese fans tended to be well mannered and reserved, but they went insane for Mano Negra,' says Bernard Batzen. The band were highly amused by Yogogi Park, where different youth cults – rockabilly, teds and punks – would dress to impress with impeccably observed detail every weekend. The Japanese couldn't get the hang of Manu's stage-diving antics, however. At one gig, the audience, seemingly as frenzied as any in Europe, politely parted when Manu launched himself from the stage and he ended up on the floor with a broken collarbone.

During the Japanese tour, Mano Negra were given use of a mobile studio truck and they decided to record a live album, *In The Hell Of Patchinko,* in Kawasaki. 'Pachinko' is the name of the zombifying slot-machine game that the Japanese love, and a convenient play on *Patchanka*, the band's patented name for their sound. 'It sounded cool to record a live album in Japan,' is the way Jo put it, 'and everyone was telling us how we were a great live band.' Recorded in a couple of days and mixed back in Paris, the album captures the white-hot intensity of the Mano Negra at their peak.

Thanks to the non-stop touring, Mano Negra had only fragments of songs which they had worked up on the bus, when they went in to record their next studio album *King Of Bongo,* at the famous Conny Plank studios in Cologne, where influential discs by the likes of Kraftwerk and Can had been created. Most of the album emerged from jam sessions, with Manu (as ever) providing the lyrics. A reworked version of "Ronde De Nuit" from *Patchanka* ended up as "Paris La Nuit" (Paris By Night). It was another early example of Manu's penchant for refurbishing and recycling songs. The lyrics, however, remained unchanged: Paris was still dying of boredom, Chirac was still immersed in political corruption and skulduggery in the mayor's office and the Apaches were still in prison.

There were journeys into ska on "It's My Heart" and dub on "The Fool", a borrowed Stooges riff on "Letter To The Censors" and an affectionate French *chanson* on "Madame Oscar", the name that Anouk, as partner of Manu's alter ego Oscar Tramor, had chosen as her guest pseudonym.

The album, while polished, sounds laboured and lacks the furious energy of the first two records. It wasn't the radical fiesta and creative leap forward that was expected, and both fans and critics were decidedly lukewarm. *Le Monde*, a centre-right national French paper that can hardly be considered a barometer of cool, wrote that *King Of Bongo* was *'un disque normal'* ('a normal record') and they missed the *'joyeux désordre'* ('joyous chaos') of the two earlier albums. Mano

Negra being called ordinary by an establishment paper? That hurt. 'We had started out with ideals about being a really alternative band,' Tom says. 'But somehow, on the treadmill of touring and releasing albums, we had gradually become a normal band.'

King Of Bongo did produce a couple of highly distinctive songs, which became Mano Negra's two biggest singles. "Out Of Time Man" explores Manu's neurosis about time (he still doesn't wear a watch), and was enduring enough to get a 2007 reworking by Nick Cave's associate Mick Harvey that surfaced on the cult TV series *Breaking Bad*. Another number which has stayed the course was the title track "King Of Bongo", a surreal tale of a bongo-playing monkey who feels alienated in the big city. In a later version, renamed "Bongo Bong", it became one of the biggest hits on Manu's solo album *Clandestino*, fitting nicely into the outsider theme of that masterpiece. 'It was about an idiot who everyone is a fan of, out in the bush,' Manu said at the time, 'but in the city everyone loves house and disco so he's lost. But he's still "King Of The Bongo".'

By the end of 1990, the atmosphere in and around the band had become darker. Antoine tried to pinpoint the reasons for this shift in mood in an interview that was filmed years later for the *Pura Vida!* DVD, which the band put together without Manu and released in 2005. He said that it was partly the global situation, especially the Gulf War, but also the increasing commercialisation of the music business. 'They privatised the channel TF1 [whose music division Santi, ironically, ended up running] and M6 – the French equivalent of MTV – arrived with its endless music videos. So you had to fit the mould and make videos that cost a fortune. Little by little the dynamics of the music business took over and changed what we were doing. We fought against it the best we could and negotiated a little freedom, but the industry was stronger than us.'

For the next two years, in a constant effort to prove that they were never going to fit the increasingly sclerotic mould of the music industry, Mano Negra undertook a trio of remarkable tours whilst they disintegrated like the tail end of a mad firework display. In fact, the word 'tour' hardly does justice to the lunatic schemes they undertook.

Their first notable and marvellous folly was a musical assault on *les banlieues*, the outlying suburbs of Paris, which are perennially stigmatised for their social dysfunction and high crime rate. As a consequence, their marginalised neighbourhoods are generally avoided like the plague by big rock stars who prefer to stick to safe, prestigious venues in the centre of the city. Mano Negra had already done their central Paris tour in the red-light district of Pigalle. Now they would play the suburbs, where rents are cheap and the poor and dispossessed immigrants, mainly of African and North African origins, are forced to live.

The ghettoisation of outlying neighbourhoods is an acute problem in Paris, especially compared to a city like London, where there is more of mix of ethnicities and a greater variety of social backgrounds in the centre of the city. Partly thanks to the policies of Chirac (who was mayor of Paris from 1977 to 1995 – and was still being pursued in the courts for corrupt deals two decades later) and his property magnate cronies, 'undesirable' social groups had been edged out to the margins of the metropolis. For Manu, it was a European version of apartheid. Apartheid-lite.

Mano Negra's idea was a simple one but it had enormous resonance, not least in the media, to whom the *Caravane des Quartiers*, as they christened the tour, was irresistible. Apart from a genuine desire to go to where their poorest fans were, and to show solidarity with oppressed communities, it was another highly effective alternative marketing strategy, grabbing the headlines and shaking up public opinion.

A TV announcer on a news clip included in the *Pura Vida!* DVD nailed it, in a statement that might have been scripted by the band, when he said, 'some groups await their audience in big venues like the Zenith, but Mano Negra prefer to go to their fans. The band has refused to give in to showbiz, and they were welcomed in the *banlieues* like prodigal sons. The concerts were sold out and the organisers had never seen such success. There was no trouble, and soon there was no stage or audience, just one big huge fiesta. They are anti-stars who don't chase fame. They may be news in New York and Tokyo, but they remember their friends in the suburbs.'

As happened on the South American tour, the eclectic mix of influences in Mano Negra's music was one of the reasons for the success of their invasion of the *banlieues*, which a close friend of the band called Walli was heavily involved in organising. The overall tour coordinator, Madani Kherfi, later commented on the difficulty of organising rock gigs in the suburbs; 'The audience here is more into rap and rai, but although Mano Negra played rock there was such a mix of rhythms and styles that they found a way in that no other rock band could have found.'

The tour hit fifteen different venues, starting at Nanterre in April 1991, and then moving on to Saint-Denis, Créteil, Champs-Sur-Marne and Montreuil. The whole project was a palpable hit and, as the TV announcer noted, the stage was invaded every night by the audience, encouraged by Manu who seemed hell-bent on breaking down the barri-ers between the band and their fans. 'When people rushed the stage it was the best,' recalls trombonist Pierre 'Krøpöl' Gauthé. 'It was a blast, a huge party.' He was glad he wasn't a guitarist, who needs to keep a constant eye on his calibrated pedal positions. 'It was OK with a trombone. It's easy to move and, if anything happens, it doesn't cost much, anyway.'

The increasing mayhem at Mano Negra shows did encour-age the band to hire their own security outfit, as conven-tional security firms were unused or unwilling to deal with the chaos (or the Chaos). They found a bunch of Parisian ex-Black Panthers dubbed Les Buffalos who proved adept at light-touch crowd control. 'We have no problem mixing it up,' Manu said at the time. 'We want to get in the audience, we want them onstage and all that we ask is that people respect our gear.' It was the opposite extreme to the hard-nosed military control of the Iggy Pop tour and, if some equipment was occasionally trashed, then Manu and the band considered it worth the aggravation.

A reflective Manu, on tour in 1990.

With their policy of constantly jamming and giving improvised performances, anywhere and everywhere, Mano Negra were adept at playing with almost anyone. A month after the Caravane des Quartiers, they found themselves playing with the Urban Dance Squad at the Transbordeur Festival in Lyons. Silvano Matadin of the Urban Dance Squad captures something of the long-lost, almost millennial fervour of the times: 'We were dreaming of bringing different cultures together, a new generation, a new energy. La Mano was the only European band who could express this kind of energy. It was something really positive. We were busy with the revolution and I was standing on the barricades.'

The band also played plenty of benefit gigs during this period, the most memorable in May 1991, when they were asked to support a large group of homeless people who were camped out on Place de le Réunion in the 20th arrondissement, after being evicted from nearby houses. Someone at UNESCO, the United Nations cultural wing, recklessly offered the band their grand and bureaucratically drab Parisian conference space for the show. Beforehand, there was a plea from the stage not to damage the hall, which was stuffed with desks, tables and assorted electronic equipment. But in vain: 2,500 Mano fans pogoing like dervishes were never going to leave a place like that untouched. It looked like it had witnessed the passage of a tornado, much to the consternation of the well-meaning but naïve employees of UNESCO.

Mano Negra were polarising French public opinion. For all those supportive fans and fellow believers who thought the UNESCO gig was a high-spirited event that just got a little out of control, there were plenty of others who increasingly saw the band as their worst nightmare: a bunch of highly undesirable anarchists, subversives, disrespecters of property and friends of dirty immigrants. The racist anti-immigrant Front National party of Jean-Marie Le Pen were in the ascendant and Mano Negra made excellent hate figures for the rabid right.

This feverish atmosphere formed the backdrop to a veritable media storm that engulfed Mano Negra's huge outdoor concert at La Défense, the largest purpose-built business district in Europe, full of shiny mirrored office blocks, that had been built in the 1970s and 1980s at the end of a grand axis that started in Palais du Louvre and joined up the Place de La Concorde, the Champs-Elysée and the

Arc de Triomphe in one straight line of urban pomp and circumstance. The *cité* at La Défense was named after the iconic statue built in 1883 commemorating the resistance of Parisians in the Franco-Prussian War.

The concert became a hot political story. The right-wing mayor of the district, Charles Ceccaldi Peynaud, tried and failed to get the concert banned before announcing he would be hiring a riot squad and 750 extra police. He then appeared on TV to announce that his measures were 'the victory of order over the possibility of disorder'. Peynaud also claimed that Jack Lang, President Mitterrand's controversially flamboyant culture minister, who had sanctioned the show, was someone that 'prefers chaos'. Lang shot back with the argument that many similar concerts had taken place all over France without incident. Manu also said his piece on TV: 'the bigger show of strength from the authorities and the more cops there are, the more likely they are to provoke violence,' a view he would later take about other risky ventures.

Santi recalls that the La Défense concert was on the TV news every fifteen minutes. 'There can't have been anyone in the backwoods of France who didn't know we were putting on a concert. We were working with Royal de Luxe and wanted fireworks and a circus aspect to the show. We wanted it to be huge.'

And it was. When Mano Negra hit the immense stage, there were 20,000 people on the steps of La Défense and about 35,000 behind them, further down the esplanade. Despite the media hysteria, everything went peacefully. As they were about to board a boat for South America, the band knew that it would be their last concert for several months in Europe. What they didn't know was that it would also be also Mano Negra's last ever major gig in France.

If the band was in danger of becoming 'normal' and stuck on the album–tour–album–tour treadmill, their next move – the Cargo Tour – threw all such thoughts overboard. Instead of setting out on the long, hard slog of international promotion in the capital cities of Europe and America following the release of *King Of Bongo* – as their manager, label and agent were demanding of them – Mano Negra decided to disappear on a boat to South America for four and a half months.

By getting away from the intense routine they had slipped into, Manu also hoped that the trip might help heal whatever tensions were simmering between band members. That first trip to South America had been an inspiration to Manu, a personal El Dorado. The continent had become – as one of Manu's French biographers, Souad Belhaddad, put it – 'his box of tricks', a richly fertile source of ideas.

As well as the flourishing of alternative rock, the 1980s had seen a parallel blossoming in France of other unorthodox art forms, especially alternative circus and performance. The French group Archaos were close friends of Mano Negra and had been re-inventing the moribund arts of the circus with their juggling chainsaws, motorbike and punk aesthetics. There was a parallel scene in Barcelona, spearheaded by the radical theatre group La Fura dels Baus, who were breaking down barriers between performer and audience with verve and frequent violence – throwing flour, water, offal or fireworks into the crowd with nerve-fraying frequency. Another theatre company posed as tourist guides and took unwary punters around the local laundrettes and slums in a glossy bus. It was subversive, funny and often spectacular.

For Manu, these new anarchic performance troupes challenged the staid conventions of live rock music. However radical your rhetoric, and even if you allowed fans onstage or dropped slogans like 'No more heroes' in interviews, rock itself was in many ways reactionary and conservative, both in the fossilised separation of star and audience and in terms of its sound. Of course, Mano Negra had come up with fertile variations on the usual rock recipe, with their spiced-up Latino percussion and brass, but that alone wasn't enough.

Manu saw a kindred soul in the alternative street theatre troupe Royal de Luxe. After starting life in 1979 in a squat in Aix-en-Provence, in 1984 Royal de Luxe moved to Nantes, where they performed in markets and train stations, doing shows like *J'ai Fait de la Publicité Urbaine,* a grotesque parody of the banality and excesses of advertising. They would build giant puppets and perform shows to a soundtrack of old washing machines, Hoovers and breaking crockery or homemade fireworks. They generally amazed and provoked passing members of the public, eliciting interest and horrified fascination among sections of the population usually untouched by the more conventional arts. Royal de Luxe's visionary founder, Jean-Luc 'Coco' Courcoult, was someone Manu regarded highly: 'Of all the people, artists or groups we met on our long tours, Royal de Luxe were the ones we felt closest to and the ones we envied the most.'

While on tour in the south of France, on a particularly insane night, Manu and the band hooked up with the theatre company at the Feria de Nîmes. 'The security guys were complete fascists,' Manu recalls. 'We were at the soundcheck and one guy with a dog said to me, "Tomorrow you are going to be the breakfast of my dog." That was my welcome onstage.' Manu complained to the promoters about the aggression of the security staff, telling them that they had to cancel the show or find another security crew, otherwise there would be a fight. 'They answered that there would be no problem. Of course, there was a big fight. There were 30,000 people in the audience, most of them drunk. Bottles were smashed; it was a mess, a real riot. There were only ten of us but some others helped out. It was like in a film.'

Afterwards, surprisingly unscathed, the band went to a party downtown, where they met up with the members of Royal de Luxe. 'One guy, really tough, an anarchist, smashed a girl's camera because she was filming and Garbancito saw what happened. He got upset because you don't smash a lady and there was another fight between us and the theatre guys, which ended up on the street. In the end we met Coco in a bar at six in the morning, completely drunk and said to him, "We should do things together," and he said "Bullshit! You have no imagination."'

Coco waxed lyrical about his latest, greatest project, to adapt an old cargo boat, sail in it to South America and

play in ports, presenting Royal de Luxe's vision of the entire history of France, to coincide with the 500th anniversary
of the arrival of Christopher Columbus. Manu was suitably
impressed with the lunacy and ambition of this grandiose
scheme: 'About a year later, Coco got in touch and asked, "Are
you ready for the story of the boat?" I said, "Of course." Coco
is totally crazy, but he's a genius.'

Having spent over a decade living in a squat and producing
shows for nothing, Coco had managed, after several years
of cajoling and charm, and a brilliant media campaign, to
persuade public bodies in France to back his scheme to the
tune of several million francs. The Mayor of Nantes provided a 10,000-square-metre hangar and there was substan-
tial backing from the *Agence Française d'Action Artistique*
(AFAA). The company started to adapt the cargo ship, building, as if on a film lot, a life size facsimile of an entire Nantes
street, complete with a *boulangerie, tabac, boucherie* and *café*,
in the bowels of the boat's cargo hold. Mano Negra came and
helped out with the building, having fun driving tanks and
yielding flame-throwers. This was the heyday of generous
and grandiose state sponsorship of the arts in France, before the rise of the health and safety culture and men with
clipboards, who would have taken one look at the whole mad
enterprise and closed it down.

The show, modestly entitled *La Véritable Histoire de France*
(The Real History of France), featured a series of vignettes
which included Roman centurions and Gallic peasants, Nor-
man adventurers, Napoleon's retreat from Moscow in simu-
lated snow, and excerpts from both world wars. There were
moments of poetry too: a Montgolfier hot-air balloon and
cannons which fired off thousands of love letters.

The plan was for the boat to dock in Caracas, Cartagena,
Santa Domingo, Havana, Rio de Janeiro and Montevideo,
before ending up with a big parade in Buenos Aires. Bernard
Batzen, who felt the tour could be disastrous for Mano
Negra's career prospects, wasn't keen at all and negotiated
a compromise. The band would play at the main cities of the

The Real History of France, presented by Royal de Luxe.

tour and fly back in between for a series of shows he had set-up, with considerable difficulty, in assorted bullrings around Europe, a concept both he and the band thought sufficiently unorthodox. His Plaza de Toros tour would promote the album and launch the band up onto the next level.

However, Manu eventually came to see Batzen to say the band wanted to stay on the boat for the entire four-and-a-

half-month tour. Batzen found himself in an impossible position and decided to resign as manager. 'As an experience, as
individuals, I understood why they wanted to do it,' Batzen
reminisced in a coffee shop in London in autumn 2010. 'But
I was their manager and I thought that the whole thing was
commercial suicide. I thought I had better bow out before I
fell out with them. I left on good terms and I still see most of
the band socially, and sometimes even work with them.'

King Of Bongo had sold around 350,000 copies, which was
respectable enough, but Batzen was sure it would have been
a million-seller if they had been willing to promote it by touring in Europe. However, he adds, ruefully, that it was possible that he and Virgin were wrong about the whole idea. By
following his instinct, Manu and the band became figures of
legend in South America and built up a huge audience that
was to stand Manu in good stead in his later solo career. This
fame and success also meant that Manu didn't have to slog
around the States when he finally decided to go back there. In
places with a large Hispanic population, like Brooklyn, Texas or the West Coast, Mano Negra's fame in Latin America
meant there was a ready-made audience. And, in countries
like Mexico, Colombia and Argentina in particular, Manu still
has a fanatical following dating back to his Mano Negra days.

When they got to Nantes, the band spent time working as
dockers and navvies rather than musicians, loading the boat,
painting, fixing things up. For some this was a welcome res-
pite from non-stop touring. Antoine in particular, who as a
teenager loved nothing better than taking apart motorbikes
and putting them back together, enjoyed the change. The
cargo ship was loaded with its own stage and lighting equipment, so that the tour would enjoy maximum autonomy and
shows could be performed almost anywhere.

Mano Negra and Royal de Luxe were joined by the dance
company of Philippe Découflé and the marionnettes of
Philippe Genty. A Grand Parade in Nantes was planned to
give the whole nautical caravan an extraordinary send-off.
Tom, Philippe, Manu and Jo dressed up as First World War

foot soldiers and had prepared some military songs to perform during the parade. Coco's critique of this initiative was blunt: 'I loved your drive and the effort you put in – but you guys really sucked. We'll have to rework it.'

The Cargo ship set sail one bright morning in April 1992. It had been christened *Melquiades*, after the gypsy-magician character in *One Hundred Years Of Solitude*, the novel by the great Colombian author, and Chao family friend, Gabriel García Márquez. Melquiades, with his restless travelling and hustling and mysticism, has more than a little in common with Manu. Márquez wrote that his hero had 'an Asiatic look that seemed to know what was on the other side of things'.

The boat steamed westwards and the band relaxed for the first time in years, watching the flying fish and dolphins, drinking *cachaça* (sugar-cane spirit) and smoking joints. After the manic speed of touring, they were happy enough to be trapped on the boat as it crossed the Atlantic at a stately pace. A couple of weeks later they sailed into Caracas, Venezuela, for the start of the adventure. A massive crowd of 120,000 attended the spectacle and goggled at the theatrics, the dancers, the puppets and, last but not least, Mano Negra, who finished the evening playing to their biggest crowd yet. And Jo got promoted to General in Coco's show.

The ten-day stopover in Caracas gave Manu time to wander about town, talk to locals in the *barrios* and get a feel of the place and its people. Often, a few of the band would give impromptu concerts in the poorer neighbourhoods, either unplugged and acoustic or hooked up to portable amplifiers. 'A Bob Marley song was like a passport,' Manu observed. 'Play something by him and the energy changes. They treat you differently.' At the next stop, Cartagena, on the Atlantic Coast of Colombia, the first person on board to welcome the band was Gabriel García Márquez himself, who marvelled aloud at how brilliant it was to bring an entire street from Nantes across the Atlantic, and then commented to Manu: 'You were a pain in the neck at the age of four, and you still are.'

With no European tour to fly back to, the band took advantage of the ship's stopovers to do concerts further inland:

Mano Negra set sail for South America on the Cargo Tour

Bogotá in Colombia, Mexico City, and Belo Horizonte in the fertile centre of Brazil. If anything, it was those gigs without the spectacular theatrics of the full-blown Cargo performance, and the numerous impromptu performances in the unlikeliest corners of South America's cities, that built up an enormous capital of goodwill for the band and for Manu himself.

It was also a very rich experience. Manu and the band were picking up musical ideas but also expanding their minds politically and socially. Their subversive reputation preceded them and fellow radicals were always sure to seek them out. Tom recalls activists working for the rights of indigenous Indians coming to visit Mano Negra in their hotel in Mexico City. The meeting had an enormous impact. When the Zapatista movement emerged over the next couple of years, with its 'spokesperson', the charismatic and masked Subcomandante Marcos, Manu became one of its most famous supporters.

That was all in the future, but an important seed had been planted. The opening track on the next – and last – Mano Negra studio album, *Casa Babylon*, which eventually came out in 1994, was called "Viva Zapata" and was to feature the chant *'El pueblo, unido, jamas seras vencido'* ('The people united, can never be defeated') over a funky groove.

The boat stopped on Cuba at Havana and Santiago de Cuba. It was the first time any of Mano Negra had ever visited the island and the experience proved significant for several members of the band, especially Manu. Jo recalls Jako hiring a car, scoring some magic mushrooms and smooching by the sea with 'a Secret Service chick'. Tom met the musicians who were to become the core of his adventurous post-Mano Negra electro-latino band P18. Antoine built some links that he developed in his later career as a producer with Radio Latina and Radio Ciudad Havana.

Manu had finally reached the country which he had often heard his communist-leaning parents speaking about, and where, according to his father Ramón, he had ancestral links. At the time Cuba was in the worst of the so-called 'Special Period'. After the collapse of the Soviet Union, the Russians, who had been supporting the country with subsidised oil and other essentials for the past two decades, pulled the plug and Cuba found itself on the verge of collapse. At one point the entire country ran out of money. Even in good hotels there was often hardly any food – a ham and cheese toasted sandwich if you were lucky – though Manu still found much to admire there.

Manu is less partisan to any particular ideology, and more pragmatic, than his father, but having seen the tough *barrios* of Colombia, he found that Cuba, in comparison, had much to be said for it. 'Go to another country in South America first, so you can compare it,' he suggests. 'Live for a month in the *favelas* of Havana and then live for a month in the *favelas* of

Bogotá and see which you prefer.' He claims that he's not a
Fidelista, and, in his view, the Castro regime has made plenty
of mistakes. 'But also victories,' he adds by way of qualifi-
cation, 'and you can't ignore that part. There isn't free expression but you risk jail or being killed if you oppose the
government in Colombia. There are no paramilitary groups
in Cuba. They don't kill street children, or throw you out of
hospitals if you can't pay.'

The free education system, and particularly the generous
free courses for foreign medical students, impressed him.
So did his visit to the Film School set-up outside Havana by
Gabriel García Márquez. 'He is considered the best writer in
South America,' Manu explains, 'and he supports the regime.
He set-up his school in Cuba, which is one of the best cinema
schools in the world, because if he had set it up in Colombia
it would only be for rich people. In Cuba it's all free.'

Manu also encountered the Afro-Cuban religion of Santeria, a hybrid system of worship and belief that mixed African
gods or orishas with Catholicism. Nearly all the musicians
Manu met wore beads of different colours, which showed
their allegiance to one orisha or another. Because the slaves
were forbidden to worship their African deities, they would
find their equivalent Catholic saints, and so these two disparate religions became entwined. The fearsome African god
of healing, Babalu Aye, for example, became associated with
San Lazaro or Lazarus, who rose from the dead. Lazaro's
saint's day, on 17 December, is also the day of Babalu Aye,
when thousands of followers walk or sometimes crawl to
the El Rincon church outside Havana in penitence, offering
rums or cigars to Lazaro.

Santeria is a very musical religion. Each orisha has its
own rhythm that is played on the sacred *bata* drums, and
devotees will be more susceptible to the rhythms of their
own orisha than that of any other deity. Sometimes they go
into a healing trance, triggered by those rhythms. Generally,
the religion is favoured by Cuba's poor black population
but many musicians, notably the much-loved diva Celina
González, are followers, as are a number of intellectuals. The

Communist Party in Cuba had discouraged Santeria, but at the time of Manu's visit there was something of a thaw in its anti-religious position.

Variants of Santeria can be found elsewhere like Haiti and Brazil, where it is called *Candomblé*. Manu became fascinated with these Afro-Catholic religions in the years following his visit to Cuba in 1992, and was later initiated into Candomblé in Brazil. While temperamentally suspicious of conventional churches and their hierarchies and hypocrisy, this magical, healing, musical expression of the marginalized, appealed to Manu's spirit.

From Cuba, the *Meliquiades* sailed on to Brazil, where they staged performances in Fortaleza, a modern city with skyscrapers, and on the beach in Ceara in the Northeast (where, years later, Manu's son was brought up). The by now ragged troupe of musicians and performers put on an explosive show in Salvador in Bahia, the old, atmospheric Brazilian capital and vibrant centre of black culture. Next stop was Rio de Janeiro, which Manu has often declared his favourite city in the world. 'It's the only place in the world where, if you walk into a bar at midnight playing a drum, they complain when you stop two hours later,' he claims.

The visit of the *Melquiades* was timed to coincide with a parade for the opening of the Rio Earth Summit, a global ecological forum sponsored by the United Nations, which made minor progress with the ratification of a climate change convention that preceded the Kyoto Protocol. Other issues on the agenda, however, such as fighting poverty and respecting indigenous rights got almost nowhere.

Protesters present at the Earth Summit included Jello Biafra, ex-lead singer of Californian punk band The Dead Kennedys and a dedicated green activist, who made a guest appearance at the Mano Negra gig. With anthems like "California Über Alles", the Dead Kennedys had been the closest thing that the USA ever got to The Clash or Mano Negra, before the band disintegrated into bitter quarrels over songwriting rights and whether their music should be used for corporate ads for the likes of Levi's jeans.

The story of the Cargo Tour spawned its own graphic novel by David Lorapido, 'A Perilous Adventure'.

Despite being the main lyricist and lead vocalist, Biafra had lost a court case and was no longer able to use the name of the band. (Manu should have perhaps paid closer attention to the story, as a similar fate was to befall him.) Biafra was a key figure – part clown, part guru of American punk. He told Mano Negra that he'd just come from a demonstration involving 15,000 people and had made his own banner, which he proceeded to unfurl onstage. 'Bush is an Eco Wimp', it read. He explained that President Bush, George W.'s father, was 'chickenshit' before launching into visceral versions of The Clash's "I Fought The Law" and the Dead Kennedy's immortal anthem "Too Drunk To Fuck". The heaving, superheated Rio crowd had to be cooled down with fire hoses.

Rock music in South America still had a radical edge, having been subjected to all kinds of harassment and abuse for decades. The Mayor of Medellín in Colombia lost his job after allowing a rock festival to take place in the city. In Mexico, rock was effectively banned for a decade after 1971. In Cuba, the *nueva trova* singer Silvio Rodríguez was fired from his official job after declaring that the Beatles were a major influence. And in Brazil, singers like Gilberto Gil and Caetano Veloso went into exile after their Tropicalia movement was hounded both by the military dictatorship and left-wingers who considered their music an imperialist invasion. According to the book *Rockin' Las Americas,* during Argentina's 'Dirty War' (1976–82) 'police routinely disrupted concerts and beat up rock followers for the sole offence of gathering to listen to music considered threatening to the military regime.'

By the time Mano Negra's Cargo Tour hit the continent a decade later, however, rock was being 'decriminalised' and the authorities were showing greater tolerance towards it than ever before. But there was still a real sense of the subversive quality surrounding rock music, unbelievable as that might seem in the current era of bland TV talent shows, branded rock bands and corporate-friendly festivals.

This was the context behind the outrage caused by Mano Negra in Argentina. After a visit to Uruguay, the Cargo Tour's last port of call was Buenos Aires at the beginning of July, where the most notorious incident of the whole Mano Negra story took place. On a TV show called *La TV Ataca,* the presenter Mario Pergolini asked Tom Darnal to define anarchism. Obligingly, Tom proceeded to get up, knock over the camera and storm out of the studio shouting *'C'est de merde. Vive l'anarchie!'* (It's all shit! Long live anarchy!).

Manu was still in Uruguay when this outrage occurred. The rest of the band had gone to Buenos Aires by plane without him. He arrived in Buenos Aires on the *Melquiades* and saw what he thought was a welcoming committee from the French Embassy down on the docks. Instead of welcoming him, however, the diplomats told him that Mano Negra had to leave Argentina immediately. 'They didn't want people like us in the country and our plane was ready,' Manu remembers. 'They advised us that we shouldn't go down into the streets because we had offended the Argentinian people and they were going to kill us. They said we would never be allowed back and our career in Argentina was over. But ten minutes later, I was in the harbour and some dockers came to me and asked me if I was the guy from Mano Negra, and they said they loved the band. When I talked to Tom, he said everyone was stopping him to congratulate him on the street.'

Just as the Sex Pistols' liberal use of swear words on Bill Grundy's British TV show had propelled them to into the tabloids and the national consciousness back in 1976 – 'The Filth and the Fury' was the infamous frontpage headline in the *Daily Mirror* – so the Mano Negra TV incident launched Mano Negra skywards in Argentina. The band, and Tom Darnal in particular, woke up the next morning to find themselves famous.

The Cargo Tour had been a success in Manu's estimation. The brilliant and spectacular entertainment on the boat, the band's exhilarating performances, firing on all cylinders, and the many life-changing contacts and inspirations, matured everyone in the band, musically, politically and spiritually.

However, the strain of such an exhausting adventure had also been enough to provoke open rebellion and the first defections from the band. Antoine had loved the technical work but was disillusioned with all the ego-tripping that came increasingly to the fore, despite all the talk of no more heroes. 'I felt almost more at home with Royal de Luxe,' he said. 'It was a good feeling, because I was getting sick of the band. I took advantage of the situation to make a switch and become a mechanic. I was happy to get my hands dirty again.' He had decided to leave the band.

Jo Dahan was the next to go. He'd always been the most purist member of Mano Negra, politically speaking, and had never wanted to sign to a major label in the first place. He joined the Wampas, whose biggest subsequent hit, ironically, was a tune called "Manu Chao", which reached the French top 20 in 2003. Its lyric went 'If I had Manu's Chao's wallet, I'd take a holiday in the Congo'.

A band on the brink of implosion: Daniel Jamet, Jo Dahan, Philippe 'Garbancito' Teboul and Manu Chao.

Daniel Jamet also decided to call it quits, partly because he was shocked by the death of Helno, the lead singer of Mano Negra's friends and rivals Les Négresses Vertes, from a drugs overdose. Shortly before Helno died, he met up with Daniel and said, 'I have everything I should need to be happy, but I'm miserable.' Daniel empathised. Life was too short to be miserable in a band in which he felt he wasn't an equal part.

The tension between the collective rhetoric and the reality of Manu's leadership was always going to be tricky for everyone to live with and accept. Manu, while egalitarian in principle, was unwilling to compromise artistically. 'If you have a guitarist that wants to experiment with his fuzz box onstage when that isn't something you rehearsed,' he told Jackie Berroyer, 'that creates a problem. Someone had to have the artistic vision.' And friction resulted from the fact that the media naturally tended to focus on Manu in interviews, not least because he was highly articulate and an accomplished interviewee. Manu claims he encouraged the others to do more media chores. 'But, in fact, they didn't actually volunteer much, although they still complained about it.'

Some members of the band were annoyed that Manu seemed to contradict himself on a regular basis. Tom Darnal quotes the example of Manu refusing to talk to the conservative press or media, but at the same time loving the idea of doing the music for a Brazilian *telenovela*, the hugely popular soap operas that gripped Latin America. The companies making these *telenovelas* were right-wing media conglomerates like Globo. But, according to Tom, the splits also boiled down to a simple human fact – 'We just got fed up with each other.'

It was the beginning of the end of Mano Negra. 'It all started with everyone sharing the same goals, and the same direction,' Manu explained twenty years later. 'But you end up compromising with what you want to do and what the others want to do – and the band were all strong characters. If you compromise a bit, you can accept that, but there has to be a limit to compromise.' Another growing problem was more personal. 'As time went on, more of the band became attached and some had become fathers and family men. Three of us were single and still wanted the rush,' Manu says. 'But it was natural for the others to have different priorities.' Bernard Batzen has his own explanation: 'Manu is an artist twenty-four hours of every day. Most of the other musicians were part-timers compared to him.'

The tension wasn't helped by the fact that there was a new album to do. *Casa Babylon*, Mano Negra's last opus, was never going to be a straightforward piece of work and the tortuous process involved in its creation is evident in that it was recorded in numerous different studios in France, Germany, the States and Argentina. There was a silver lining, however; the album is reckoned to be Mano Negra's greatest, both by the critics and the band itself.

What happened to the Cargo boat? The Nantes street was reconstructed at a museum in Normandy, while the boat was sold to Greek shipbuilders to transport materials for the reconstruction of Beirut. Meantime, South America was calling again. Coco and Manu had dreamed up an even greater and crazier scheme.

CHAPTER 7:
PRÓXIMA ESTACIÓN –
VIOLENCIA

'We're not going to make politics; we just want to give something free for the people.'

Manu Chao

Colombia, November 1993. 'The guerrillas wouldn't shoot a bunch of clowns, would they? I mean, where's the propaganda value in that?' Manu was praying his intuition was right. They had been offered protection by the army, but Manu had turned it down. Then, four hours outside of Santa Marta, a group of masked men with AKA sub-machine guns held up the train. They were hardened men, trained killers, who were used to fighting the army and ambushing military patrols, but on this occasion it was difficult to say which party was the most shocked. The guerrillas were confronted by a train pulling twenty-one carriages, full of a hundred unwashed punks and hippies, assorted other vagabonds and, as their protection against slaughter, a handful of clowns.

There was also a cage wagon for Roberto, the giant metal flame-throwing dragon (or possibly iguana, no one was sure about that); a yeti wagon, which unleashed snowstorms; a museum wagon full of frozen sculptures; and a fairground wagon. Other wagons housed a tattoo parlour set-up by Tom

Darnal, a studio for the Colombian broadcaster Caracol Radio, who were one of the sponsors of the trip (the guerrillas eyed Caracol's satellite dish with great interest), and a performance stage for the musicians. The ice sculpture idea only worked sporadically because some *narco-traficantes* had stolen a truck containing a large ice-making machine. Having no clue what to do with it, they later dumped it in a ditch.

After plenty of confusion, and an intervention by Manu, who explained that the whole idea of this caravan on rails was to put on free shows for the people, the guerrillas let the train pass, even offering to take over from the clowns as tour security for the rest of the trip.

One of the passengers on the train was Manu's father Ramón Chao, whose evocative memoir of the trip was published under the title *The Train of Fire and Ice*. Ramón felt his paternal presence might magically protect his offspring. 'As long as I was there, no harm would come to him,' he claimed, somewhat self-importantly. When he first asked Manu if he could be part of his son's latest adventure, Manu said that he wasn't the organiser but that Ramón could come along by all means. But could he try and make what he wrote more readable? 'You mustn't use too many literary references,' he told his father. 'Your last novel was too ornate. I couldn't finish it.'

There have been some legendary rock'n'roll train trips. Nigel Williamson summed up their history in *Songlines* magazine: 'The Grateful Dead and Janis Joplin once took a ten-day train trip across the Canadian prairies, stopping every night along the route to jam and drink the local saloons dry. Gram Parsons and the Flying Burrito Brothers undertook a similarly debauched coast-to-coast US train tour in 1969, landing their record company with a $100,000 tab from the bar and restaurant car. Yet there has surely never been a ride quite like the one Mano Negra took across Colombia in 1993.'

Initially, the train was Coco's idea. Flushed with the success of the Cargo Tour, the majordomo of Royal de

Luxe approached Manu with his latest scheme. It had been inspired by the time he'd spent time travelling in Colombia after the Cargo Tour. 'I saw train tracks everywhere but never trains,' Coco remembers. 'I asked about it at Bogotá central station. The engines still worked, but none of them ever left the marshalling yards. Hundreds of towns that had been served by trains in the past had been cut off, leaving them hostage to the army, drug traffickers and guerrillas. I told myself something needed to be done. But what? So, to make people talk about something other than terror in Colombia, I conjured up the idea of a train reconciling the two hereditary enemies – fire and ice.'

It turned out that the longest and most significant railway line that Coco and Manu could revive was the old Sun Express from Bogotá to Santa Maria, which passed through Aracataca, Márquez's birthplace. *One Hundred Years Of Solitude* is a fabulist's account of this town's history, a tragicomedy woven from the epic story of a local family, which opens with the line 'Many years later, as he faced the firing squad, Colonel Aureliano Buendia was to remember that distant afternoon when his father took him to discover ice.' This was a sign, Manu and Coco decided one stoned evening. It was written in the invisible book of fate. They would call their transport *The Train of Fire and Ice* – which also forged an elegant link with the cargo boat which had been named *Melquiades*, after the gypsy in Márquez's novel who brought ice to Macondo (his fictional name for Aracataca).

For Manu the idea was particularly potent. 'After touring there,' he explained, 'I realised in fact that there are two countries in South America. The big border is between the cities and the countryside. There are two universes, which are totally different. With the Cargo we went to all the big cities and with the Train, the idea was not to play the big cities but to play for the people of the deep-down country, which is another culture, another people.' The train with its vagabonds and gypsies wasn't going to stop at cities like Cali or Medellín, but at small places like Gamarra and

Bosconia. Meanwhile, it would give a publicity boost to the railways, which were increasingly under threat.

Initially, railways had been built in Colombia primarily for the transport of single products, linking the coffee-growing areas to the sea, for example. The United Fruit Company had its own railway to freight bananas from their huge farms to ports on the Caribbean coast. It had been impossible for the humble citizen to cross the country by rail for more personal and mundane purposes. Aware of this shortcoming, the government poured millions into developing an interconnected network between 1922 and 1934. But in the following decades, and especially under the dictatorship of Rojas Pinilla, 'an offensive against the Labour movement led to the dismantling of large state enterprises', according to Ramón Chao. Bus and truck companies, the domestic airline Avianca and other private companies emerged as savage competitors to the state railways. By the time of the Colombian train adventure, there were only 1,600 km of track left in use, and the authorities had allowed them to deteriorate to such an extent that derailments were commonplace. Ramón quotes the president of the rail company as saying that 'the average speed this year has risen to twenty-three kilometres an hour, and we've had 1,000 derailments'.

It took more than a year to prepare the *The Train of Fire and Ice*, with Coco, the 'irresistible' production manager Cati Benainous and Manu straining to convince the Colombians that the idea was feasible and searching high and low for backers. A decent tranche of seed money – 550,000 francs – was provided by AFAA, the French arts organisation directed by Jean Digne, who believed culture was to be found as much in the streets as the Paris Opéra, and had already backed the Cargo Tour in 1992.

For Manu this planning stage was just as fascinating as the actual trip itself. 'One village was run by guerrillas, another was paramilitary, so we had to say, "In six months we want to come and give a concert. Of course, we ain't gonna come if you're going to kill, kidnap or rape us." We told them we were musicians and clowns. "We're not going to make politics; we're not coming with the government. We just want to give something free for the people." So we had to negotiate all that.'

Manu remembers the advance guard, 'in a little car, on the train, with a few friends, like in a Western, going from village to village'. In each one 'there seemed to be so much violence daily. Within families it was like Yugoslavia, where one brother might be a paramilitary and another a guerrilla. In every village they seemed to burying somebody.'

The trickiest part, recalls Manu, was to explain to the Colombian authorities that they didn't want any soldiers on the train. 'The army wanted to put soldiers on the train for our security. We had to spend months explaining to them that our only security was for them not to come, because we had to be neutral. That was the only way to be safe. If they came, we'd be dead, it would be war.' In the end, there weren't any shootouts at the shows. 'That's the thing we are really proud of with this train. Everywhere we stopped, in every little place, for maybe one week, there was no war. Everybody partied instead.'

It took a couple of months to customise the train, and whoever happened to be around was expected to lend a hand. 'There were no roadies or technicians. Mano Negra was a democracy, so everyone had to join in,' recalls photographer Youri Lenquette. 'When I arrived, I thought I was going to take pictures. Instead I was given a hammer.' With only a fraction of the funding promised for the trip, a train that was only half railworthy and no guarantees they would get out alive, 'anyone with any sense wouldn't have tried, let alone gone ahead with it,' said Yenquette. 'But Manu had a dream.'

After a month with all hands to the wheel, the train left Bogotá on 15 November 1993, with a motley crew of around a hundred souls on board. It trundled along at about 15km an hour, and within a day it had its first derailment. At least the slow pace meant that the passengers could climb on the roof and take a piss into the air rather than in the insanitary toilets, though that was a trickier job for the women.

Manu 'the Jesuit' tried to impose some rules. First, no guns on board. Secondly, with the French media already running stories with sly headlines like 'French band take a line through Colombia', he also tried to ban drugs, but it was a losing battle in a country where coke was 3,000 pesos a gramme and the infamous *punto rojo*, the powerful ganja from Sierra Nevada, was also ridiculously cheap. It might have been a good idea, though. The drugs fuelled a pervasive sense of paranoia about the various armed factions whose territory they were encroaching on.

Even the most basic knowledge of politcial and guerrilla factions in this war-torn country would have required levels of sophistry beyond anyone on the train. Even Ramón, who was a well-informed and experienced political journalist, found it a challenge at times to work out who was who on the merry-go-round of death that spun bewilderingly all about them. The chief protagonist in the conflict was the FARC (Revolutionary Armed Forces of Colombia), which was founded in 1964 as a guerrilla offshoot of the Communist Party. Their political idealism was soon muddied by the need to raise cash, which they did by kidnapping and imposing 'revolutionary taxes', even on poor farmers. Many of its leaders were killed by hitmen in the employ of the big landowners who formed their own death squads with names like MAS (*Muerte a Secuestradore*s – Death to Kidnappers) and other paramilitary groups, often backed by the CIA and other foreign agencies.

The Colombian Army periodically tried to impose order, with decreasing results and increasing bloodshed. Into this confused and bloody situation came the *narco-trafficantes*, or *narcos* for short, the drug barons who had bought up large swathes of land on which to cultivate coca crops. Peasant farmers would sell cheap when confronted by this cauldron of violence, and then move away, adding to the overcrowding in the large cities. The *narcos*, of course, hired their own killers and maintained their own private armies.

If all this wasn't confusing enough, there were also many splinter groups, an alphabet soup of destruction: the PRT, the

Manu entertains a Colombian street kid on El Treno.

ELN, the EPL and the PP to name but a few, each with their own operational territory. There were vigilante groups with names like Vampire, Trigger, Alpha 83, some dedicated to eliminating street kids, others, such as the self-explanatory Death to Homosexuals, with more specific missions of violence. With grim irony, there was even a small paramilitary group called Mano Negra. And then there were freelancers, who belonged to no organisation, like the *sicarios*, teenage gunmen who would, for a minimal sum, shoot whoever their bosses had fingered.

In 1992, a film made by Víctor Gaviria in Medellín called *Rodrigo D: No Futuro*, told the story of ten teenage *sicarios* who ran errands for local drug barons. By the time the film was released, nine of its stars were dead, and the film's director feared for his life, declaring that the equivalent of US $50 was enough to get him killed. In Colombia, the punk slogan *'No Futuro'* was more than just the rallying cry of bored teenagers. It was simply, for too many, a statement of fact. Measured by its homicide rate, Colombia was the most dangerous country in the world. In Medellín, the murder toll was ten times that of Los Angeles. In the year before Manu's train trip, there had been 25,000 murders and 800 political assassinations in Colombia.

In this world turned upside down, where life was cheap, some of the big drug barons became popular folk heroes. Most notable among them was Pablo Escobar, who had spent some of his ill-gotten millions on building cheap housing and, on one occasion, handed out a thousand keys to a thousand lucky families in a single day. He also built schools and even a fabulous zoo, with free entry to the people, stocked with tigers, lions, rhinos and elephants, which had been flown in from exotic locations and housed in gilded cages. There was an ulterior motive, though. Elephant dung, when smeared on packages of cocaine, was apparently the most effective way of confusing police dogs. But, compared to most of the other actors in Colombia's violence, Escobar was seen as a man of the people. He was killed while Manu and his cohorts were on the train, and his death was mourned far and wide.

Ramón Chao's book *The Train of Fire and Ice* is subtitled *Mano Negra in Colombia*, but, as Manu points out, the subtitle was highly misleading. 'I blame the publishers rather than my father. The band was effectively finished by the time of the train trip. We'd spent a year setting up the project, and they only decided to come at the last moment, and even then most only stayed a few days for the first concert.'

According to Tom Darnal, the one other member of Mano Negra who stayed on board for the whole trip, Manu was hoping for a 'miracle'. He had no thoughts of pursuing a solo career at this point, far from it. The train trip was to be make or break, a kind of endurance test of the band's mettle and capacity to survive the most loaded odds. The trip was less well organised than the Cargo Tour, and had almost no money at its disposal, but if the band members were committed to Mano Negra they would come, or so Manu believed. In a sense, it was also a way for Manu to ask his comrades the question, 'How much do you love me?'

There were other musicians on the train who were possible new Mano Negra recruits, notably Fidel Nadal, a rapper the band had met in Argentina, who was to appear several times on Mano Negra's final, posthumous album *Casa Babylon*. There was Jean Michel Gambit (also known as Gambeat), the giant, friendly bass player from The French Lovers, who played *trashguinguette*, a kind of unplugged French punk music hall mixed with formulaic rock'n'roll, which sounded as if it had been played without mics or amps in bars and dance halls throughout France and arranged by a psycho.

Like Les Casse Pieds, The French Lovers were alumni of the school of the Paris metro. 'We met hanging around the neighbourhood. We used to talk, play music and then crash at six in the morning at Mano Negra's office,' recalls Mano. 'I decided we had to bring The French Lovers along, especially as we didn't know if Mano Negra would come. I was determined about that and somehow we found some francs to make it happen.'

The first show was in Santa Marta, on Colombia's luminously green Caribbean coast. Five thousand people wandered from Philippe Mazaud's Ice Exhibition to the Light Tent via the Brazilian capoeira dancers who provided an exotic counterpoint. Tom Darnal set-up his tattoo parlour, and his most popular designs were Jesus and Roberto the Dragon, who was the biggest attraction of the whole *feria*, with his projector eyes, smoke-spewing nostrils and ten-foot-long jets of fire which were expelled over the crowd to the sound of a special theme tune written by Tom. The French Lovers played a set and when Xoumoul, their guitarist, cut his finger and needed stitches, Manu took his place.

Members of the public were always asking where to buy tickets, even though the show was free. But as crowd control swiftly became a pressing issue and unmanageable crushes built up at some attractions, it was decided to issue slips of paper which, in a parody of bureaucratic form-filling, were obtainable from the Office of Human Desires. Each applicant had to write down their passions or dreams for the future on the slips, which could then be handed in at the Ice Show as entrance tickets. A huge queue developed at the Office of Human Desires and local entrepreneurial types immediately started selling slips for 1,000 pesos. The written desires of the audience included winning the local beauty contest, or the lottery, or a motorbike, as well as the return of lost parents, the end of violence and Colombia winning the World Cup.

From the start the train had its stowaways – many of them lost street kids who boarded and refused to get off. In Santa Marta a black teenager called Rondelle, appeared onstage, dancing and singing with incredible panache, and then started drumming before rolling offstage. Manu befriended him and managed to find an organisation that helped young people to take him under their wing. He even thought about adopting Rondelle and bringing him back to France. But when Manu tried to contact him again, he had disappeared, and the charity had no idea what had become of him.

Mano Negra didn't play on that first night in Santa Marta but took to the stage the following evening. Gambeat took on bass duties and Fidel Nadal rapped in Spanish at machine-gun speed, providing a brilliant and novel counterpoint to Manu's baritone voice. Fans came from all over Colombia. Many had caught the band on the Cargo Tour and they treasured this unforeseen opportunity to see them again at this strange and wonderful *feria*, celebrating and dancing late into the humid night. Some new *Casa Babylon* material was premiered and the evening offered intriguing glimpses of a potential new direction for the band. But, from the band's point of view, the sound was terrible – there were problems with the backline and they couldn't hear what they are playing. And it turned out to be the last gig that Mano Negra ever played.

For several members of Mano Negra, the train trip was the last straw. Here was Manu dragging them into another quixotic scheme, for no money, in terrible conditions, as some kind of loyalty test. By the time the train trundled in to Márquez's birthplace of Aracataca, where the gypsy Melquiades had revealed his block of ice, a stop ironically billed as the climax of the whole trip, Santi, Philippe, Pierre and Jean-Marc, the trumpeter who had been brought in to replace Antoine, decided they were bailing out and going home. The defection of the drummer, percussionist and brass section was the irrefutable end of Mano Negra, even if some of them helped to finish *Casa Babylon* back in Europe.

The band who had revolutionised French rock died there in Aracataca, the birthplace of magic realism. It was a disaster for the train trip. They were the big draw. How were Manu and Coco going to appease the funders from AFAA, who happened to be present? Or the press? 'It's not serious if some of Mano Negra leave,' announced Cati, putting a brave face on the whole affair. 'Manu is staying and so are Tom and Fidel.' But no one was convinced.

There was a meeting to decide whether the Train would actually carry on with its journey. Ramón describes how the railway workers swung the argument. One of them, Diablito, put the case for continuing with sincere passion. 'You don't realise the hope this train brings to the villages we go through. It makes them dream of peace, of developing the country. Disappointing them will do a lot of harm. It would have been better not to start.'

So the train staggered on, through small towns like Bosconia, Barrancabermeja and Dorada, before returning to Bogotá, much to the appreciation of the locals. 'Imagine the ambience – it was crazy,' says Tom. 'Half the train was on coke, half the crew had left, the money ran out completely, Coco lost a bundle.' There was one Colombian whose job was to sit at the front of the train looking out for bombs. 'At certain points they thought a bomb would be likely, and we all had to travel in the last wagon.'

The conditions were atrocious. 'There was no chance to take a shower, no water, terrible hygiene, forty-degree heat and your clothes sticking to you,' Tom remembers. 'Sometimes you are pleased to remember such adventures in hindsight, but in the case of the train, actually, even to remember is painful.' So why did Tom stay on board when the other Mano Negra guys jumped ship? 'It's my character,' he explains. 'You go to the end unless you have a really good reason to leave.'

The end of the line for Mano Negra: Youri Lenquette's classic image.

Coco was hospitalised with an eye problem and most of the train-goers were afflicted with some kind of illness or other. But for Manu it was 'maybe the greatest adventure I ever had'. His and Coco's grandiose dream of reviving the railways in Colombia might have come to nothing. But the fact the train existed and got to the end without fatalities was a small miracle.

Back in France, there was still an album to finish. Manu wasn't going to let that slip. *Casa Babylon's* wild-style mix was more focused on Latin America, with large doses of reggae, the added raps of Fidel and pure rock'n'roll on tracks like the football terrace chant of "Santa Maradona", a paean to the great football demigod (or demon, if you happen to be English and remember the 'Hand of God' incident in which his hand-ball goal knocked England out of the 1992 World Cup).

Despite its fragmented gestation in different studios in the years leading up to and after the train trip, *Casa Babylon* was a great artistic leap forward. The sincere regret of Philippe and others is that the breakup of the band robbed them of the chance to perform the material live. 'It took three months to recover from the Cargo Tour. We should have stopped, taken some time off to think about it, maybe do nothing for a year after all the touring. But no one considered that option,' Philippe remembers. As for the train, 'It was a tough experience, crazy, but real. We all cried – I mean, we suffered.'

Partly as a result of Manu's experiences in South America, the songwriting on *Casa Babylon* was deeper and more mature. Unlike some of the other Mano Negra material, the songs still sound absolutely fresh and strong. On tracks like the mid-tempo "Señor Matanza", Manu, singing in Mexican Spanish slang over an implacable salsa-reggae groove and an insidious descending organ line, takes on the big, corrupt authority figures who own the town, the land, the bars, the *jineteras* (hookers) and have the power of life or death. Manu went back to Bogotá on his own to film a clip for the song, with the faithful François Bergeron, as ever, directing.

On "Sueño De Solentitiname" (Dream Of Solentitiname), Manu dreams of Guanajuato, Guatemala and Panama during a night of unrest, asking the 'beloved world' for a cure to his pain. On "Bala Perdida", people 'boil night and day on the avenue', seething with 'expensive cargo' and *'guajira* blood'. There are characters who reappear from earlier albums, like the little urban monkey who 'speaks his mind.' Then there's a track featuring Super Changó, the Yoruba God of Thunder, a key deity in Cuban Santeria and Brazilian Candomblé, reborn as a cartoon superhero – Batman from south of the border. Manu went on to develop this character in a story he used as a basis for *Clandestino*.

The album was described as 'a masterpiece of kinetic aural globalism' by Josh Kun, a writer specialising in *rock en Español*, who highlighted its use of samples, spoken-word snippets and atmospherics recorded on the road – all of which looked ahead to Manu's solo albums, *Clandestino* and *Próxima Estación: Esperanza. Casa Babylon* was a parent to those twin siblings, with Manu's hand firmly on the tiller. With Mano Negra in ruins, the album is often seen as his first solo work, to the annoyance of the other musicians who took part, though it's not a claim Manu ever makes himself.

While the band had disintegrated, Manu was in the studio every day. 'The others came and went,' he remembers. At times he did go off on his own, booking studios and paying for them himself if necessary. 'The band still owe me money for that,' he claims. A couple of tracks towards the end of the album, "La Vida" and "Sueño de Solentiname", were recorded in this way.

From Manu's point of view, with his work ethic and driven nature goading him on, and with the dysfunctional collective playing only an erratic role, it was up to him to bring the album to fruition by any means necessary. Tom, stalwart to the end, resented the fact that Manu would finish mixes without telling him. 'I'd start a tune and leave it and by the time I came in the next day it had become something else, a Manu song,' he recalls.

Nonetheless, Tom was responsible for injecting a valuable boost of energy: the opening of *Casa Babylon* is a storming track called "Viva Zapata", the first musical testimony to the new political movement of the Zapatistas. Tom had been in Mexico in January 1994 when the the Zapatista Army of National Liberation emerged out of the jungle in the Chiapas region of Mexico to occupy the important regional centre of San Cristóbal de las Casas. The Zapatistas were named after Emilio Zapata, the leading figure in the Mexican Revolution of 1910. Both Tom and Manu found their campaign inspiring and both became involved in the cause with its demands for indigenous land rights, political equality and self-government. Tom later spent a few weeks in the mountains in the Chiapas. 'They said they wanted a foreign person to look after a school far into the mountains in a small village and look out for planes.' Manu also sought out the Zapatistas out a couple of years later and ended up jamming with their charismatic leader Subcomandante Marcos, who always appeared in a mask to keep his real identity secret.

Something that appealed to Manu and Tom was the Zapatistas' style, notably the playful communiqués of Marcos, full of metaphors, jokes and poetry. Marcos was a postmodern media-savvy trickster. He styled himself Subcomandante because he deemed himself to be 'under the orders of the people' and rejected the idea that he was a leader.

'The Zapatistas were the first ones I came across who really explained the politics of globalisation to me, before the French intellectuals,' says Manu. 'And that the economy rules the world and politicians mean nothing. The Zapatistas have a good analysis of what modern society is and how it works. We felt very involved with them. Their messages were the exact same things I was thinking, and there aren't many examples of messages like that coming at you in the world. Also, they never said they were fighting for power, nor wanting to be president. They want dignity.'

Manu's support for the Zapatistas has continued ever since, both financially and otherwise. 'It was, like, finally there is someone we can trust,' he said. Marcos himself declared that 'Music holds roads that only the knowledgeable know how to

walk and builds bridges that bring worlds that otherwise you wouldn't even dream about, closer together.'

When *Casa Babylon* was released in May 1994, it went into the top 10 of the French album charts and was a minor hit across Europe. But with no live band to promote it, it was yet another missed opportunity for Mano Negra to go truly global. Nonetheless, while the album enjoyed only modest success in Europe, it had an electrifying impact in South America. Josh Kun attests to scores of bands who cite *Casa Babylon* as a major source of inspiration. In Mexico, particularly, it inspired a whole generation of bands, including Tijuana No!, Plastilina Mosh, Café Tacuba, Maldita Vecindad and El Gran Silencio. In Argentina, it galvanised established bands like Los Fabulosos Cadillacs. There were even rock venues on the continent, like the one in Córdoba, Argentina, described in the introduction to this book, who changed their name to Casa Babylon.

'The album has grown over the years into a sort of unofficial template for Latin American rockeros looking for models of New World collision,' wrote Kun. The Colombian philosopher Oscar Guardiola-Rivera, whose book *What If Latin America Ruled the World?* examines the region's growing influence on the international stage, said that, for him, as for a multitude of disaffected youth at the time, 'Mano Negra were our band more than any other. And Mano Chao was a visionary.' The shy boy from Sèvres had become the Subcomandante Manu of Latin rock.

Manu is well aware of *Casa Babylon's* far-reaching influence: 'It was something from outside that gave people permission, in a certain way. We were listening to the same things, and reading the same books. But the album showed that rock needn't be in English. It was a bridge between rock'n'roll and the folkloric.'

After *Casa Babylon*, there was only one other brand-new Mano Negra product that ever saw the light of day, although the intervening years have seen a slew of compilations and tribute albums. It was a book called *Mano Negra Le Boukin*, which was put together by Tom Darnal – a scrapbook of album covers, articles, newspaper clippings, playbills, all wrapped up in kitsch ethnography and erotica, in the distinctive Darnal style. 'I delayed finishing the book,' Tom says with a melancholy smile, 'because I knew, as soon as I had handed it in to the publishers, that was the end of the road. It was all over.' It is a wonderful and chaotic celebration of Mano Negra, well worth seeking out; a few of the scraps and photos have been included in this book.

If Manu's musical future seemed confused and unclear in 1994, things soon took a decisive turn for the worse. At several meetings of the Patchanka SARL 'board', the other members of Mano Negra turned on him – every single one of them. Manu well remembers Tom, his friend and fellow traveller for the past decade and half, alienated by the imperious treatment he felt he had received from Manu during the *Casa Babylon* sessions, saying, incredibly, 'you would be nothing without us.'

In contrast to the other 'real' families that various members of the band had started in recent years, Manu had come to believe that Mano Negra was his family, his band of musketeers who had taken on the world and almost won. He had invested five years of his life and every last joule of his energy and dedication in those friends and in the band of his dreams, France's potent answer to The Clash, and now those same friends sat around the table slicing him with their words. It felt as if the house which he had painstakingly built, piece by piece, was being dismantled. And what about all the jointly owned property, like the famous Mano Negra black hand logo? Manu was not allowed to use it. 'This was the original symbol I'd made in the basement in Sèvres, with my own hand, as a teenager,' he says, still deeply hurt by the memory. What about all the unused recordings? 'I had thousands of hours of studio recordings, tons of songs I recorded personally. I couldn't use any of them.'

The final, heart-breaking scene was played out by the band when they voted – democracy in action – that unless five members of the original band were involved in any future project, then the name 'Mano Negra' could never be associated with it. Manu answered with the terrible, Lear-like statement that 'If I can't use the name Mano Negra, I will never make any music ever again.'

And, at the time, he meant it. He felt cast out into the wilderness, betrayed by those closest to him. To make matters worse, his relationship with Anouk had also become merely platonic. The rumour on the train was that she was having an affair with Fidel. Manu and Anouk would work together again, but the romantic spark was gone. He found himself, aged thirty-five, horribly alone, his career over, in despair. Over the next few years, his wandering existence was often accompanied by depression and suicidal thoughts.

Manu's dark night had begun.

CHAPTER 8:
THE LOCO MOSQUITO

'A cow saved my life.'

Manu Chao, recalling a night in Rio

anu hit the road and hit rock bottom. 'I decided to end my life in Brazil,' he says. 'It really was a depression. It was very bad. Not that I wanted to kill myself, exactly, but I thought about it every day. It was my first thought of the day. That's the song "Dia Luna ... Dia Pena" on *Clandestino*. "Day of the moon, day of pain – with no reason". That's the terrible thing about depression, it's a sickness – you have to find a reason to live, *quick!'*

At his lowest point, Manu found himself in a bar in a shanty town – a *favela* – in Rio when a cow walked in. It was raining. 'I got face to face with this cow, which was lost like me. Just looking at the cow's eyes I felt good. There was something immensely tender in her eyes. After that I started to meet cows in very strange places, so I figured the cows wanted to say something to me. Since then I realise why cows are sacred in India. One day I will go to India to say thank you to them.'

Manu was in a strange, unbalanced state of mind. 'I was crazy and unable to make any decisions about my personal life or my professional life. But it turned out that to be so lost was also good because I was always recording – and *Clandestino* is the result of the recordings from this time. I didn't know I was making a record – it was pure therapy.'

Out of the chaos and madness, Manu's biggest record was born, even if he had no idea of that at the time. With his damaged ego, his debilitating conviction that his career was over, and his experimentation with drugs, Manu cast his net deep into the water of his subconscious and pulled out a masterpiece. 'The album came out of hundreds of projects that didn't work. It was a baby of those years lost in the century.'

When he was at his worst, his mother Felisa gave him some sage advice. 'She told me that for you, life is *pena*. But it's good to go to the end of life for one reason – curiosity. Even if it's hard.' One of Manu's greatest characteristics is an insatiable curiosity. The word 'curious' is a favourite of his.

The period from 1994 to 1997 was a lost weekend for Manu that ended up lasting three years ... and became a part of his mythology. 'He went missing-in-action ... an insurgent Parisian-Basque nomad who travelled the Americas without an identity,' as the writer and academic Josh Kun put it.

As part of the quest he took peyote in Mexico, became convinced that a witch had put a spell on him in Brazil and travelled down to Galicia on a motorbike with his father. He entertained children in the Zapatista villages in Chiapas. He trudged the streets of myriad cities. He found it impossible to stay in any one place for more than a couple of weeks. 'I had a bad addiction to travel,' he admits.

Contrary to what people around him predicted after the breakup of Mano Negra, what Manu missed most wasn't the performing, it was the travelling. 'With Mano Negra, I never spent more than three days in the same town in five years. It took me eight years to be able to stop in one place for more than a month. Wherever I went on the planet I had to leave, I felt claustrophobic. I couldn't make my life anywhere because everywhere I went my body needed the fix of another place. I didn't have a home for seven years. I had my things at my parents' place and always slept at friends' places.'

Even so, staying for a longer period of time in one place compared to the constant motion of touring in a band (when time contracted) was a revelation to Manu. 'I'm a shy guy.

I was so happy to be in the crowd and not be the one who goes up onstage and sings. You have to be sharp and very wise to get rid of the invitation of the conservative rock'n'roll circle bullshit. Every disco is more or less the same all over the world. But go around the train station or bus station and the central market, you can meet people and feel the city. The market is the place I really like.'

It wasn't only the end of Mano Negra that Manu was grieving; it was also the end of his long relationship with Anouk, the love of his life. 'It was the end of the band, the end of personal things, a thirty-something crisis, which maybe is normal enough, no?' Having been burnt by love – 'being in a band is also a question of love', he says – travelling was also a convenient way of avoiding become so again. "Trapped By Love" is the title of one of the songs on the album *Próxima Estación: Esperanza*, but which was written around that time. 'When you are Trapped By Love, so much in love with a girl and she says stop and everyone knows it, you are fucked!' is Manu's terse précis of the lyrics.

Manu wasn't the only one to go off the rails after the breakup of Mano Negra. 'It was a strange family story, a violent split,' remembers Frank Mahaut, the lighting guy who was very much part of the Mano Negra collective. 'Two brothers shouting at each other. Everybody became crazy. But, for the years we were together, it was my band. Afterwards it was hard. I tried to work with other bands but it was so boring in comparison. I became a junky for five years.'

Tom Darnal was also bruised and battered. 'When you are king of the world, what do you do after that?' His view of Manu's state of mind was that 'If you have good people around you, like Emmanuel de Buretel at Virgin, who believed in him, and enough money, you can go deep into your depression. If you don't, you can't permit yourself to go down'.

Although that might sound unsympathetic – Manu's black feelings were real enough – Manu himself has some sympathy with Darnal's point of view. 'One thing I came to respect was meeting people who had nothing, who had to look after a family, who retained their optimism and hope. They couldn't afford to get depressed; they hadn't got the time. So they were some of my best professors.'

These meetings with the lost and marginalised people that he met on his journeys through Europe, Africa and South America, the disenfranchised and dispossessed, many of them displaced by exile, migration and xenophobia, were essential to Manu's emerging vision. He became a poet and critic of a new globalisation that meant a playground for the rich, and freedom of movement for some, but increasing barriers and exploitation for the rest. Manu, of course, with money to buy plane tickets (the one genuine luxury for a man allergic to expensive hotels) was only too aware he belonged to the privileged. 'I met so many people who couldn't travel. I couldn't invite them to my home, even if I had one. They didn't have a passport, so there was an inequality in my friendships because of the bureaucracy.'

Even if Manu is exaggerating when he says that *Clandestino* was the result of a hundred different projects, his lost weekend was populated by numerous, mainly abortive, ideas. He thought about starting a circus in Rio. He began recording a techno album in Naples. He collaborated with bands in Tijuana and Brazil, and he jammed with musicians in myriad bars in at least three continents. He explored assorted political movements and found himself on a spiritual quest, particularly in Brazil and Senegal.

He had finally managed to build a promising career by the age of twenty-eight, but at thirty-three he felt as if he had slid on a snake all the way back to square one. As depressives go, he was a manic one. Rather than retreating into his shell and disengaging from the world, his appetite for the world cranked up to an almost frenzied level. He still had *Deprisa, Deprisa* ('Hurry, Hurry') tattooed on his arm.

Manu doesn't recall the exact, dizzying itinerary of those *loco mosquito* years under the radar, and it would be impossible to be exactly sure of precisely where he was at any particular moment, but there were numerous key moments in amongst the weeks and sometimes months that he based himself in one city or another.

PARIS 48.9°N 2.3°E

Manu's spent the immediate post-Mano Negra weeks back at square one, in Paris, a city he had been trying to escape from since he was a teenager. He jammed with Gambeat, the bassist from the Colombian train trip and avoided the other members of Mano Negra. Another close Parisian friend at the time was Aldo, a man after Manu's heart. 'He's an important man, a free man. He lives on the street, he has no clothes, no ID, no papers. We didn't really have a place to stay except for my parents' house. Gambeat and Aldo were my family in Paris.' They used to sleep regularly in the record company office, leaving early in the morning before anyone else arrived.

Aldo was someone even less concerned with material possessions than Manu, someone he could emulate. Furthermore, according to Manu, he was a visionary who had special powers. 'He predicted things like the economic crash exactly two years before it happened. He's extra lucid, that's for sure.' Gambeat, christened Jean Michel Gambit, was to be in all manifestations of Radio Bemba, Manu's post-Mano Negra outfit, and became a more level-headed influence.

LONDON 51.5°N 0.1°W

Manu had become more and more interested in techno, house and electronica, thanks in part to the influence of Tom Darnal. The context of this fascination was a brand-new dance movement, fuelled by the drug Ecstasy, that had had sprung up over the last few years, all over Europe but particularly in Britain. Inspired by the house music coming out of Detroit, 1988's 'Second Summer of Love' saw young ravers trancing in urban clubs like Shoom! in London and thousands of revellers dancing until dawn in fields in the middle of the countryside, at events with evocative names like Spiral

Gambeat, shirtless as ever. A veteran of the train tour, he remains a fixture in Radio Bemba. This photo, with Manu, was taken on the first Clandestino tour.

Tribe or Raindance. These young ravers linked up by means of the then-novel mobile phone, connecting with strangers as equals in a state of Ecstasy-fuelled bliss, to the sound of minimal, euphoric, pumping, four-to-the-floor house, techno and trance music, often pursued by the police.

The police's excuse was that they were cracking down on drugs and the illegal use of property, but there was a strong sense at the time that this movement was something subversive that was threatening to the established order. It had a star-free egalitarian ethos that appealed to Manu, even though it was soon commodified and star DJs and clubs like Ministry of Sound became highly profitable enterprises.

It was a moment where a youth music culture unified a whole generation with anti-authoritarian energy, and even if it was more hedonistic than political, Manu was fascinated. But musically, his experiments with electronic dance music never really gelled. In London, he had a brief musical fling with Leftfield, one of the emerging electronic dance groups, who later had a punk-electronica hit with John Lydon, the former Sex Pistols singer. A few aborted days in the studio, mostly hanging around, came to nothing.

NAPLES 40.8°N 14.25°E

In Naples, Manu's collaboration with the electronica band Kwanzaa Possee progressed far enough for a for it to earn a name, Treize à Table (Thirteen at the Table), after the lyrics of a Jerry Lee Lewis song. That old love of rock and roll still burned in Manu.

Thirteen proved to be an unlucky number for Manu and although the project was sufficiently promising for Emmanuel de Buretel from Virgin to come and investigate, it came to nothing. 'I was a little concerned about Manu,' remembers De Buretel. 'I knew he'd taken the break up of Mano Negra very hard, he seemed to have lost his confidence. But I also knew he had incredible energy and talent. But then in those years he went off the radar for months and months – then, as now, he hadn't got a mobile. You have to wait for him to contact you.'

BOGOTÁ 4.6°N 74°W

Over the next few years, in between his pinballing around Europe and Africa, Manu spent most of the time in the continent that had provided him with so much inspiration since the earliest days of Mano Negra. He went back to Bogotá to film a clip of two of the strongest tracks from the final Mano Negra album *Casa Babylon* – "Senor Matanza" and "Sueño se Solentiname". It was Manu's last duty for Mano Negra and he was in a dark state of mind, which wasn't helped by de Buretel's assertion that, had he been able to keep the name Mano Negra, he would have been offered a major new deal, and his new band would have been a worldwide priority for Virgin. But the other members of Mano Negra had successfully barred Manu from using the name and so he had no idea if or when he would ever record an album again. Even if he did get a new band.

Manu went back to Colombia on his own to film the videos with the ever-faithful director François Bergeron. The song "Senor Matanza", with its lyrics about the power of corrupt Mafia types, hit a nerve in South America and eventually became one of Mano Negra's best-loved tracks. Amazingly, Manu tracked down one of the kids who had danced on the train in Colombia and persuaded him to star in the video.

Almost everywhere he went, Manu collected the names and numbers of friends, musicians and fans he had met on the road, and he received many offers to stay, to play in bars, to disappear under the radar. But he soon moved on to Mexico, where he spent much of the next few months off his head on hallucinogens.

MEXICO CITY 19.1°N 99.4°W

When Manu hit the vast, sprawling, chaotic and vibrant metropolis of Mexico City, he mitigated his pain with peyote. It became his drug of choice and he claims 'opened me up in a certain way. It's an interesting drug, a professor. And it's not like a dictatorship that you depend on. You can still experience what you learned on peyote, without having to use it.' He had been introduced to the drug by Tom Darnal. 'The ancients say you should experience it in nature,' Manu says, 'as part of a ritual reconnection with nature. But I was brought up in the big city and, for me, the city is nature.'

Manu based himself in the *barrio* of Tepito, a neighbourhood where most European tourists would be in a state of constant paranoia. But he never had any problems. 'Every day I would take peyote down town in the rough *barrios* of Mexico City, places it was usually very hard to go. Peyote was a good protector for me. It may be stupid but it's true. Peyote put me in a good harmony with the old guys of the neighbourhood.

Señor Matanza – Manu's last video for Mano Negra, with one of the streetkids (left) who had been on the train tour.

Everyone smiled at me. I don't know how, but it worked like a kind of magic passport.'

The Tepito neighbourhood is well known for its open-air market, which is Mexico's central exchange for counterfeit goods, or *fayuca* in the local slang. If you want branded alcohol complete with packaging, often from China, you go to Tepito, and the *barrio* is notorious for selling everything from drugs to pirate videos and weapons. Hijacked trucks and their entire cargo have been known to simply disappear in Tepito in minutes, dismantled by experts. Robbers will observe what you are buying and then hold you up. But there's also a pride in the neighbourhood. Many of Mexico most famous boxers and wrestlers, such as the legendary

Místico, came from there. As the saying goes, 'Everything is for sale in Tepito, everything except for dignity.'

The peyote passport also had other effects. 'It opens up your sensitivity for the present moment. For example, you get a feeling whether something good or bad will come in the door. You sense the energy before it happens. You are totally in the present, rather than part of a schedule or planning your week or your life. It helps you position yourself in life and reach the right place at the right moment.'

Above all, peyote opened up Manu's imagination. 'I began to write songs again.' The first notable tune to emerge from this period was "El Hoyo" (The Hole), which eventually appeared on *La Radiolina* in 2007 and remains an essential part of his live set. The opportunities for football-type chanting afforded by the song's title – EL HOYO YO-YO – helped its consolidation into the live set. The refrain *'yo vengo del hoyo'* ('I come from the hole') makes reference to *'Tepito Fayuca'* and describes his favourite *barrio* as a *'hirvinete caldera'* ('boiling kettle') but also as his *'bandera'* ('flag').

Another song that emerged from Manu's time in Tepito is the Oedipal ditty "La Marea" (The Tide): *'Hoy tuve miedo de mi sombrita / So me tumb bajo el sol / Mamala marea va subiendo / Mama ... va subiendo hay que marea / Nada es para siempre'* (I was scared of my shadow / So I fell down under the sun / Mama the tide is rising / Mama ... it's rising, oh what a tide / Nothing is forever). Again, he recorded it several years later, for his second solo album, *Próxima Estación: Esperanza*.

The fact that some of Manu's songs often emerged years, sometimes even decades, after Manu wrote them is indicative of his working methods. Manu really felt more and more like an "Out Of Time Man", as the Mano Negra song goes: 'Time don't fool me no more / I throw my watch to the floor'. He had indeed thrown away his watch, as though time itself was one of the conventions he was trying to give up.

In Mexico City, with its Aztec echoes and hints of the future, Manu had the impression that all continents were flowing together, all centuries colliding. The peyote helped, but Mexico was a place where the globalised world really was shrinking distances and the past and future seemed to intermingle promiscuously.

TIJUANA 32.5°N 117°W

On the road again, Manu investigated a city that was to play an even more crucial part in the creation of *Clandestino*: Tijuana, up on the border with the great Satan itself. 'Tijuana is a central point in the planet's fever,' Manu says. It's a place where thousands of workers who cannot legally cross the border pursue crushingly low-paid menial labour in so-called *maquiladoras* or sweatshop factories, owned by Americans, to make goods for export to the States. According to Manu 'Tijuana is the best and the worst.'

Along with Juarez, the city is ground zero for drug trafficking and ruthless gang warfare. In the 1980s and 1990s, before the extreme violence of recent years, it was also a party destination for North Americans who come over the border in search of hedonistic fun. For Manu, it became an emblematic place where desperation, corrupt politics, violence and wild fiestas collide – both in reality and in his music. 'The problems are concentrated there. From the North they came to party, for the cheap beer and girls and drugs, and from the South it's the end of the line. It can be hell.'

In some ways, things hadn't much changed since 1939 when Graham Greene, in *The Lawless Roads*, described the excitement of the gringo crossing over the border to an illicit playground, where everything is permitted and death is to be scorned. 'The border means more than a customs house, a passport office, a man with a gun ... Life is never going to be quite the same again after your passport is stamped and you find yourself speechless among the money changers.' The tourist, however, 'lived in a different world' according to Greene. 'They were impervious to Mexico.'

Manu is perhaps the first artist to have been in a position to really report on Tijuana from both sides of the great divide, as a privileged gringo who also knew the harsh realities behind the flashing neon and the souvenir shops selling sombreros to the *yanquis*. Tijuana was a 'fever point', a place that illustrated various sicknesses. It was full of extreme if often humorous inauthenticity (all those sombrero shops), a place where the cruelty and absurdity of immigration laws were in stark evidence. 'They are totally hypocritical,' Manu asserts. 'The businesses in the States need workers with no papers, because they have no rights and can be hired and fired at will and paid poverty wages.'

But the border has a particular energy, a kind of suspended existence. For a local writer like Rafa Saavadra, the city, not-Mexico but still Mexico, was a laboratory of postmodernism 'too real to be a simulacrum ... it moves and is moving, that is why it is difficult to label her'. It was perfect for Manu.

The *Clandestino* album begins with the title track, in which Manu crosses the border as lawless *mojado*, or 'wetback' (as the migrants who get wet trying to cross the Rio Grande are known). He feels like a paperless outlaw, 'lost in the heart of the great Babylon'. At the end of the album, on "El Viento" (The Wind), he morphs into the wind and crosses the border unseen. Midway through is "Welcome To Tijuana", with its refrain of *'tequila, sexo y marijuana'*, a song that is more fun than deep, but offers hints of the dark side of the migration in lines like *'con el coyote no hay aduana'* ('with the coyotes there is no customs'), the 'coyotes' being the slang for the traffickers who transport Mexicans illegally across the border.

Manu had already visited Tijuana with Mano Negra, going over the border during their first American tour of 1990. The band played at Iguana's, a club which was basically only for an American audience. There they were rescued by Luis Güereña, one of the singers of the band Tijuana No!, who was, according to Manu, 'quite angry we were playing that place, so he showed us something of the real Tijuana'.

Tijuana No! were a rock/punk/ska band, who were originally known by the simple and nihilist name of No! They were one of the many bands in South America who were inspired by Mano Negra, and Manu became friends with Luis. When he returned to the city, he stayed with him in La Coahuila, the main avenue that runs through the

Luis Güereña – welcome to Tijuana No!

Zona Norte, the drag where many of the most notorious strip shows are to be found. 'I'm never gonna forget living with Luis; it's an important little part of my life,' Manu remembers.

Luis played a key role in Tijuana's music scene, promoting bands like The Dead Kennedys and Black Flag to a punk-deprived Tijuana youth. His own first band was called Solucion Mortal, and, as his bassist had no papers, they had to smuggle him across the border to play gigs in San Diego or Los Angeles. Luis would show people the scars on his belly and claim they were inflicted by a knife-wielding border guard.

Luis's flat, where he lived for twenty years and housed Manu, was an underground one-bedroom box at the rear of a chain-link-fenced parking lot. He bootlegged his water and electricity from the neighbouring water plant. The decor included posters of The Clash and a photo collage of friends captioned 'Fuck Authority'. He was a provocateur and clown, goose-stepping onstage, wearing an Uncle Sam hat and a Hitler moustache, haranguing the audience, bawling that Mexicans were ugly and that he didn't want them in his country. If audiences reacted angrily, and they did, then so much the better.

Luis was one of a trio of singers in Tijuana No! The others were the warmer-voiced Teca García and the more melodic Cecilia Bastida. The band ended up, like The Clash and Mano Negra, signing to a multinational, BMG, but remained stridently independent. Their song "La Migra" included samples of helicopters and the conversations of US Border Guards and ends with the slogan 'Fuck The USA!' Another song, "Travel Trouble", could almost have been penned by Manu: 'Travel, travel like money does / Travel, travel, like narcotics do / Travel, travel like pollution does / Travel, travel like corporations do ... Know the countries, know the world / Cross the oceans, cross the roads / Jump the fences, break the gates ... '

Besides the Mexican politics and references to national heroes like Zapata and Pancho Villa, the group did songs about Soweto and the Mothers of the Disappeared in Buenos Aires, and lent support to the Peruvian revolutionary group Tupac Amaru Revolutionary Movement (MRTA), leftist insurgents who opposed the Shining Path and were strongly rooted in the indigenous population.

Mano Negra had operated as what Josh Kun calls a 'galvanising node in a dissenting globalist circuit of musical activists' that included Tijuana No!, Bad Brains in Washington DC, Todo Los Muertos in Argentina (with Felix Nadal, who had performed on *Casa Babylon*) and the Basque separatists Negu Gorriak, whose singer Fermin Muguruza, an old Manu pal, ended up producing an album by Tijuana No! in San Sebastian in the Basque country. That record, *Transgresores De La Ley*, includes guest appearances by members of several of the above bands and was dedicated to the Zapatistas, the EZLN 'and no one else'. It featured a stirring version of The Clash's "Spanish Bombs" and used samples of speeches by Subcomandante Marcos, something Manu was to use on *Clandestino*. Manu himself contributed a skanking track called "Borregos Kamikazes" (Kamikaze Rabbits) about the flatterers encircling a corrupt nameless president known as *'el gran ladrón'* (the big thief).

Tijuana left its marks all over *Clandestino*, not least in the repetitive sound of a plastic whistle that sounds like a falling bomb and comes from a keychain popular with the city's street vendors, which Manu recorded on his portable recorder. As for Luis Güereña, he died of a heart attack in his underground bunker in 2004. Whilst Manu was on marijuana and experimenting with peyote, Luis had picked crystal meth and heroin – the wrong drugs. Someone put a microphone and the first demo tape of Tijuana No! in his coffin.

Tijuana embodies a possible future, which, when he's feeling pessimistic, Manu thinks could take hold of the rest of the world. When he was in Tijuana in 1995, the big guys were

the Narco Juniors, who would swagger around town with a girl or two on their arm. But they had some remnants of a kind of macho morality; it was not the done thing to kill women or children, for example. The newer *narcomafia* groups have no such restraint and go in for ever more vicious and frequent slayings and gruesome mutilation. Most of these killings happen along *la frontera* and Tijuana and Juarez have become the most dangerous cities of the Western world. The days of Mexico's frontier towns being the destination of choice for carefree gringos are finished.

CHIAPAS 16.4°N 92.4°W

In Mexico there was also a more positive 'fever point', which suggested another future: the Zapatistas. In 1995 the group had retreated into the mountains of the Lacandona jungle and renounced offensive violence. There, they issued proclamations of a 'fourth world war', the third being the Cold War and the fourth the assault of unrestrained capitalism, which would drop 'financial bombs' and destroy the livelihoods of minorities. Their prediction that the gap between rich and poor would grow ever wider, and their warnings about the dangers of unfettered globalised money markets, have proven all too accurate. Their struggle for land rights and their critique of the new economic world order captivated (and still inspires) Manu. Their analysis that the real power is in the hands of the multinationals, and that elected politicians have limited room for manoeuvre, chimed in harmony with his own thoughts.

What also appealed to Manu was the anti-hierarchical structures of the Zapatistas, with Subcomandante Marcos, the self-styled Delegate Zero (imagine a punk band with a singer with a name like that), the frontman and mouthpiece, a postmodern Che Guevara with the media savvy of a Malcolm McLaren. In his mask, smoking a pipe, with his parrot, Marcos had mystique to burn, and having abandoned the armed struggle, words had become his weapons. For someone like Manu, who had been brought up on Don Quixote and Gabriel García Márquez, Marcos's communiqués were full of poetry and fascinating stories, as well as political analysis.

Marcos was a shape-shifter, difficult to pin down. Once a *guerrillero*, he was the author of stories and had invented a character called 'Marcos' in stories written by Marcos. The fact that the Mexican authorities have announced that Marcos is really Rafael Sebastián Guillén Vicente, born 19 June, 1957 in Tampico, Tamaulipas, to Spanish immigrants, may or may not be true. Manu was attracted by this blurring of factual and fictional personas. When his level of fame jumped a league after the release of *Clandestino* and the media tried to pin various labels on him – anarchist, socialist, terrorist, punk, hippy – he too tried to keep a bit of distance between himself and the character 'Mano Chao', to keep some mystique and keep them guessing.

Back in 1994, Marcos had written to a ten-year-old girl in Mexico City, who had sent him a drawing. In his response, he conjured up a fable introducing a beetle and knight-errant called Don Durito de la Lacandona. The ensuing 'Durito' communiqués and tales told the story of the Zapatistas' struggle, revealing their organisational history, their critique of traditional politics, and the reasons for their opposition to neoliberalism. Marcos's most clear critiques of the capitalist system are told through his beetle.

Tom Darnal, who had been even keener on Marcos and the Zapatistas than Manu, had already spent a couple of weeks guarding a school in Chiapas, watching out for planes. 'Actually, it was the most boring two weeks of my life,' he remembers. Manu also paid a visit and played songs to the kids in the village in Chiapas. 'It was strange, it was in the dark, in a hut. A man picked us up and we met Marcos. We looked at the other Zapatista commanders. "I'm terrible at the guitar," Marcos said to me, "but you are going to compete with Tacho." And we launched into an all-night duel of songs ... '

Subcomandante Marcos (left) with Manu's guitar-duel partner Comandante Tacho in La Realidad, Chiapas, 1999.

Inspired by the indigenous Indian tradition of respect for Mother Earth goddess Pacha Mama, Manu wrote a key song on *Clandestino*, "Por El Suelo" (Dirt Cheap) in Chiapas. *'Pachamama te veo tan triste / Pachamama me pongo a llorar / Esperando la ultima ola'* (Pacha Mama I see you so sad / Pachamama I'm going to cry / Waiting for the last wave).

Manu also sampled Marcos's own words on *Clandestino*. In the song "Sol Y Luna" (Sun And Moon) there's one of the few palely hopeful lyrics on the album: 'Looking for an ideal / When will it be? / When will the sun come through?' It is followed by a recording of the Fourth Declaration of the Lacandon Jungle, read by Subcomandante Marcos, which translates as:

> *We were born of the night*
> *In her we live*
> *And in her we will die*
> *But in time the light of truth will*
> *Be for the many*
> *For all those who the night brings to tears*
> *For those to whom the light of day is denied*
> *For everyone the light*
> *For everyone everything*

Manu also liked Marcos's subversive humour. When a footballer from Inter Milan, Javier Zanetti, expressed his support for the Zapatistas, he received a letter in return from Marcos: 'I challenge you to a match against a team from the Zapatista National Liberation Army,' it read, 'at a time and a place to be determined. Given the affection we have for you, we're not planning to submerge you in goals. As we wait for your reply, we'll continue with our rigorous training regime.' Marcos also proposed a match in Cuba and one against a Mexican transsexual team.

By the time he had finished in Mexico, it seemed to Manu there were two possible futures for the world: a Mafia future, in which the Señor Matanzas of this earth, the gangland bosses, would take control alongside the newly unfettered bankers and undemocratic corporations with no thought for the fragile health of Pacha Mama. Or a version of a Zapatista future. The choice was Manichean; the angel of justice versus the devil of money. It informed Manu's politics thereafter, and when *Clandestino* turned out a success, he gave part of the royalties to the Zapatistas.

RIO DE JANEIRO 22.9°S 43.2°W

Manu's next destination was a city he had loved when he first visited it on the Cargo Tour, Rio de Janeiro. He avoided the tourist hot spots of Copacabana Beach or chic Ipanema and opted instead for the bohemian neighbourhood of Santa Teresa, halfway up the hills to the poor *favelas*. There he found rooms with a *capoeira* teacher called Sorriso, who lived with his daughter Valeria in a funky apartment strewn with cushions, hammocks, drums of assorted sizes and the one-string *berimbau* instrument used in *capoeira* ceremonies.

Capoeira combines music and martial arts in high-energy balletic movement and aerial acrobatics. It was first developed as a form of self-defence by communities of escaped slaves in the seventeenth century, and was banned, on pain of prison or torture, until the 1930s. These days most big cities have a *capoeira* centre and plenty of foreigners come to Brazil to learn the art. It also has more philosophical dimensions, including the trickster element of *malicia*, a quality that enables the *capoeirista* to detect deceit and to sense a person's real motives. *Capoeira* practitioners are supposed to gain deep levels of insight and even an understanding of the basic forces of the universe.

A related and also historically suppressed part of black Brazilian culture is Candomblé, the Afro-Brazilian religion that is a close cousin to Santeria in Cuba and Voodoo in Haiti. Manu was fascinated and thrilled when a Candomblé priest pronounced him a Son of Changó, the Yoruba God of Thunder. He was intrigued because he had already written songs which featured Superchango, his own cartoon version of the deity, and had spent evenings cooking up the fable of

Manu in Rio, partying on the street in the *barrio* Santa Teresa, 1997.

Superchango and his nemesis Cancodrillo (a half-dog, half-crocodile beast), which he later said was the mythical basis or back-story that underpins *Clandestino*.

Manu spent three months based in Rio but his restlessness drove him to explore the rest of Brazil. Among many trips, he made one to the great music and religious centre of Bahia, Salvador. Many different expressions of religion flourished there; groups like the Irmandade da Boa Morte (Sisterhood of the Good Death), a secret society of Afro-Brazilian women whose philosophy, as their name suggests, urges everyone to face death whenever it comes, without regrets, having forgiven and been forgiven all sins. Ever since encountering the group, at the end of each day Manu tries to do a reckoning of those he has offended and, if necessary, ask forgiveness, to keep his soul clean. He also claims to be ready to face death whenever it should it come.

Later, he went to Manaus, deep in Amazonia, and took a boat down the black, silky Rio Negro where he tried *ayahuasca*, probably the most powerful natural hallucinogen known on the planet, considerably more potent than peyote. Nearly everyone gets physically sick from *ayahuasca* and the visions that the drug provokes can last for days. But for Manu 'it is a way to confront your demons'.

Politically, the group that appealed most to Manu in Brazil was the Movimento dos Trabalhadores Rurais Sem Terra (MST), the landless movement that fought for the redistribution of land in favour of the impoverished in rural areas. He visited a couple of MST squat settlements, whose legality they based on the most recent Constitution of Brazil which states that land should fulfil a social function. MST also points out that, based on census statistics, Brazil is one of the most unequal countries on earth, with three percent of the population owning two-thirds of all land.

The movement started in 1985, when 2,500 landless families arrived in trucks, buses and motorbikes to occupy Fazenda Annoni, a 9,500-hectare plot of land in Rio Grande do Sul. By 2010, around 400,000 families had appropriated some 35 million acres. Often they were brutally evicted, and hundreds of squatters have died in the process. But like the Zapatistas, the MST encampments gave the squatters a voice. They were organised as participatory democracies, in which women were given an equal say and environmental concerns were taken seriously.

In Ceará, the parched northeast of Brazil, Manu spent a few days on the road with the Repentistas, the troubadours of Northern Brazil, who are known for their ability to improvise a song on the spot and survive on the lethal sugarcane liquor *cachaça* and little else. Later, in Sao Paulo, Manu sang on a track called "Sem Terra" (Without Land) with the Brazilian band Skank, an upbeat number whose tempo belies its subject matter: 'Who wants to ignore them / Who suffer and have already suffered / In Paraná, in Pará, in Espírito Santo'. The music was a Jamaican dancehall

pop-ska mix and the album *O Samba Poconé* on which it was eventually released in 1996, became a sizable hit, selling over a million copies.

Rio was confirmed as Manu's favourite city in the world, and Santa Teresa became his 'special' neighbourhood. Manu became the guitar player of the *barrio* bars. The old guys didn't know who he was, but every time he went to them they would encourage him to stay and play for hours. One of the only times that Manu appeared in the media during his 'long weekend' was when he gave a short interview to MTV Brazil and answered questions posed by his friend Sorriso. He looked tanned, relaxed and untroubled.

Santa Teresa has many artists, the most famous of whom was the Chilean-born Jorge Selarón (who died in January 2013), whose trademark pictures of African pregnant women can be found in local restaurants. He was celebrated for the dazzling mosaics installed in an obsessive labour of love up the 215-step staircase between Santa Teresa and Lapa. Manu would pass by the toiling artist and exchange a few words on his way to Lapa's atmospheric bars, which specialise in *chorinho* (little cry), the first, and very charming, urban jazz music pioneered in Rio, traditionally played by a trio of flute, guitar and the four-stringed *cavaquinho*.

Manu also wrote a touching love song in Santa Teresa and dedicated it to Valeria, who had become his girlfriend. It appeared on *Clandestino* as "Minha Galera" (the title can mean 'My people' and also 'My Boat'). In it, he describes Valeria as his *cachaça*, his *capoeira*, his *flamenga* (female follower of the Flamengo soccer team), his vagabond, his waterfall. It's a simple and beautiful song, one of his successful 'list' songs – like "Me Gustas Tú", a compendium of things he loves, which eventually became his biggest hit.

Rio was a beautiful existence in many ways, but Manu was still torn up inside, trying to invent his future, feeling that he had lost his instinct. He experimented with various kinds of music, with the drums and *berimbau*, with a kind of new *capoeira* music, and, in the spirit of Royal de Luxe, he even dreamed of starting a new circus, but he was unable to turn such ideas into anything solid.

Rio was and remains the dreamlike *cidade maravilhosa* for visitors, but Manu saw another reality in the slums: 'There are some people who romanticise the anarchy of the *favelas*, but life there is dangerous and violent.' Outsiders, like Manu, were tolerated if they knew the right people, but there was always the danger of getting caught in the cross-fire of inter-gang rivalry or the frequent shootouts between drug dealers and the police.

Manu, however, would wander through the huts and door-less concrete shells that stood on top of each other in the

Favela Baronesa, next to Santa Teresa, talking to the kids and playing his guitar in the open-air beer shacks. And, while he had found a nostalgic charm in the *chorinho* of Lapa, here he encountered a new music called *funk carioca* that sounded positively futuristic. It was based on minimal loops by Miami DJs, which were mixed with the occasional brass stab and rap or vocals, mainly in praise of sex or drug gangs. When Manu was in Brazil, the style was still in its infancy and he saw it as kind of tropical energetic punk, with a brutal freshness. In wasn't until the 2000s that the music was exported, by DJ Marlboro and others, and appropriated by hip artists like Diplo and M.I.A.

Then, one rainy day, he found himself in that favela bar when the cow that would change his life came loping in. The way it looked at him ... He was sure there was some wisdom to be gleaned from the oceanic depths of its compassionate gaze. Caught in a kind of purgatory of indecisiveness, he told himself, 'Manu you are so lost, be crazy now. If I see a cow it's yes, if I don't it's no. I lived for two years like that and everything went OK. Better anyway.'

A little later, in one of Lapa's bookstores, he discovered the *I Ching*, the ancient Chinese book of divinations, over which you throw stalks or dice to highlight particular passages which have relevance at a particular time. Questions are answered, usually in an ambiguous manner. 'This book became one of my favourites. It's a book that can talk to you. I did the process, and the first time the text said, "Follow the cows and you will find fortune." I was very happy. This day was very important to me because I said, "I'm not crazy." By treating the cows good, I did find fortune. I made *Clandestino* and found fortune. For money, for my life, for everything ... that's the story.'

It was time to return to the old continent.

CHAPTER 9:
CLANDESTINO

'Me gusta Malasaña ... me gusta la mañana'
___
From "Me Gusta Tú"

MADRID 40.4°N 3.7°W

Manu was back in Europe early in 1995. He recalls that it felt like a 'slow moving old tanker compared to the swifter boats of South America'. But in Madrid, where he was based for a few months in the first part of the year, he found a sympathetic ambience and energy in Malasaña, a gloriously bohemian neighbourhood that had been the centre of the *movida*, the hedonistic countercultural movement that sprang up after the death of Franco in 1975.

In the post-Franco euphoria of the 1980s, taboos were broken daily. Late-night bars, nudist and bondage clubs, punk and goth venues and stylish boutiques appeared as if from nowhere, accompanied by the open use of recreational drugs. Spanish pop-punk bands like Radio Futura and Nacha Pop gained a national audience, fashion designers such as Ágatha Ruiz de la Prada pioneered an eccentric but sexy *movida* style, while filmmakers like Iván Zulueta and most famously Pedro Almodóvar, chronicled the sense of messiness and freedom that prevailed during those years.

The *movida* was already history by 1995, but the bars and the attitudes remained. In Malasaña you could hang out at bars like the Pentagrama (El Penta) or La Via Lactéa and be flirting or deep in conversation with photographers, actors or musicians till the early hours. Manu and Gambeat, his Parisian friend and bassist, both moved to the neighbourhood and became friends with a guitarist called Madjid Farhem. Madjid could play both *flamenco* and rock, and Manu rated him almost as highly as his hero Paco de Lucía. Manu, Gambeat and Madjid formed a trio and, augmented by different local musicians, did a few tentative gigs, playing old favourites from Los Carayos and Mano Negra numbers and some of Manu's new songs.

There was finally some light at the end of a long, dark tunnel. 'It was beautiful,' Manu says. 'It was the start of something.' Manu had found a new gang and Madjid and Gambeat were to remain his key musical partners in Radio Bemba, the name he used for all his groups from then on. The world *'bemba'* is Cuban slang for 'gossip' and 'word-of-mouth' and was adopted by Castro's rebels up in the Sierra Maestra mountains during the early days of the Cuban revolution.

Manu also began to plot a new happening – an event he called *La Feira de Las Mentiras* (The Festival of Lies), which would include circus, food, politics, and music. Unlike the other schemes he had been dreaming up, this one eventually did take place in Galicia in 1998 and was to be a worthy follow-up to the Mano Negra spectaculars like the *Caravane des Quartiers*, if not quite as insane as the Cargo Tour or the Colombian train ride.

Manu also met a gorgeous, spirited actress called Paz Gómez – the girl who would appear in the video of "Me Gustas Tú", on his second solo album. In the song, Manu namechecks his everyday passions, Malasaña among them.

Things seemed to be looking up, although Manu was still feeling unsettled and indecisive about reviving his musical career. Maybe, he thought, he should just give it all up and live in Africa or Asia as a social worker, or follow the family trade as a journalist. There was a nagging sense that, no matter what he did, the black cloud would never lift. He had a

persistent intuition that the problem was that someone, perhaps one of the Candomblé priests in Brazil, had put a black
magic spell on him, which he couldn't shake off.

GALICIA 42.8°N 8.5°W

Manu's father, Ramón, was planning a motorbike trip from
Paris to his birthplace in Galicia to research a book he was
writing on the pilgrim route to Santiago. Concerned about
his son's state of mind, he asked him to come along. Ramón
was turning sixty that year and used it as gentle leverage.
The two needed some father and son bonding after Manu
had been AWOL for a couple of years in South America.

Ramón's book, *Priscilianio de Compostela*, which was
published in 1998 in Spanish and Galician, propounded the
subversive theory that it was not Saint James the Apostle
whose remains are in the ancient Cathedral of Santiago but
a Galician heretic called Priscilian, who had been executed
in the fourth century, the first recorded Christian to have
been executed by the Christian authorities for heresy. The
precise nature of Priscilian's offensive doctrines is lost in the
Galician mists, but Ramón writes that he and his followers
allowed women to read the scriptures, had a great faith in
nature, used apocryphal biblical texts and held mixed-sex
retreats in the woods. Their opponents accused them of
indulging in sex orgies and pagan and Satanic rites.

Ramón's book is a shaggy-dog story that mixes the politics
and doctrines of the early church with his own motorbike
pilgrimage, in which Manu – named Oscar after his Mano
Negra pseudonym, Oscar Tramor – plays a supporting role.
Ramón rides a small Honda, Manu a larger Yamaha 500TX
'with aviator helmet, leather jacket, trousers cut off at the
calf, and his bag and guitar at the sides'.

'Manu was depressed,' Ramón recalls, 'and had said that
maybe his salvation was in Galicia. To begin with he was in
his shell, but once in Galicia he started writing songs.' As he
puts it in the book, *'Je ne sais si l'eau ou les mystères Galicians,
mais Oscar renait au fil des heures'* ('I don't know if it was the

Manu with his brother Antoine and father, Ramón

water or the mystery of Galicia, but Oscar was reborn with the passing of the hours'). By the end of the book, Ramón is satisfied that Oscar is 'going through a resurrection'.

A key part of the trip was when father and son stayed with the Pinto family, neighbours of Ramón's family in Bastavales, a village close to Santiago. Since her husband had died, Joséfa Pinto looked after the family farm – cows, of course – along with her daughter Nina. According to Ramón, they were 'true examples of Galicians in a perfect state of conservation'. Ramón went back to Paris and his work commitments, but Manu remained there for some weeks, the tranquillity of the surroundings aiding his recuperation.

Joséfa was 'a teacher of life, a force for happiness', according to Manu. She also knew many Galician folk tunes and played the local drum. Although in her sixties, she would jam with Manu until the early hours. Manu also had other friends in the area, including the band Os Diplomaticos, from Monte Alto in La Coruña, and he would sometimes go off for days with them. This trait led Joséfa to give Manu the nickname *el desaparecido*, the disappearing one – which prompted him to write the song, which became a keystone of *Clandestino*, in her kitchen. Manu says it is his one true autobiographical song. It is certainly juicy with resonance, particularly the line *'Deprisa, deprisa a rumba perdido'* (Hurry, hurry down the lost highway), which namechecks the Carlos Saura film about vagabonds that Manu had tattooed on his arm. The phrase *'rumba perdido'* echoes another of Manu's mentors: Hank Williams, the hillbilly Shakespeare and his classic song "Lost Highway". There are also political resonances in the song – to the 30,000 supposed 'subversives' whom the rightwing Argentinian junta of the late 1970s and early 1980s 'Disappeared', though Manu insists the politics in the song were accidental.

Manu also wrote other songs at the Pintos' house, including "Bixo Do Coco", a *bixo* being a local word for an insect that gets in your head. It was a fertile time. Joséfa's rural retreat, her care, the healing breezes and abundant green nature of Galicia were probably just the therapy that he needed.

PARIS 48.9°N 2.3°E

For all Ramón's talk of Manu's 'resurrection', it was a gradual recovery. But he did go back to Paris, where he reunited with his ex-love, Anouk. Even if they weren't together as a couple, he felt great tenderness for her.

One day, when he was at the Khelifas' family house, where he sometimes still stayed, tragedy struck. Anouk's grandmother was run over and killed in an accident. In Anouk's garden, he played some soothing music on his guitar, including a new song called "Clandestino". Those simple but powerful chords rang out, carrying Manu's song of heartfelt empathy with struggling Peruvians, Bolivians and Nigerians with no papers, whose *'vida va prohibida'* (life is forbidden). They were destined to move ceaselessly, like the *'raya del mar'* (manta ray). *'Correr is mi destino,'* sang Manu, *'perdido en el gran Babylon'* (to run is my destiny, lost in the great

Anouk – the love of Manu's early life – on the solo album he produced.

Babylon). Although Manu, of course, could travel as he liked, two things remained 'illegal' in the chorus: marijuana, which made him a criminal, and Mano Negra. The final chant of 'Mano Negra – illegal!' made it clear that the legal prohibition on using the band name still rankled painfully.

Anouk was one of the people Manu felt he could trust, and who he felt understood him. He decided rather impulsively to ask her to become his manager and she accepted. Manu could also help her. During the years she had worked to promote Mano Negra, Anouk had always harboured desires to make her own album. She had sung backing vocals for Mano Negra and Manu loved her unaffected voice. She asked him to help her record her songs. Virgin were happy to release her album, *Automatik Kalamity*, possibly thinking they would get some kind of new Manu album.

But Manu didn't hijack the project, self-effacingly helping her to realise her vision, adding guitars even when the songs like "Mauvais Sang" seemed to be aimed at him: *'Quand arrive la nuit / L'autre je connais / La distance qui nous sépare / Dévoré la passion /Résidu d'amitié / Je connais la couleur / Des jours de mauvais sang'* (When the night arrives / I know the distance which separates us / the passion is devoured / Just a residue of friendship / I know the colour / Of the days of bad blood). On another song, "Je Ne T'Aime Plus", which ended up on the *Clandestino* album, Anouk and Manu sing a poignant public farewell to their relationship: *'Tellement j'ai voulu croire / Parfois J'aimerais mourir / Je ne T'ame plus, mon amour'* (I so wanted to believe / Sometimes I want to die / I don't love you any more, my love).

The album, with a downbeat pop-reggae vibe, sounded as if it might have commercial potential, but it barely troubled the charts.

Working with Anouk, and dealing with Virgin again, got Manu thinking about what he could do with the songs he had accumulated on his travels. The black dog of depression hadn't stopped his prolific creativity. 'What had really got to me,' he later reflected, 'was that I had become cut off from my instinct.' He had always followed his gut feeling before, in both his professional and personal life. 'Every time I tried to act in rational way, I thought things through too much, and it came to nothing.'

Since Galicia, he was feeling a little more connected. There was a sense of possibility rather than nothingness. The rust had burnt away. While he was working on Anouk's album, some Sèvres friends introduced Manu to a young sound engineer called Renaud Letang, who had worked on spectaculars with Jean Michel Jarre and others. Although ten years younger than Manu, the two had plenty in common, and Letang became Manu's pivotal musical co-pilot. He had been born in Tehran but brought up in Sèvres and, having also lived in Venezuela and Indonesia, had a cosmopolitan worldview. The two met up in a café in Sèvres and Letang passed a kind of test when

Manu left him with over fifty songs he had written on the road. The ten that Letang suggested they work on were more or less the same ones that Manu thought were the strongest.

Working once again in the cave-like garage under the Chaos' house in Sèvres in June and July 1997, *Clandestino* started to take shape. One big artistic question for Manu was how prominent the electronica and techno elements should be. Just as Mano Negra had created an impact with what they called *patchanka*, an innovative mix of punk, rock and Latin elements, Manu was wondering whether a similarly unique mix of his songs with electronica might work.

In the end, it was an accident that made up his mind and changed the course of the album, his career and his life. The audio software on Letang's computer developed a bug, which accidentally stripped out the electronics and drums, leaving the music naked, spare and beautiful. It was like an old painting covered in layers upon layers that had been stripped bare to reveal a masterpiece. *'Le hazard est mon ami,'* Manu likes to say. Chance was his friend.

'We felt we had given birth to a UFO,' Letang remembers. For even though they could tell they were on to something, it didn't sound like anything that either of them had ever heard before. Manu gave Letang a lot of leeway to work on mixes, much to the astonishment of the members of Mano Negra, who were used to Manu's studio control-freak perfectionism. When it came to decide on the final versions, Manu and Letang played them to the children of some Sèvres neighbours, who were aged three, five and six. 'The ones the children liked were the one we chose,' Manu claims.

On the finished album, Manu's musical odyssey though the *Grande Babylon* opens with two, spare classics. Manu is lost in the century, running is his destiny: "Clandestino", the opening track, is an instant classic, with the weight of inevitability. Then comes "Desaparecido", the song he had composed in Galicia, with its insistent refrain of *'cuando llegare?'* (when do I arrive?) that is never answered. Manu and Letang spent a large amount of time giving the acoustic guitar the right amount of attack and the voice the right sinuousness on these songs. Manu was plugging into a bigger picture, empathising with the lost and the oppressed, whilst singing about being lost himself. Its sound had to match that – and not a personal, singer-songwriter vibe.

The next track, "Bongo Bong", uses the lyrics of the Mano Negra song but with a new bouncy, quirky and highly catchy backing track (Robbie Williams was amongst those who later did a cover version). The song tells the story of a monkey bongo player who's a big shot in the jungle but moves to the big city, where he is ignored. The stoner lyrics no doubt appeal to that universal grievance of not getting due recognition for one's perceived talent and general brilliance and the song segues into "Je Ne T'Aime Plus", the strange, heartbreaking duet with Anouk.

Another twist and we are in the bleak world of "Mentira". 'Everything in this world is a lie,' goes the song, with politicians a firm target of course, but also promises of love. Then there is "Por el Suelo", the song he had written about the

Renaud Letang – Manu's producer and collaborator on *Clandestino*.

172

poor in Chiapas, with its haunting phrase *'Esperando la Última Ola'* (Waiting for the Last Wave), a nihilistic end-of-millennium surfing image, a dark mirror to the sunny optimism of the Beach Boys. Manu used it as a doomy subtitle on *Clandestino*'s album sleeve. All that's left for the world is the *'tequila, sexo, marijuana'* of "Buenvenido En Tijuana", as Manu's smashed voice flirts with death and tries to obliterate the pain with sex and drugs, in the border between Mexico and the US and between this world and the next. In 'Dia Luna ... Dia Pena' there's no reason to live any more.

"malegría" is one of Manu's new invented words and, like the song, "Lagrimas De Oro" (Tears of Gold), it describes and finally celebrates the bittersweet nature of life. Then, at last, in "El Viento" Manu magically becomes the wind itself. There was a crazy wisdom about the song-cycle and something of the weight of a prophetic vision as well.

By autumn Manu and Letang had a version to play to Virgin. The only person in the company who actually thought it would sell, according to Manu, was Emmanuel de Buretel. 'Manu came round to my house one evening,' Emmanuel remembers. 'His father was there, too. I told him I thought the album was fantastic. A killer. Some of the songs were for the ages.' Ramón also loved it: 'I was impressed by Mano Negra but I didn't understand them. With this album, I really thought Manu was a poet, a true artist.'

The fact that a record company executive, a classical-music-loving sixty-year-old Marxist, and some three-year-old neighbours all loved the record hinted at its potential universal appeal. But most music professionals, and Manu himself, were sceptical. It was a personal record that didn't fit any radio station format. The general opinion was that it would sell a few thousand to loyal Mano Negra fans, but that its lack of rock energy might alienate as many as it attracted. There was also no regular band to promote the album and Manu knew that its acoustic approach with electronic elements, not to mention the samples of Subcomandante Marcos, would in any case be a challenge to reproduce live.

Manu was fairly convinced that *Clandestino* would be his swan song. He was impressed, however, that Virgin were willing to promote it by funding and helping to produce his *Feria de Las Mentiras* (Festival of Lies) in Galicia, the project he had dreamed up in Madrid. Although people assume Manu hates all corporations, he acknowledges that there can be good, adventurous people working for them, and Virgin's backing of the festival was one such case.

But Manu's lack of confidence in *Clandestino* was clear when he met the old Mano Negra manager Bernard Batzen at the Festival Mediterranée a couple of weeks before the release date. Manu gave him a copy and self-deprecatingly said it was a *maquette*, a demo, rather than the finished article.

Clandestino came out in April 1998, and, with a low-key promotion, it crept into the lower reaches of the French charts, reaching number 19, where it stalled. A couple of low-budget but effective video clips were filmed – as ever, by François Bergeron – for the songs "Clandestino" (with faces of different nationalities either full of hope for a new life, or in despair at being blocked from travel) and "Desaparecido" (a simple performance framed by Bergeron's hallucinogenic Inca images).

As the marketing people at Virgin had thought, the main radio stations in France such as RTL2 or NRJ failed to see how *Clandestino* could fit with their programming format. De Buretel also says that references to marijuana in a couple of the tracks was another excuse for the established media to steer clear. Meanwhile, Les Têtes Raides, an indie folk-rock band that included ex-Mano Negra member Pierre Gauthé, released their album *Chamboultou* the same week and it sailed into the French top 10. The comparison was depressing.

The reviews and reactions were more encouraging – and not just in France. Ernesto Lechner of the *Los Angeles Times* wrote, 'it is inspiring to see an artist like Manu Chao reach out in so many different directions and pull it off, because the record is extremely cohesive. Besides all the ideas and the concepts and the lyrics, it's just a very, very beautiful record to listen to from beginning to end. It's really almost a concept album. It's a cycle of songs.' The song-cycle was a favoured format in the nineteenth century, reaching its zenith in works like Schubert's *Winterreise*. Manu was revisiting it with his own pre-millennial 'winter journey' in song.

And Manu managed to pull off the *Feria de Las Mentiras*, which became a ten-day extravaganza. 'The inaugural parade will be chaired by a monumental octopus, the God of Lies,' read his proposal, 'embodying the contradictions and hypocrisy of the world past and present. There will be confusion between background cries of sea gulls and brass band music. There will be an inhuman monster's lair ... of the terrible Octopus. To enter, each will pay, after telling a lie. Inside, everything is flashy, attractive, false and illusory. All weekend its doors will be open to the public. It's the world of television, advertising, charlatans, hucksters, swindlers and thieves of all kinds. In short, the world today. One motto: everything must be profitable, consumable, disposable.'

François Bergeron's Inca-hallucinogenic video for "Desaparecido".

For the street parade, scheduled for the sixth day, Manu proposed that 'The bands of Galicia will mix the drums of Venezuela, Colombia, Brazil and Senegal to recreate the ambience of a grand carnival. Children will be the heroes of the Court of Miracles. Miscegenation and recycling will be the watchwords.'

Manu was using the experience of working on the Cargo Tour and the Colombian train trip, and combining it with his love of fiesta and carnival to create a communal event he thought could be an antidote to the increasingly commercialised music festivals sprouting throughout Europe, with their overwhelming corporate presence and overpriced food and drink.

The event ran from 7 to 12 July, 1998, and it was a great success. Manu invited sympathetic bands like the Latin hip hop crew Sergeant García from Paris, Amparanoia from Barcelona and his local friends Os Diplomaticos from La Coruña. Joséfa Pinto supplied the Galician folk. Some improvising Brazilian *repentistas* came from the province of Ceará to compete against the local *refuegista* storytellers. There was cheap good quality food, drumming, football and a true carnival atmosphere. It lost a lot of money, however, and plans to replicate it elsewhere were shelved.

CHAPTER 10:
DAKAR, BARCA ...
INSH'ALLAH

'Clandestino *has spawned an exchange of*
hope. Something strong and tender.'

Manu discovers what he has created

After the Feria in Galicia, Manu was left with a feeling of anticlimax. He had few expectations of *Clandestino* becoming anything more than a modest commercial success – and even if it did, he didn't have a band to promote it. With the album dispatched, he was again at a loose end, tormented about what to do next. He was thirty-seven years old. The other members of Mano Negra were mostly family men and happy fathers by now. Manu himself was alone without a lover or any prospect of children. He'd given music a good shot, but perhaps it was time to think of doing something else. He decided on travelling to Africa, seeing what was really happening, and maybe helping out, becoming some kind of social worker. Also, he had a vague idea for another musical train trip in a similar vein to the Colombian trip, this time between Bamako, the capital of Mali, and Dakar, the capital of Senegal.

Within three months, he was married and living in Dakar. And he'd converted to Islam. And, equally extraordinary, within a year, almost entirely through word of mouth, and through constant play in clubs and beach bars, *Clandestino* had become a worldwide phenomenon, and Manu had on his hands the biggest-selling album in French rock history.

DAKAR 14.6°N 17.4°W

Like those other Manu favourites – Havana, Rio and New Orleans – Dakar is one of those rare cities where the air itself seems to hum with music. The car horns, the shuffle of people through the busy markets, the shouts of street vendors, all seem to be part of some urban symphonic pattern. People sing as they go about their business, and even if they are just talking to each other or into their mobiles, still a novelty back in 1998, they talk in a singsong Africanised French or the equally lyrical local Wolof language. There are flower-sellers who wear baskets on their heads, which make them look like their hair is made out of flowers, as if in a surrealist painting. Everything is imbued with movement and energy.

Dakar is also a stylish and fashion-conscious city, where local *sapeurs*, with threads modelled on the latest Paris styles, or at least convincing Parisian knock-offs, gild the local bars and boulevards. Manu frequented the rougher clubs, some of which only open at around 4am, where you can hear *djembe* and talking drum jams that totally rearrange your ideas about rhythm. He was also fascinated by the *griots*, the praise singers who have the histories of important families going back centuries fully memorised but can also be found at local wrestling matches bigging up the fighters. Even stranger were the groups singing Hindi film songs in the Peking district, using West African grooves rehashed Bollywood-style, with Indian playback singers like Lata Mangeshkar reincarnated in the form of a six-foot Senegalese goddess.

Of all the countries in Africa, Senegal has the greatest mix of musical connections, plugged in to the Arab world, Europe and the Americas, and the variety and pulse of the rhythms on display is unmatched. A nation of nine million souls, it has a musical impact way above its size, and when Manu arrived it boasted international stars like pop-mystic Baaba Maal,

Afro-salsa groups like Africando and a genuine superstar in Youssou N'Dour, who, when not touring, appeared regularly in his own Club Thiossane in the La Médina district.

But, like those other great musical cities so beloved by Manu, Dakar also had its B-side of corruption and poverty. Manu had no intention of being a mere tourist and preferred to mingle with the people down on the streets and so he found lodgings with a Senegalese family in downtown Dakar.

Senegal is on the outer edges of the Islamic world, which in those days before al-Qaeda in the Maghreb seemed very far from the strict, desert puritanism that holds sway in Mecca and the Arabian Peninsula. Senegalese music stars like Cheikh Lô and Youssou N'Dour follow differing mystical Sufi-inspired forms of Islam. For Youssou it's a combination of being a Mouride (a devotee of the Senegalese Sufi mystic, Amadou Bamba) and a follower of the Tidjani Brotherhood (of Moroccan origin), while for Cheikh Lô it's the Baye Fall, a sect whose devotees look like Rastas with their exuberant dreadlocks and multicoloured patchwork tunics. The Baye Fall also revere nature, believe in the purifying benefit of work and also follow the path of the Senegalese saint Amadou Bamba. In many ways, Manu felt on their wavelength.

Living with an Islamic family, in a predominantly Muslim nation, Manu became drawn to Islam. The fact that this faith was demonised by the West only made it more appealing to him. If Islam was the spiritual path of millions of poor people through North and West Africa, and of all his Senegalese musical heroes, with a strong tradition of poetry and music, it was worth investigating. Manu was still searching for a path that might bring him peace of mind. 'I loved to pray with the locals and go to the mosque,' he remembered later. 'It was very good to stop your everyday life five times a day to reconnect and think. But to begin with, while the family was praying in a Muslim way, I was praying in my way.'

Used to musicians' hours and rising late, Manu found himself enjoying the duty of getting up at six in the morning for prayers. But the path to Allah wasn't easy. 'When I went to the mosque and became a real Muslim,' Manu recalls. 'The free part of myself said, "No, I don't want to learn something I don't really understand by rote." For me, being raised in Europe, the position of women in Senegal was very difficult. When I asked, "What does it mean?" the family tried to teach me. But they couldn't explain enough for me to understand. I respect that, and Islam too, but I realised that my real religion is my own one. In Brazil, in Africa, I learned that there is not only rationality in life.' Manu says he has also learned a lot else from his fellow Muslims, including cleanliness. 'I learned to wash the body five times a day. In Europe we are pigs.' But once you become a Muslim, you're a Muslim for life, so Manu remains a Muslim, despite his heterodox views.

Manu also appreciated the slow speed of life in Dakar. Haste comes from the Devil, slowness comes from God, as they say in Morocco. 'That was something they didn't teach me in school either,' Manu says. 'I had to go to Africa to learn that. I'm a speed addict and that's one of the terrible things in my life. It's my culture and I need speed and kicks, but I also know it's a drug.' Manu says he also found the same slowness in other countries, but to a lesser extent. 'In Colombia, they say if you are in a hurry you are already dead.'

In Dakar, in the middle of his Muslim phase, Manu did something which most people would consider a big deal in their lives. He got married.

One of the families that Manu was staying with had an unmarried mother and the community was censuring the entire family because of it. Manu for his part was seen as an anomaly, being single at the advanced age of thirty-eight, and it would hardly be possible for him to become a normal Muslim and remain unmarried.

At the family's suggestion, Manu offered to marry the mother and happily went through with a Muslim marriage ceremony. He was still battling with depression, but if he could help someone by committing such a selfless act, then why not? At the time, he genuinely felt it would give him the stability he desperately sought. He certainly didn't hold any resentment against the woman for being an unmarried mother, as others did, and, if anything, the idea of becoming an instant father appealed. It wasn't as if he had had any great belief in marriage as an institution until then, in any case. And, to really give Islam a try, he would go along with its norms in his own determined, sometimes foolhardy, way.

The Senegalese don't necessarily view marriage as a romantic union, in the Western sense. Just as in many other countries, it's considered to be more of an practical solution, an alliance between families. and for Manu, too, the arrangement was something he accepted quite casually, as a part of regular, everyday life. What the legal status of the marriage in Europe would be was not entirely clear. Traditionally, it's very easy for a man or a woman to get divorced in Islamic countries.

One thing that impressed Manu was the cohesion of family life in Dakar. 'I discovered family in Africa,' he claimed. 'I hope one day I'll be the father of a family, but in an African way, living in a neighbourhood, not in a European way, which is too narrow. The European way scares me a lot. It's like a prison, a little flat with your kids. I will never be a family man in an occidental way. I don't want a European or nuclear family ever. Never say never, of course ... I want kids and to be a father, but with other rules.' In Dakar, the whole notion of family seemed to involve a lot more freedom and space. 'My kids would be living in the neighbourhood,' said Manu of his theoretical family, 'running around and being taken care of. I can take care of the kid of my neighbour; she can take care of mine.'

After his marriage, Manu travelled through the country and stayed in villages, helping when and where he could, handing out money for good causes, perhaps a school roof or a set of new water pumps. But whatever the richness of the musical and other experiences he was having in Senegal, his pockets weren't infinitely deep, and his one solid project idea – a musical train ride between Bamako and Dakar – was proving hard to organise.

Nonetheless, he decided to give Virgin France, his record company, a call to see if funding might be available for the

Manu plots his next move.

train idea. He had been out of touch with them for some months, not wanting to learn any more disappointing news about his stalled career, or of any residual recriminations from the rest of Mano Negra. However, when he put the call in to Virgin Paris, he was astonished to learn that rather than fading away into the sunset like the swan song he had anticipated, *Clandestino* was notching up healthy sales in France and beginning to move in Belgium, Germany, Mexico and elsewhere around the world.

The news was astounding. Despite the seemingly wild and fanciful predictions of Emmanuel de Buretel, Manu had been convinced that *Clandestino's* intimate acoustic sound would confine its appeal to a cult singer-songwriter fan base and Mano Negra diehards. He was wrong. The word-of-mouth excitement generated by the album was extraordinary. The album seemed to gain its first international audience among backpacking and globetrotting types, who were cast in much the same mould as Manu himself, and in that summer of 1998 it became the soundtrack of choice in hip beach destinations from Koh Samui to Puerto Escondido to Ibiza. Travellers would come back with fond memories of their summer adventures and turn their friends on to the music in their heads, namely *Clandestino*. Its power lay partly in its *malegría*, that Manu Chao neologism that mixes the words *'mala'* ('bad') and *'alegría'* ('happiness') and expresses a happy-sad bitter-sweet quality in both life and music. It was a soundtrack to the moment when the sun goes down, echoing the transitory nature of life, reflecting the truth that sadness and loneliness exist even in paradise.

By pure chance, Virgin's modest and low-key marketing approach, with its anti-consumerist aura, proved to be perfect. *Clandestino* was something that people discovered for themselves, through their network of friends, rather than on an advertising hoarding or in a TV commercial, and it was appreciated all the more for it. The trajectory of the album was most unusual. In 1998, the year of its release, it sold 300,000, the nineteenth best seller of the year in France; in 1999, it sold 500,000 and was the fifth best seller. It was only in March 1999, almost a year after its release, that *Clandestino* entered the top 10 of the French album charts, where it stayed for the entire summer. But then, rather than slipping away, *Clandestino* just carried on selling and never left the charts for the next four years. The same pattern played out internationally, and the album ended up selling more than five million copies worldwide. No doubt the real figure was double that, if you include all the pirated copies.

Only in the Anglophone world did the album remain something of a cult success, popular among a smallish audience with an ear tuned in to what was happening in France, Spain and the rest of the world. And this was despite the fact that Manu had signed to the prestigious UK label Palm Pictures, set-up by Chris Blackwell, the man who had previously founded Island Records and 'discovered' Bob Marley. In the rest of the world, despite a slow start, *Clandestino*'s eventual success was simply immense.

Even though *Clandestino* didn't fit into any existing genre or format, a relatively new and growing interest in the catch-all cubbyhole of 'world music' put some wind in its sails. It's an artificial marketing category that Manu rejects as absurd, though he has benefited from its existence. There was at the time a growing interest in music from Africa, the Caribbean and South America, fired in part by a search for authenticity among Western audiences fed up with pre-packaged formulaic pop. In the years leading up to the new millennium, there were more and more radio shows, magazines, websites, record-shop space and general coverage dedicated to world music in all its indefinable variety.

Coincidentally, *Clandestino* was released in the same month as *Buena Vista Social Club*, that sepia-tinted hymn to the glory days of Cuban *son*, which sold over eight million copies. That album was also discovered by word of mouth and burned slowly before receiving huge exposure by Wim Wenders' film of the same name. More than any other albums, *Clandestino* and *Buena Vista Social Club* opened the ears of European and North American rock fans to musical styles from outside the West and brought in other listeners in their slipstream, who ended up exploring other musical styles, notably from Cuba and West Africa. Despite Manu's misgivings about classification, these two albums spearheaded the 'world music' boom and they remain the category's biggest sellers.

By the autumn of 1998, it was becoming clear that in France alone *Clandestino* would sell at least 300,000 copies. That was a healthy tally for any album, and was enough for Virgin to commit to a follow-up, as well as to invest money in a band to play live shows. After all the snakes of recent years, a ladder had propelled Manu to the top of the board. The rudderless months and years, underneath the radar, *desaparecido, clandestino*, were coming to an end for Manu. It was time once again to return to the old continent.

BARCELONA 41.4°N 2.1°E

First of all, Manu had to decide where to live. Paris was still a city he felt the need to escape from, with its cold winters and cold heart. If he had to be based in Europe, it would be southern Europe. Barcelona was an obvious choice, with its alternative artistic and musical community and its noble history of republicanism, not to mention the most stylish and brilliant football team in Europe. Manu recalls that he opted for the Catalan capital when a cow appeared before his eyes as he was mulling over the question. That swung it. The cows had been leading him out of his personal and professional nadir. Why break a winning streak?

He felt confident enough about his choice of Barcelona to buy a place near Plaza Real in the heart of the old town, the Barri Gòtic. Apart from anything else, he needed somewhere to store his possessions, which were scattered in Madrid, Paris, Rio and elsewhere. He bought a basic apartment. He didn't need a patio, because he would eat out and live as much as possible outside, using locals bars like the Mariatchi as his office and a place to jam late into the night.

Then there was the question of a follow-up to *Clandestino*, which Virgin were beginning to clamour for. Fortunately,

Renaud Letang was available to help Manu trawl through all the other songs that he had written on his travels and both agreed that there was enough for the basis of a second album. As a working title, or subtitle, they called this *Próxima Estación: Esperanza* (Next Station: Hope), words that Manu had heard on the Madrid metro, as the announcement just before a stop called Esperanza. Manu's recording of this made it on to the album – unwisely, as it turned out, as the train announcer later successfully sued Virgin for payment.

However much Manu disdained the conventional rules, creating a record loved by millions was an immense boost of confidence. Whatever doubts he had that his music career was over were dispelled, and a renewed certainty and purpose urged him on as he grappled with the task of putting together the follow-up. The two co-pilots, Renaud and Manu, whittled down Manu's songs, knowing, this time, the sound and the direction it would take – and knowing it would work. This confidence and easy atmosphere translated on to disc. *Próxima Estación* would be a lighter album than *Clandestino*, with more brass and more humour.

Manu began to dream, too, of a new band – one that might have the impact of Mano Negra, or perhaps even surpass it. Once again, he focused on the task with the devotion of a football manager picking his crack squad. The core of the team was to be the bassist Gambeat, his Parisian friend; Madjid Farhem, the guitar wizard that Manu had met in Madrid; and Philippe Teboul, the percussionist from Les Casse Pieds and Mano Negra, who had been with Manu ever since they busked together on the Paris metro. To this core was added David Bourguignon on drums; B-Roy on accordion; Roy Paci on trumpet; Gianny Salazar on trombone; Gerard Casajús Guaita on drums and percussion; Julio García Lobos on keyboards; and a rapper called Bidji.

As the band starting rehearsing and gelling miraculously fast, however, clouds began to gather on the horizon from Manu's past. Virgin – as might be expected – wanted to captialise on the success of *Clandestino* by putting out a *Best*

Of Mano Negra album. Manu was resolutely opposed to the move. Just when he was forging a bright a fresh creative future, this seemed to him to be a very backwards move and a bald attempt to cash in on his unexpected success. But Mano Negra's implacable democratic system outvoted him. The best he could do was to ensure that a small proportion of the profits from this unwanted release went to charities supporting the indigenous people of Chiapas in Mexico. If the Zapatistas were to benefit, it would at least mollify his pain and embarrassment.

But an even deeper and more emotional shock was in store. Manu's long friendship with his ex-girlfriend Anouk was sundered, at least partly due to his sudden success. Manu had given her a co-writing credit for the song "Je Ne T'Aime Plus" on *Clandestino* (and she had appeared on the video for the song), but she wanted a further percentage of the album royalties for the period when she had managed him. The case ended up in the hands of the lawyers. Manu chose not to fight and settled out of court. His father Ramón was among those who thought he should have fought harder but, for Manu, squabbling over money with his former love was just too painful.

These experiences crystallised Manu's determination to change his whole approach to music and business. The new band, Radio Bemba, would be under his control – creative and organisational democracy had proven too traumatic. Furthermore, to ensure this, he would hire his musicians on a tour-by-tour basis, for the duration of each tour only and with no further commitment. He also realised that attempts to operate either without a manager, or with a friend and ex-lover like Anouk, or a family member like Santi, had all ended disastrously. Instead, he asked Jacques Renault, co-founder of the management and touring company Corida, an old-school showbiz hand who had looked after French alternative pop group Les Rita Mitsouko and promoted tours by Dire Straits and Eric Clapton, to look after his affairs.

The band is assembled – Manu, Madjid (with the glass, centre), Gambeat (in the white T-shirt) and the rest, on the road in Mexico.

MEXICO CITY AND ALL POINTS SOUTH

After several weeks of rehearsals, the new look Radio Bemba was ready for the road. The idea was to do some try-outs in Mexico, the country that had always been good to him and where both *Casa Babylon* and *Clandestino* had taken off in a big way. In fact, the band were thrown right in the deep end when they were booked to headline a massive free concert at the Zócalo, the huge square in Mexico City's historic city centre, encircled by the National Palace, the cathedral and the ruins of an Aztec pyramid.

After the Zócalo concert, Manu realised, with somewhat mixed feelings, that whatever fame he had known with Mano Negra had been ratcheted up several levels. Even though the

free concert was not properly publicised, over 150,000 fans rammed the square. The band played both new songs from *Clandestino*, like "Bienvenido a Tijuana" and "Por El Suelo", with harder, rock-reggae arrangements, and some older Mano Negra numbers including "King Kong Five" and "Mala Vida". There was a disparity between the more acoustic album versions of the *Clandestino* songs and their raucous high-energy live renditions that has been a characteristic of Manu's live show ever since. The balance between the horns and the sonic dynamics provided by percussion, brass and accordion seemed to work magically well.

Even though Manu was almost crippled with nerves before the show and the band were 'still in diapers', as he put it, any fear that he had lost his ability to win over and electrify a large audience melted away during the euphoric set. Camille

T. Tiara of the *San Francisco Bay Guardian* caught the show in Tijuana a few days later: 'Seething with energy after hours of anticipation, the audience reacts in unison to the music,' she wrote: 'impromptu slam pits pop up throughout the auditorium floor, and bodies roll overhead as soon as the band brings up the beat.' A lower-key benefit in the Chiapas followed, in front of an altogether more impassive Indian and Zapatista crowd, before the band took off to perform elsewhere in South America.

Everywhere, Manu was overwhelmed by the reaction. 'The album *Clandestino* has spawned a beautiful thing,' he told a Mexican journalist. 'An exchange of hope. It wasn't so much about selling or not selling, but about having such a response from the people, which I've never had in my life. Something strong and tender. It's fabulous!'

Manu was also developing a new style of agitprop art. At each stop of the tour, he did what he had promised if ever he had the chance to 'use the microphone' again and publicised the struggles of the oppressed. Often he plugged into a local struggle or movement and would hold his obligatory press conference at a venue relevant to that struggle. 'I was lucky, I was used by history,' he told a reporter from *Le Monde*, though he was also careful to avoid presenting himself as some kind of political messiah. 'I'm like you,' he continued, 'lost in the century. I always seek the *Tumba de Don Quixote* (Tomb of Don Quixote). Here and there, I see little lights, points of fever, like the Chiapas. But I'm a musician, I sing a little, talk a little ... '

Like Don Quixote, Manu was a scatterbrained knight-errant, stumbling upon aspects of the truth, tilting against the windmills of world politics. In Mexico City, he had dedicated the concert to local students who had been arrested for protesting against hikes in tuition fees. In Mendoza, Argentina, he declared: 'I come here because it is a way to break the monopolies of information,' offering his support to the local *barrio* of La Gloria and its community radio station Cuyum, as well a library threatened with closure.

In Bolivia, the tour coincided with a protest over water rights in and around the town of Cochabamba, high in the Andes. There were riots, arrests and protests, and a seventeen-year-old youth was shot and killed. With its slogan *'Agua es un derecho, no una mercancia'* (Water is a right, not a commodity), the protests pitted local people against an American-owned company that had taken over the local utility. Manu was able to use his press conferences to highlight the issue and get international publicity and the company eventually withdrew. Manu could claim, in small part at least, to have helped achieve this outcome.

One stop in Uruguay combined politics with r'n'r. Manu held a press conference at Cabo Polonio, a delightfully bohemian coastal spot that was threatened with development. Cabo Polonio is a famously chilled beach village which back then had neither electricity nor running water, a landscape of shacks and shifting sand dunes, a single lighthouse, with Rasta-coloured flags of red, gold and green serving as wind vanes. To get there you had to take a pick-up truck or go on horseback. Nightlife was lived by candlelight, and animals wandered around freely. It was an eccentric place that Manu loved and he decided to stay there for a couple of weeks. One day there was an eclipse and a whale was washed ashore, as if disoriented by the sun's occlusion. Then, as he was waking up the next morning, a cow nuzzled its way into Manu's shack. He knew he was in the right place.

CHAPTER 11:
SHOT BY BOTH SIDES

'The nail that sticks up is the one that gets hit by the hammer.'

Japanese proverb

The second year of the shiny new millennium was a brilliant and successful one for Manu. He found time to complete his follow-up to *Clandestino* – *Próxima Estación: Esperanza* – and attracted a huge following on tour, mostly in Europe this time. His band consolidated their fearsome live reputation, as evidenced on a triumphant live CD, which in the old vinyl days would have been a generous double album, with its twenty-nine tracks.

Yet 2001 was also the year when Manu's political opponents – both on the right and left – cranked their vilification into overdrive. Several of his concerts were cancelled in controversial circumstances by authorities who saw him as an anarchist 'leader'. Meantime, as the world's most famous 'millionaire backpacker', Manu became a target for purists in the alternative movement. As the Japanese proverb goes, 'The nail that sticks up is the one that gets hit by the hammer.'

The live album was recorded by Virgin in July at La Grande Halle de La Villette in Paris. The recordings were released in 2002 as a CD called *Radio Bemba Sound System* and a DVD called *Babylonia En Guagua*, a reference to the Bob Marley live album *Babylon By Bus*. Both showed that Manu had created a band with a power approaching, even surpassing, that of Mano Negra, except that this time Manu was securely in the driving seat, with his hands on the controls. A backstage documentary entitled *Babylon's Fever*, which was released with the live DVD, shows a rather introverted Manu, the quiet boss with his mind on the taxing job of keeping his crew happy and productive, sitting at the back of the bus, occasionally jotting down new song ideas while the others get up the usual rock'n'roll hi-jinks; scoring dope, jamming merrily and chatting up the *chicas*.

The musical dynamics were certainly impressive, with Manu's increasingly assured tenor voice given a counter-point – and an alternative focus onstage – in the rapper and singer Bidji, and a rich texture created by the three piece brass section, B-Roy's accordion, David and Gerard on drums and percussion.

Manu could be quietly confident that the studio album, *Próxima Estación: Esperanza,* would do well. For the first time since the early days of Mano Negra, all the ducks were lined up for a professionally marketed, properly backed release, with priority support from Virgin and a hot new band to tour behind it. Arriving in the wake of *Clandestino's* success, this new disc was likely to be a million-seller. In the end it sold 3.5 million copies at home and abroad. Manu saw it as 'the little sister' of *Clandestino* – more female in character, while *Clandestino* was more male.

Several of *Próxima Estación's* backing tracks were, to the confusion of some critics, but in typical Manu fashion, recycled. Both "Homens" and "Mr Bobby" use more or less the same track as "Bongo Bong" on *Clandestino*. According to Manu, "Homens" was 'simply a practical solution'. He had been trying to write a piece of music for his old girlfriend Valeria in Rio, but she didn't like it, so Manu suggested using the backing track for "Bongo Bong", which he happened to have on his computer. On top of it, Valeria rapped gently in Brazilian Portuguese that men, whether black, mulatto, creole or white, whether *gordo* (fat), *safado* (horny), *careca* (bald) can make a woman happy, so long as they show respect, preferably have money and are *bom de cama* (good in bed). Manu might have been nicknamed 'The Jesuit' by the other members of Mano Negra, but you couldn't call the content of his albums puritanical.

"Mr Bobby" was a tribute to Bob Marley, Manu's 'professor of simplicity' and a key figure in his life, a saint of the global underclass, whose music travelled everywhere. Bob Marley's lyrics are graffitied all over the walls of cities in Africa, the Caribbean and most other points of the globe. Manu's provokes the same coverage in Spain and Latin America. The language Manu uses in this song and elsewhere is not exactly that of a native-born English speaker: *Tonight I watch through my window / And I can't see no lights / Tonight I watch through my window / And I can't see no rights*. Like many of Manu's songs, "Mr Bobby" is double-edged, optimistic and yet also despairing, full of *malegría*.

The most immediately catchy song was "Me Gustas Tú" (I Like You), a simple, almost childish ditty that lists some of the things that Manu likes, ranging from the gifts of nature (the sea, the light, the wind) to his favourite haunts of La Coruña (the town in Galicia where his father comes from) and Malasaña (his adopted *barrio* in Madrid), to guitars, reggae and marijuana. The song is a slacker generation's version of the *Sound of Music* classic "My Favourite Things".

The song's refrain of *'que horas son, mi corazón'* – which translates as 'what time is it my (sweet)heart?' or, with more resonance, 'what times are these my (sweet)heart?' – pops up again both on the song "La Primavera" (The Spring) and on *Próxima Estación*'s final track, "Infinita Tristeza" (Endless Sadness). Once again the idea is simple. Manu asks what time it is in different parts of the world – Mozambique, England, Japan, Washington. The effect is to create an instant web of connections across the world and the feeling that we're all in this together, economically, politically, ecologically and musically.

The multiple global references, musical styles and languages that interweave throughout the album provoke a feeling similar to that experienced by frequent travellers at the moment when they wake up, in a state of semi-consciousness, forgetting where they are. The opening line of "La Primavera" claims that we have been deceived by the spring. 'Politicians are always promising a bright new future,' explains Manu, 'a new spring, which, of course, never comes.'

In a profile some years later, the *New Yorker*, having quoted Manu as saying that he writes songs 'as therapy, to address the rage I feel about this world,' added that 'on the whole he is too smart to simply telegraph his feelings and theories'. In fact, the most overtly political song on *Próxima Estación* is "Denia", which is sung in Mahgrebi (North African) Arabic. Most listeners won't have a clue what the song is about: 'My heart aches to watch you / Poor Algeria / Life through your eyes / Life as lie / Life swarming with police / Life soaked with mothers' tears'.

Whilst the album glows with a generalised sympathy for the downtrodden in Mozambique or Algeria and for the state of emergency in the world, its atmosphere is much more upbeat than that of *Clandestino*. The addition of brass and bleeps and bleats adds to the crazed cheerfulness. Tracks like "Papito" and "La Chinita" are jolly to the point of mania. "Promiscuity" ('Too much, too much promiscuity / Can drop to insanity') is another quasi-burlesque number about the emotional dangers of sleeping around, that could have come straight out of the music hall. Then there's the jaunty Franglais of "Le Rendez-Vous", in which Manu takes a date to a French movie.

Overall, *Próxima Estación* was less obviously political than his more engaged fans might have expected. This was a conscious move for Manu. 'I'm aware that rebellion has been co-opted as a marketing device,' he said at the time of the album's release, citing the pictures of Che Guevara that were use to advertise Absolut Vodka. 'But maybe because I'm nearly forty, just complaining about what's wrong with the world isn't enough.'

"Mi Vida", which means 'my life' but which can also be a term of love and endearment, is the saddest and most beautiful song on the album. It features some evocative and surreal poetic imagery: *'mi vida lucerito sin vela / mi sangre de la herida / no me hagas sufrir mas / mi vida bala perdida / por la gran via / charquito de arrabal / no quiero que te vayas / no quiero que te alejes'* (my life bright star without a candle / my blood from the wound / don't make me suffer more / my life a stray bullet /along the Gran Via / a puddle in the slums / I don't want you to go / I don't want you to leave.)

Manu loves those rare moments when a song arrives almost fully formed. The ones that just appear like that are always the best. "Mi Vida" came to him one night and was recorded the next day.

The song "Trapped By Love" is an archetypal Manu composition. He had written it in the aftermath of his break-up with Anouk, and the disintegration of Mano Negra. But it was an enduring motif. 'I love this song,' he later elaborated. 'I couldn't be trapped by a city, by a person, by nothing. I was a *loco mosquito*.' Recently, Manu had met a Senegalese girl called Nadine who ran a shop in Barcelona selling imports of clothes and other trinkets from West Africa. They developed a serious relationship that was to last seven years. At one point they tried living together, but Manu found that level of domesticity and routine impossible.

With the huge success of *Clandestino*, Manu was in a position to make serious demands of the record company when it came to marketing *Próxima Estación*. Instead of plastering the Paris Metro with posters in the traditional way, Virgin agreed to rent an entire station in Manu's favourite quarter of Ménilmontant and stage a kind of art event there, as well as an album launch at his friend Johnny McLeod's Babel Bar. Manu vetoed the idea of doing any TV advertising.

Outside Paris, marketing reverted to more textbook hard-sell methods. A reporter from the *Wall Street Journal* was amused to see the effect of this strategy in Nîmes. 'There are Manu Chao billboards on the roads. A life-size Manu Chao "tower" at the entrance to the FNAC department store. And at electronic dealers, TV sets can be seen broadcasting Manu Chao. Thanks to a global corporate giant, the face of one of the best-known anti-globalisation protestors hangs over this French town.' Concert-goers even got the words 'Manu Chao' stamped on their wrists. But the reporter also added that 'Mr Chao is the first to recognise the contradiction between his lucre and his politics. Working for a multi-national corporation, he says, disqualifies him from being a symbol of anti-globalisation.' He quotes Manu saying that: 'The dictatorship of the world economy will mean, if it continues, collective suicide. I'm just trying to help – although it's true I do have a lot more means to do so than other people.'

Manu was, in fact, set to earn several million euros from *Próxima Estación*. Its success also put the wind back in

Clandestino's sails and kicked it back up the charts. 'Money', concluded Manu, 'is a problem that has been solved.' But that in itself brought other, albeit lesser, problems in its wake.

The album reviews were generally positive, which was a boon, although it must be said that *Próxima Estación* had such momentum behind it that it was in effect critic-proof. *Le Monde*'s review of the album was entitled *'Les collages euphorique de Manu Chao'* and went on to describe the project as mad, glorious and miraculous.

The few negative grumblings focused on the fact that the album wasn't as innovative as *Clandestino*, and that, in fact, it was just more of the same. 'He's made the same album,' observed a puzzled Charlie Gillett when chairing the BBC's annual World Music Awards. Which was almost true, but missed the point, for the soundscapes and emotional atmosphere of *Próxima Estación* were different and more positive: there was less of the *malegría*, more of the fun. In retrospect, it feels like one of Manu's most fully realised and cohesive albums – and a career milestone.

Próxima Estación was propelled up the charts by "Me Gustas Tú", which became a top 10 single in France and several other European countries. Manu was particularly pleased that buskers throughout the continent adopted the song, often modifying the words to their own desires. At a time when every computer buff was banging on about the future being interactivity, this was the kind of interactivity that he could appreciate and enjoy.

There was also some disappointment from Manu's more radical fans that the album wasn't more directly political. In Peru, a critic for the newspaper *La República* regretted that Manu had not 'sparked a Molotov to set fire to the rock stage once and for all, to light the fuse of rebellion against the old order'. But that wasn't a role Manu felt was for him. Indeed, in 2001 he avoided an opportunity, consciously, to take overt leadership of the anti-capitalist movement and become something of an 'alternative world leader'.

GENOA 44.4°N 8.9°E

A month after the release of *Próxima Estación*, from 18 to 21 July 2001, the G8 summit of world leaders took place in Genoa. It was the cue for massive anti-globalisation protests. Three weeks before the summit was due to begin, Manu and his band Radio Bemba played at a festival in the city. Half the price of each ticket sold went to the Genoa Social Forum, which organised the anti G8 demos and to the building of a Clandestino bar in the city, which gave water, apples and other basics to the demonstrators free of charge.

Then the band played a massive free show at the Duomo in Milan, 'in the heart of Berlusconi country', as Manu put it. And the night before the protest they played another rousing show, the proceeds of which went into a fund to pay for the legal fees of any arrested protestors.

A few cynics applauded this piece of radical-chic marketing for Manu's album. The authorities thought differently. A few weeks before Genoa, an Italian police squad had descended on Virgin's office in Milan, seeking evidence to back their assertion that, in their own words, 'Mr Chao's music encourages the drug trade', and when the band played the Treviso Festival, the army turned up and 30,000 people were forced to pass through the entry gates one by one, delaying the concert for three hours. Paulo Varesi, head of the Rinnovamento Sindicale, an Italian police officers' union, declared that 'Mano Chao is sending out a deviant message, which can be interpreted as an appeal to engage in warfare.'

On the eve of the summit, the Italian Minister of the Interior declared on TV that he wanted to negotiate the security of Genoa with Manu. Manu rebuffed this idea. Meanwhile, over 200,000 anti-capitalists – socialists, communists, anarchists, greens and others – descended on Genoa. Rejecting the legitimate right of the eight world leaders to decide the trajectory of the planet's economy, they saw Genoa as an opportunity to highlight the evils of globalisation, hopefully in a festive, non-violent spirit. The authorities, and, most vocally, the Italian Premier Silvio Berlusconi, argued that attempting to blockade the meeting was an anti-democratic and violent act in itself.

The G8 meeting was held inside a 'Red Zone' in the centre of Genoa that was declared off-limits for non-residents and surrounded by a fearsome barricade, which cut the pro-testors off from the summit delegates. Fears of a 'terrorist attack' led to a militarised atmosphere, with anti-aircraft missiles and helicopters hovering above. Only one activist, Valerie Vie, a secretary of ATTAC, managed to get through the barrier, but she was immediately arrested. (ATTAC is a French-based anti-globalisation pressure group and Manu was one of its founding members. Originally a single-issue movement that demanded the introduction of the so-called Tobin tax on currency speculation, ATTAC now devotes it-self to a wide range of issues related to globalisation.)

Manu was in the thick of the action. In a sequence that is included in the *Babylonia En Guagua* DVD, he declares: 'There are a thousand different ideas for the future: I want to respect them all. The important thing is to stay united and say no to the future that is being proposed.' He says this with passion and then adds, waving to the sky, 'and say no to the fucking helicopters!' The video shows Manu with trumpeter Roy Paci playing joyously amongst a good-humoured bunch of protestors as they follow the march. It continues with Manu condemning the 'dictatorship of money' and pointing to the barricade, saying, 'That wall could fall in six months. The system seems really solid but actually it's fragile, because money is virtual and exists in computers. Another crash in Singapore or Wall Street and', he mimes dominoes falling, 'everything collapses'. He was ahead of his time.

This was an unusually relaxed moment of the demon-strations, which rapidly turned ugly as the police raided social centres, media hubs and union buildings, not just in Genoa but across Italy, arresting three hundred demonstra-tors. An English journalist, Mark Covell, described how an armoured police van broke through the gates at the Diaz

Manu on the march with Gambeat (left), during the anti-G8 demonstrations in Genoa, 2001.

Pertini school building in Genoa, where he was staying with a group of protestors. They cracked his head with a baton, knocking out sixteen teeth before he passed out. Almost all the demonstrators were beaten. Blood was everywhere. 'It was like a Mexican butcher's shop,' Covell said. At least four hundred protestors and a hundred security forces were injured in the clashes.

On 20 July, a 23-year-old activist called Carlo Giuliani was shot dead during street battles with the police. 'Everyone is stunned by the violence,' Manu posted on his website. 'It makes you want to become violent, the violent way we were treated.' However, he felt that the over-the-top brutality of the police was designed to provoke a like-for-like response from the protestors and cautioned against being manipulated and allowing the authorities to portray the protestors as violent terrorists.

Perhaps the last word on Genoa should go Haidi, the mother of Carlo Giuliani, the dead protestor: 'What is at stake is the equilibrium of the planet, along with all the people who inhabit it, its animals, plants, the sea, the land, the air we breathe, the art and culture built up over millions of years, the billions of people who have patiently and tirelessly created it. We can't just abandon everything to the drabness of indifference, the arrogance of a few men, or the stupidity of blind greed.'

Manu returned to Genoa a few days later and went to Piazza Alimonda, where Carlo Giuliani had lost his life. 'I went on foot and felt waves of emotion. I met my dad there who said a beautiful sentence: "We cannot force them to tell the truth about the G8, but we can force them to lie more shamelessly."

In subsequent years, Italy became the country where the authorities were most antagonistic towards Manu. In the public imagination, he was an anti-Berlusconi – an idealist, eco-activist and supporter of the marginalised. That made him a threat. His name was further blackened by an interview with the French communist newspaper *L'Humanité*, in which he said he had friends among the black bloc, an anarchist grouping that dressed in black at protests, which included members who believed that violence was justified.

'Everywhere in Italy at that time I really felt the heat,' Manu remembers. 'The press was saying, "Here comes the worst of culture, the drug addict, let's fight him!" Police with very aggressive dogs come to the shows. When we played the local shops closed down, very scared because the press would say that the vandals are coming. But of course the kids and everyone came to the shows and it wasn't like that. It was the opposite to what they say in the press. The shops opened afterwards and admitted they were stupid to believe what the press said.'

In the town of Ferrara, there was even a pirated poster of Manu. 'It was the worst picture of me,' he says. 'It just said

"This man is not welcome in our town."' Manu still has that poster at his home in Barcelona. He might not have enjoyed the heat from the authorities, but he was still enough of a rock'n'roller to get a kick from being an outlaw.

Manu and Radio Bemba played other more surreal gigs in Italy around this time, including one at a prison in Volterra, a picturesque Tuscan hill town south of Pisa. The Renaissance exterior of the prison is on the town's tourist trail, right next to the Etruscan gate and a magnificent fiteenth-century fortress built by Lorenzo the Magnificent. When the band arrived in Volterra, they were received like a notorious gang of gunslingers in a Western film. The good folk of Volterra had been whipped up into a panic by Berlusconi's papers. All the shops were shut and boarded up. The relatively liberal authorities who ran the local prison had given permission for the prison band to open Radio Bemba's show in the town, but

Manu with participants at the event at the Volterra prison event.

at the last minute a message came from Milan forbidding the prisoners to play.

Manu then persuaded the prison chief to allow Radio Bemba to play inside the prison walls instead. It was a maximum-security jail, full of lifers, murderers and other criminals deemed to be amongst the most dangerous in the land. But once a year they had a prison theatre day, and this time Radio Bemba were going to provide the music. 'It was like a Fellini film,' recalls Manu. 'There were murderers dressed as women. Other guys dressed up as Nazis, another one like a pilot. It was totally insane. But a great gig, one of the most memorable.'

SPAIN: JAI ALAI KATUMBI EXPRESS

The problems in Italy spread to Spain in 2003, when Manu decided to put together a tour with Radio Bemba and invited

his old friend, the Basque punk-radical Fermin Muguruza, along as a guest. As they would be performing several of Fermin's songs, they decided to go out under the slightly unwieldy name of Jai Alai Katumbi Express, '*Jai Alai*' being Basque for 'Merry Festival' and Katumbi another of those favourite Manu neighbourhoods – in Rio de Janeiro. Songs like Manu's "Merry Blues" were mixed with Muguruza tunes like "Maputxe" – most of them joyful and infectious ska workouts that Radio Bemba could gel with instantly. Starting off in small venues

Public enemy – Fermin Muguruza.

and rooms, the band ended up playing arenas a few months later.

Muguruza was a political activist and member of the militant Herri Batasuna party in the Basque Country, whose goal was total independence. Some of its members were pro-violence, although Muguruza did not share that point of view. Manu's own take on the independence of his mother country was at best ambivalent, 'There are enough borders already, why do we need any more?'

The tour ran into trouble when the Association for Victims of Terrorism (AVT) denounced Muguruza as a 'terrorist', on the basis of a song called "Surri, Surri" – a hit for his old band Kortatu in 1985, which had revelled in the escape from jail of a couple of ETA members. There was a firestorm in the press, particularly in Málaga, where a local politician called José Maria Martin Carpena had been assassinated by the Basque separatists ETA in 2000. Muguruza was banned from performing by the local authorities in Málaga and Murcia and, when Manu refused to play the concerts without his friend, he in turn was accused of being an 'apologist for terrorism'.

'I have spent years saying I am against violence of the ETA,' declared Muguruza in his own defence, 'but it seems no one believes me. Yes, I am a leftist and in favour of independence. But this is a witch hunt, an ideological persecution to delay any political solution.' Manu regretted 'the stigmatisation of people trying to find a peaceful solution to the Basque problem', while pointing out that Fermin's offending song had been released eighteen years earlier.

These attacks were especially painful to Manu due to the memory of his beloved grandfather, Tomás Ortega, who had fought against Franco. Didn't Franco's general Emilio Mola say that it was 'necessary to spread terror, eliminating without scruples and hesitation all those who do not think as we do'. That meant democrats, Reds, Jews, Freemasons, Muslims, trade unionists, gays, 'free' women, socially conscious priests and other deviants, all of whom were victims of Franco's calculated campaign of terror. 'In my neighbourhood, it was hurtful to be branded as some kind of terrorist,' recalls Manu, 'but, for the sake of my grandfather, I answered the press, saying, "I was born in France, I'm a republican and a democrat."'

Just as he was dealing with these caricatures from the right, Manu began to be attacked on his left flank, particularly by voices emanating from his native Paris. Thanks to his enormous success and profile, he had become a target for the moralising left. Manu's manager Emmanuel de Buretel believes the reason was simple jealousy: 'Out of the optimistic alternative scene in the 1980s, Manu was the only one who really made it worldwide.'

An infamous barb came in 2003 in the form of a catchy punk song called "Manu Chao" by Les Wampas – a band that Daniel Jamet, one of Mano Negra's guitarists, had gone on to join. Over a riff that owed a fair debt to "I Wanna Be Sedated" by The Ramónes, the song had a chorus that translates as: 'If I had the wallet of Manu Chao / I'd go on holiday to the Congo / If I had the bank account of Louis Armstrong / I'd take a vacation until at least Easter'. It appeared both as a single – which went top 20 in France – and on an album pointedly titled *Never Trust A Guy Who Having Been A Punk, Is Now Playing Electro*.

'What bothers me about people like Manu Chao is that, while they protest, they live lives of the elite, who criticise the system while taking advantage of it,' Les Wampas lead singer Didier Wampas explained. 'The song isn't a settling of scores, the chorus just came to me like that. Maybe it's because of my communist education, but I do have some trouble understanding how you can be a billionaire and still be criticising. When you are selling albums at 140 francs, you accept the system. You're in. When you are Manu Chao, you could sell your albums at 30 francs and still make money.'

The argument elicits some sympathy from Manu. 'I did fight with Virgin 20,000 times to make the discs cheaper,' he says, 'but the distributors just say "Super! Manu Chao lowers his price, that means more for us." The public end up paying the same. Artists don't have that much power to intervene in the price, even when they're signed to an independent.'

In any case, these days, Manu makes the reasonable point that filesharing allows people to consume his music for nothing. He has declared openly that he's not worried if people download his music for free. 'If I was a fifteen-year-old with no money, it would be really stupid not to get the songs I like on the internet.' This, of course, generates the counter-accusation that Manu doesn't support independent labels, for whom piracy can mean life or death. 'I didn't actually say I was pro-piracy,' Manu clarifies. 'The Senegalese you see selling CDs on the street are actually part of a mafia to whom they pay ninety per cent of their takings and who control that market. It's pure exploitation. There's nothing worse for me than these kinds of mafias.' He does recognise that piracy can be the ruin of a small label: 'The public has to be responsible and buy the discs from independent labels. For me, I'm earning good money, so it doesn't really matter.'

More problems and flak came flying Manu's way after he guested on a track by Noir Désir, one of the most revered groups in the story of French rock. The song was called "Le Vent Nous Portera" (The Wind Will Carry Us), a pleasantly melancholy tune that features Manu's distinctive guitar sound. Manu came into the studio and laid down a guitar part as a favour to the band. 'It was done very casually,' he remembers. 'It maybe took twenty minutes.' The band asked about credits and payment and Manu said he would be happy with the standard union rate for the session and a credit as one of the musicians, nothing more.

When the song came out, it was released as a single with a sticker flagging up the Manu Chao involvement. This strategy proved especially effective in Italy, where Manu's fame far outstripped that of Noir Désir. Their album went on to sell a million, largely due to the fact that "Le Vent Nous Portera" became a hit single. Both Manu and his manager Jacques Renault were upset that Noir Désir and their record label had cashed in on the Manu Chao name in order to sell their own record, and that what had originally been a simple friendly favour had been turned into the cornerstone of an entire marketing campaign. So Renault contacted Noir Désir to demand a royalty over and above the original session fee.

Shortly afterwards, Bernard Cantat, the lead singer of Noir Désir, beat up his girlfriend, the actress Marie Trintignant, during an alcohol-fuelled brawl over infidelity in a hotel room in Vilnius, Lithuania. The following morning she was found in a coma and died a few days later. A post-mortem revealed she had suffered multiple head injuries. Cantat admitted hitting her, but said that she had received the fatal blow when she fell and hit her head on a radiator. A Vilnius court found Cantat guilty of manslaughter and sentenced him to eight years in prison. It was a notorious scandal in France, where opinion was divided between those who thought the episode was a tragic accident and those who saw Cantat as a murderer.

At this point, Manu might have been better advised to withdraw his legal demand for royalties. Perhaps it was that streak of Basque stubbornness that made him stick to his claim. But his stance generated considerable ill feeling, which Noir Désir's record company mischievously stoked into controversy. Still, the cash that Renault extracted from Universal went towards setting up Manu's charitable foundation – which he has since used as an end for other bad money, for example, a settlement from HSBC when they used a track of his without authorisation.

PARIS-BAMAKO: AMADOU & MARIAM

An entirely new musical avenue presented itself in 2001. Manu had first heard the Malian musicians Amadou & Mariam whilst on a visit to Paris from Barcelona. As he was driving around the *péripherique* ring road late one night, he happened to hear their breakthrough track "Je Pense À Toi" on the radio. 'This song burst out and grabbed my attention,' he remembered. 'I was instantly hooked. I didn't know who the song was by. When I sung it to my friends, they said, 'Everyone knows that – it's Amadou & Mariam!' I rushed out and bought all their CDs. Every day I'd put their records on at home and when I started singing along I'd add to them. All these ideas for backing vocals and melodies came into my head. It became a game I played every day.'

Manu loved the blues-rock edge to their music. 'The blues came from Mali,' he explained. 'John Lee Hooker's ancestors must have come from there. But I also loved the immense amount of humanity, the strong sense of sweetness and gentleness in their music.' Amadou & Mariam also appealed to Manu on a philosophical level. The lyrics of tracks like "Tout Le Monde Est Troublé' (The Whole World Is Troubled) bemoan war, brothers falling out and disease, but are undercut by driving, positive music, a disconnect which seems to imply that there may be terrible problems in the world, but that doesn't mean we can't dance or celebrate. 'We sing about finding beauty in the face of hardship,' says Amadou Bagayoko. 'We want the audience to be happy, and to dance. We don't want them going home and committing suicide.'

Amadou & Mariam's own personal history mirrors the triumph of courage over adversity expressed in their songs. The couple are both blind – they met at Bamako's Institute for the Young Blind in 1975, where they were brought together by their mutual passion for music. Mariam lost her sight to measles at the age of five, but a year later started singing at weddings and baptism parties. Amadou became blind as a teenager, but was already an accomplished musician, and he later played with Les Ambassadeurs du Motel de Bamako, one of Mali's leading groups, whose ranks included Salif Keita, an albino with one of Mali's greatest voices who became one of the first global world music stars in the 1980s after the release of his extraordinary and inventive album *Soro*.

Amadou & Mariam began to make a name for themselves in Mali and beyond during the 1980s. Owing to the lack of good studios in Mali, they moved to the Ivory Coast for four years, where they released a series of cassettes, which brought them to the attention of African music lovers in France.

It had been four years since Manu had been in Africa, and he felt the music drawing him back. 'Throughout all that time I'd missed the place,' he says. 'It was a physical sense, I felt it in my guts. You don't just walk away and forget Africa.'

It turned out that Manu knew Amadou & Mariam's manager, Marc Antoine Moreau, from the heyday of the alternative indie-rock scene in Paris during the 1980s and they met again at a concert in 2001. Manu mentioned that he would be thrilled to work with the duo, though it wasn't until September 2003 that their calendars coincided sufficiently for a meeting to take place in Paris. 'We went into the studio for a day to mess about and have a bit of fun,' Manu recalls. 'But we ended up working so well together that we stayed on in the studio for six days.'

All those hours of 'homework' that Manu had put in listening to Amadou & Mariam's music paid off. 'We didn't have to spend months together in the studio to get a vibe going. There were songs that Amadou & Mariam had written and others that we came up with in the studio. It all happened very spontaneously and everyone was surprised that we got the basis for an album in one week.'

Manu had some useful backing tracks to work with for the opening song "M'Bife", and cooked up another couple of songs called "Taxi Bamako" and "Senegal Fast Food", the later an effervescent ditty with its Manu-esque globalised lyrics, *'Il est cinq heures à Mali / quelle heure est-il au Paradis?'* (It is five o'clock in Mali / What time is it in Paradise?). In addition, he roped in old cohorts Philippe Teboul on percussion, Pierre Gauthé on trombone and Roy Paci on trumpet for the Paris sessions, to help fashion a wonderfully driving backing track to Amadou's song "La Réalité", with its signature message, *'C'est la triste réalité, mais ... dansons ensemble'* (That's the sad reality, but let's dance together anyway).

In January 2004, before resuming work at Amadou & Mariam's place in Bamako, the capital of Mali, Manu and Marc Antoine Moreau travelled to the Festival in the Desert, an event which, since its founding in 2001, had rapidly become an annual gathering of mythic proportions. It took place on the shores of an ancient lake, in amongst talcum-white sand

A serendipitous trio – Manu onstage with Amadou & Mariam at the Festival in the Desert, Mali, 2004.

dunes, sixty kilometres west of Timbuktu. In other words, the middle of nowhere. Manu performed several times and spent hours jamming around a campfire with the desert blues band Tinariwen.

Once at Amadou & Mariam's house in Bamako, the album began to take an African shape with the help of local musicians like *djembe* player Boubacar Dembélé and the Ivorian afro-reggae superstar Tiken Jah Fakoly, who sang lead on a lament about corrupt politicians entitled "Politic Amagni". The track included a chant written by Manu that was reprised in the song "Politik Kills" on his next album, *La Radiolina*. It tells how politics needs ignorance and feeds on blood. For the final track on the album, Manu recorded a lovely, touching love duet between Amadou & Mariam called "M'Bifé Blues".

Manu loved being back in the heat and chaos of an African city, and he regularly escaped to the roof of Amadou & Mariam's house to drink mint tea and smoke joints. He also met and jammed with the couple's son Sam and his rap crew SMOD (the initials of the group's four founding members) up on the roof. The young rappers' refusal to slavishly employ either American or European rhythms and the social awareness in their music appealed to Manu. 'Hip hop in Europe is all about bling bling, about money and girls,' Sam says. 'Most hip hop in West Africa isn't like that at all. We have problems and so we can't just talk about having a big car. There's no point in copying the Americans. Right now, Africa needs to talk. Africa must stop crying.' Manu was sufficiently inspired by SMOD that he agreed to play on their next album (*Ta I Tola*, released in 2004), and to produce an album with them as well. Thanks to the constant traffic of projects coming Manu's way, the geographical distance and his wayward working methods, it would take another six years before that album saw the light of day.

If there's a subtext running through *Dimanche À Bamako*, as the Amadou & Mariam album was eventually called, it's a comparison between the chaos of modern Bamako and the gentler city that the couple remembered nostalgically from their childhood days. As Mariam reminisced to writer Andy Morgan: 'When I was young, Bamako was like a little village. We'd go into each other's houses and tell stories. We girls would go out in the moonlight to the riverbank and have fun. Nowadays they don't do that because they are just watching TV.'

Nonetheless, life in Mali has improved in other ways, especially the treatment of the disabled. And the fact that blind Malians enjoy a much greater level of care is partly due to Amadou & Mariam's tireless support of the Institut des Jeunes Aveugles (Institute for Blind Youth) in Bamako, and to their own elevated profile, which reached unimagined levels after the release of *Dimanche À Bamako*.

The *Dimanche À Bamako* album was an immediate hit in France, reaching number 2 in the charts and becoming the soundtrack to the summer of 2005. The album won the

Victoire De La Musique, the most prestigious music prize in France and an accolade that meant a great deal to the couple. 'Back in the early days in Mali we would always listen to the broadcasts from the prize ceremony. So when we won the prize ourselves, it really touched us.' It was a hit with the critics in Britain, too, with the *Observer* newspaper calling it 'the fizziest Afro-pop ever bottled' and including it in their list of the best albums of the decade.

Whereas previous Amadou & Mariam albums had sold 15,000, this one went past the 600,000 mark, and its success put their careers on a new sky-high trajectory. It led to the couple meeting with the idols of their youth, like Dave Gilmour of Pink Floyd or Robert Plant of Led Zeppelin, and to an invitation to play at President Obama's Nobel Peace Prize award ceremony in Stockholm. Amadou & Mariam not only became cultural ambassadors for African music in general and for Mali in particular but also an inspiring role model for the blind and disabled.

Yet even this triumph created some sourness in Paris. There were mutterings that Manu, who didn't need the money, was overcharging the couple for his services. In fact, according to their manager, the deal that was struck after some robust negotiation, was 'perfectly fair'. And in any case, back when Manu first started working on the project, it seemed unlikely that it would ever become a major hit. It was a gamble for all concerned.

People also accused Manu of filching some of the material on the album from other sources, most notably the "Soul Fire" chant from a song by Lee Perry. Throughout his career, Manu has often been accused of plagiarising songs. They always say, where there is a hit there's a writ: strike lucky with a song, and someone somewhere will claim to have written something similar. This hasn't happened to Manu, which suggests any borrowings haven't been blatant. Or, at least, according to Manu's manager Emmanuel de Buretel, nothing that would stand up in court. 'There are websites dedicated to how Manu has borrowed music,' he says. 'But we've only been involved in one court case, the one with the guy whose voice was sampled on the Madrid metro saying, *"Próxima Estación: Esperanza"*. All the other samples we can we have cleared.'

That was one of the mysteries of Manu. He had an above average voice, but you couldn't say he was one of the great singers; and he admits to limited technical ability as a guitarist in a firmament of technically brilliant players. Likewise, some of his songs didn't seem that original – surely they must have been plagiarised from somewhere?

It's a thought that occurs to many songwriters themselves. Paul McCartney famously woke up with the tune of "Yesterday" already written in his head; singing it to others, he was convinced it must be a standard he had heard somewhere? He was lucky enough to dream it. Manu says that's how he feels about some of his songs, especially the ones that arrive 'already written'. They may be simple (they are performed by buskers the world over), but the best of them have that sense of immediate familiarity, as though Manu, like McCartney, was merely an amanuensis, an aerial tuned into some Akashic realm of the collective unconscious where all songs have already been written.

PART TWO

OTROS MUNDOS

In search of Manu

CHAPTER 12:
BARCELONA – THE NEIGHBOURHOOD GUY

'The only Guru is yourself.'

Manu Chao, Barcelona, 2005

On the release of *Próxima Estación: Esperanza* in 2001, Manu agreed to interviews with reporters from the main European papers, including *El País*, *Le Monde* (whose reporter, Paul Moreira, found Manu 'still a humble vagabond, the same fire in his eyes, the same stubborn faith') and the UK's *Daily Telegraph*. The latter, in their wisdom, commissioned me – and so I set off for my first meeting with Manu, at the Café Glaciar, a stylish hang-out, decorated with black and white jazz photos, in a palm-lined square in the old Barri Gòtic quarter of Barcelona.

Looking back, I'm a little surprised the interview was not my last. In part because it was the *Telegraph*, which, with its conservative politics, must have slipped under Manu's radar when he accepted the publicity schedule. But more because of my own particular line of questioning. I had a theory at the time that when interviewing a rock star you should try and unsettle them a bit, disturb their sense of being in control, so they won't unload the same warmed-up anecdotes that they give to all the journalists. It was a strategy that had worked nicely with Lou Reed, who is famously monosyllabic and hostile to interviewers. So I kicked off by asking Manu if recycling his old material meant he'd lost his inspiration, and then suggested, 'Your lyrics all sound like they were written when you were stoned, as if you wrote the first thing that came into your head.'

Manu wasn't bothered in the least by either question. On recycling, he answered that newness was overrated, society was neophiliac, and capitalism was entirely fuelled by making people feel insecure so they kept buying new things. The recycling of riffs and tunes happened all the time in reggae and dancehall, so it was no big deal. 'Why this obsession with the new? I wear the same trainers usually till they fall apart. Let's make more use of what we have.' And, on the question of his lyrics (which are, of course, often highly poetic), he just paused, laughed and then said, with disarming frankness, 'Yes, that's exactly how I write.' I laughed, impressed at his lack of defensiveness and gave up trying to be provocative.

Most of the time, as a music journalist, you feel you have your subject more or less figured out before you even meet them. You've already clicked where they are in the scheme of things. That didn't feel at all the case with Manu. For one thing, there were those eyes. The only way I can put it is that it seemed as though he had seen things that most of us haven't, and maybe he had really seen more than most people. He had jumped between worlds, from the most extreme of the Brazilian *favelas* to the gilded landscapes of the A-list rock star life, where he's been feted by presidents and loved by millions. Or maybe it was just the drugs: he had spent weeks off his head at a time on peyote and other powerful hallucinogens.

Five years later, I'm sitting in the same café, possibly the same table, watching the same hot ebb and flow of downtown Barcelona life, waiting for Manu Chao. Since our first meeting, he has become a genius loci of the city, the bohemian puckish spirit of the Catalan capital.

I'd actually seen Manu a few times since that first meeting in 2001. The first was at a Radio Bemba concert only months later, in Paris, the week after '9/11'. It was a strange time, in which the gods of celebrity had been temporarily deposed. The world seemed to be spinning momentarily on a different axis. Vacuous stars had been on TV to raise money, attempting to look serious and concerned, whereas Manu seemed to possess the weight and moral vision to cope with the madness and calm us all down.

Then there was a concert at London's Shepherd's Bush Empire in March 2002. The performance was a rousing one but also memorable because I'd run into Joe Strummer backstage, together with his wife, Lucinda. Strummer was trying out his bad Spanish on Manu, despite the fact that Manu speaks perfectly good English. 'He adored Manu's music and they were good friends,' Lucinda said to me, some time after Strummer's vulnerable heart gave out suddenly in December 2002.

I'd also met Manu briefly in London, again in 2002, in a café near Brick Lane. He was with a couple of students who ran political websites, in the midst of a conversation about how new archaeological digs were revealing the complexity of indigenous Amazonian culture, when a rep from Virgin Records, his label at the time, arrived breathless to inform Manu that he had secured tickets for the Brit Awards, which was taking place that very same night. Manu would meet David Bowie and Robbie Williams (who had covered Manu's song "Bongo Bong"'). 'I'm spending the evening with some friends,' was Manu's polite but dismissive reply. Taken aback, but undeterred, the Virgin man added that he had also landed a spot on an influential TV show the following week. Manu wasn't having that, either. He explained that he was splitting up his group at the weekend and going off backpacking.

Now, five years on, I had managed to secure another interview with Manu, having no idea that the meeting would lead to this book and a ringside seat at several of the most significant moments in the next few years of Manu's life, watching him record with patients at a mental asylum in Buenos Aires, jam under the desert skies in Sahrawi refugee camps, perform to monstrous crowds in New York and Boston, headline the Glastonbury Festival, DJ at a London squat ... become initiated into the Macheteros of Atenco in Mexico.

When Manu finally turns up at the Glaciar, on an antique bicycle with no seat, he looks bronzed and fit, like a Galician peasant who has been working the fields. Those three-hour gigs of his were clearly aerobic. He begins by complaining that trendy, overpriced bars are pushing out his favourite neighbourhood haunts. The little street-level co-ops and associations, which he uses as an office, and the concert halls where he would go into battle with his 50 euro guitar, the cheapest on the market, were being closed down. Buskers are being arrested in the street, which still remains a favourite rehearsal space.

I talk about our previous meetings, the Shepherd's Bush Empire concert, and meeting Joe Strummer – something of a heroic figure to both of us. Manu says he isn't against meeting heroes, or stars, in principle: 'Sometimes, I'm quite interested in getting to know them because they're part of the world and I'm curious. I like my position because I can be in the ghetto or in the street meeting people one day and talking with stars the next. I'm curious to know about these guys and how they manage their lives.' But Manu is careful to add, 'I prefer to meet stars I don't care about.' The ones he admires always let him down.

The only exception is Joe Strummer. 'Joe has been like an uncle to me,' Manu says. 'We met and played together in the time of Mano Negra and he used to send little letters or postcards. I met him the last time six months before he died, at a festival in Japan. He was staying in the campsite, washing in the river. I saw him at six in the morning and he was changing a little tape, organising the music, making sure everyone at that little party was in the right mood. He taught me another lesson. I was lucky to be around him. God bless Joe.'

Manu, Gambeat (right) and other members of Radio Bemba, with Joe Strummer (centre, in black), at a party in Granada, Spain.

I'd heard Manu's line about Bob Marley being a 'professor of simplicity'. Something in that resonated, like a key to understanding Manu the man, and his success. At my cheap, bohemian hotel off the Ramblas, there was a copy of the *Tao Te Ching* by Lao-tzu, who had written the spiritual masterpiece sometime around the sixth century BC whilst wandering around China with a dancing girl. Flicking through the book, I happen across this phrase: 'Manifest plainness. Embrace simplicity. Reduce selfishness. Have few desires.'

I find myself thinking of the contradictions between Manu's success as a pop star and his attempts to keep things basic, both in terms of material possessions and music. I have the notion that the name 'Chao' could easily belong to some oriental wise guy and Manu certainly has the wiry cat-like litheness of a kung fu merchant. Something disorienting you do notice is that sometimes Manu seems much older than his years, then, minutes later, much younger

I broach the subject of simplicity with Manu by quoting the poet, filmmaker, sometime opium addict and boxing

manager Jean Cocteau: 'A true artist has to go through complexity to reach simplicity.' 'Yes, that's true,' answers Manu.
'But try explaining that to a twenty-year-old. You must first
complicate your life and then simplify it.'

Another essential Manu characteristic is his nomadism.
Travel, says Manu, is both his drug and his school. I'm also
a compulsive traveller and we talk about the way in which
travel can lead to a kind of innocence. You find yourself
someplace new, where everything is a little strange: the language, the music, the buildings, the people. The effect is to
make you feel like a child again, trying to figure things out.
Many artists try to reconnect to the creativity of childhood
and travel is one way of doing it. And when you're forced to
notice your surroundings because they're unfamiliar, time –
or at least memory – slows down. There's an illusion that the
inevitable black express train to oblivion coming your way
might just be delayed for a little longer. We agree that travel
can also be an antidote to depression, especially if indulged
in short bursts. Every moment seems to be significant, every
trip a narrative.

I tell Manu that listening to his albums is a little like
travelling, in that you get different views of the same thing,
repeated in different ways, as if you were moving over a
landscape. His music is perfect for listening to on planes and
trains, with its exhilarating pulse of forward projection and
shifting horizons. He talks of how technology has allowed
him to indulge these passions, music and travel, at the same
time. He recorded his two solo albums using a portable
studio. 'In the old days,' he said, 'you had to go into a studio
for a couple of months. Now I have a portable studio, which I
can take as hand luggage. I treat technology like a kid does; I
enjoy making mistakes.'

It's possible that travel is hard-wired into the human soul
and that being on the move is more natural than living a
sedentary existence. I tell Manu that I've been reading Bruce
Chatwin's *Anatomy of Restlessness*. He claims that wandering
is a human characteristic genetically inherited from the
vegetarian primates and those nomadic genes are more

prominent in some of us than others. Chatwin also makes the point that nomadic art is more instinctive than rational, and those with nomadic tendencies are naturally averse to piling up possessions. Both observations seem apt in Manu's case.

I'd been told that Manu had no fixed abode. It was one of many legends that floats around him. And yes, he tells me, for seven years he did indeed have nowhere, but now he has a permanent base, a flat in Barcelona. 'I had musical instruments and other stuff in Madrid, Mexico, Paris, Rio ... ', he says. 'It wasn't exactly efficient for making an album. And I love the street life here. There's still a strong anarchist tradition and in my neighbourhood there are lots of immigrant musicians from South America, and people from North Africa and Pakistan.' The Pakistanis ride around on scooters banging a can to let people know they have gas for sale, a sound which Manu had used on *Próxima Estación: Esperanza*.

I push Manu to define his politics and he says the vital key for him is the neighbourhood. It's essential to his world-view. The late DJ Charlie Gillett used to call Manu 'the neighbourhood guy'. 'You cannot change the world, I cannot change the world,' Manu asserts. 'I cannot even change my country, even if I know what my country is. But everybody can change his neighbourhood. I try. That's a responsibility of everybody. I hope the solution is there. I don't believe any more in one big revolution that's going to change everything. I believe in thousands and thousands of little neighbourhood revolutions. That's my hope.' In fact, he believes that revolution starts with changing yourself, which is 'by far the hardest part'. Then, maybe, you can change your family or your neighbourhood.

Who to vote for is always a problem: 'I've never voted for anyone, only *against* people. There's never been someone I really believe in. In any case, the problem with democracy is that politicians don't have the power they used to have. The corporations have more power.' He says there is more power, in voting terms, if you are a shareholder of a corporation.

Manu sets out in Barcelona, cheap guitar strapped in place. The collage illustration is from the book *Manu & Chao* by Jacek Wozniak, the artist who created Manu's logo and with whom he often collaborates.

You can't pin an easy label on Manu – anarchist, socialist, ecologist, Marxist – all are wide of the mark. Like so much about him, he can't be put in a straitforward box. What matters is neighbourhood action, consumer action, and support for the underdog, the marginalised and the oppressed. He feels that his personal responsibility is 'to use the microphone' that he has as a celebrity to broadcast the inequalities he sees around him. But he also repeats that he is just a musician, without the answers, lost in the century like everyone else.

Manu looks up at the clock and tells me he was supposed to be at a bar to meet a Russian promoter, about an hour ago. 'Come for a beer,' he says, and we set off through a warren of walkways until we reach a wall lit up by a red painting of a woman entwined with a snake, with the legend 'El Mariatchi'. The bar is a favourite of Manu's – one of several drinking dens in his *barrio* set-up by *okupas* or squatters. It is furnished with unmatched plastic chairs and battered tables and the speciality of the house is the Hydro-miel, a potent cocktail of honey and assorted spirits. It turns out the honey for the liqueur comes from bees owned by Manu. He's bought some hives. That I hadn't been expecting, but Manu enthuses, saying one of his escape fantasies is retiring as a beekeeper.

Manu is immediately surrounded by numerous friends, a guitar materialises and he sings "Mr Bobby". Then others start to sing, and half the bar joins in on bottles or whatever percussive objects are to hand. Manu plays a few numbers from an as-yet-unreleased album with a Brazilian theme, the most memorable being a song to his son, Kira. Later he explains to me that Kira is six years old and living in Fortaleza in northwestern Brazil, the result of a short-lived relationship with a Brazilian woman. He usually manages to see them for a month or two around the New Year.

At the bar, there is a CD on sale called *Mariatchi Boogie* with a track by Manu and others by various local musicians, which buskers can sell to make money. Donating the tracks is an example of Manu's generosity but also his preference for encouraging self-help. Clearly, the scruffy Mariachi bar is a place where Manu feels at home and where he gets inspiration: 'The number of songs that came to me in bars, listening to stories of guys who had drunk too much and became unbuttoned ... '

It's getting late, but I have to ask him about the cows – which he sees as portents that guide his decisions and 'saved his life' in Brazil. 'It's important to see the signs, but it's not good to see the signs everywhere,' Manu says, enigmatically. 'I'm not anxious to see the signs; I know they are coming. After you get involved in this game, there are signs everywhere, so you have to take care. When you get signs in life they are very, very clear.'

'People in the Occident get lost in the cocoon of mysticism,' he continues. 'There are a lot of charlatans there. It's like food in Barcelona or London. Ninety percent is dog food, ten per cent soul food. There's 90 per cent bullshit, ten per cent knowing what they are talking about. If that. So beware of the gurus,' he concludes. 'The only guru is yourself.'

Sometime around midnight we leave the bar. Out of the Barri Gòtic gloom, someone in the warren of alleyways whispers, 'That guy looks like Manu Chao.'

CHAPTER 13:
NEW YORK – INTO THE HEART OF THE BEAST

'I've met the devil in person … twice.'

There's a dangerous storm and it's heading our way. Backstage at the Prospect Park Bandshell, Brooklyn, the computer screen is locked on to the weather channel and it's telling us that the deluge will strike right at the start of the concert. On the first truly hot day of the summer, with temperatures pushing one hundred degrees, there's a tangible pre-gig, pre-storm electricity in the air. Six thousand Manu Chao fans know they are in for a memorable night, under the open sky, in the rain. Tickets are so hot that the *Village Voice* has run an article about the strategies and scams people are trying out on Craigslist to get one. Cash on its own won't work. Claiming you were employed by an NGO or a homeless organisation stands a better chance.

As the band prepare to rush onstage, there are hugs and prayers, the psychological armour of gladiatorial troubadours. You can sense the tidal power of the crowd, baying for entertainment. A couple of music business types, pale courtiers, are talking quietly in a corner about units and demographics. I wish the band *mucha mierda*, the customary

Electricity in the air – Manu onstage at Prospect Park, June 2007.

Spanish encouragement, and take up a perch at the side of the stage, looking out over the crowd. The rush of energy is exhilarating. I'm on a precipice, looking on, suffering from vertigo.

The United States is 'the devil in the eyes of the rest of the world', according to Manu. Although he has toured South America extensively, both with his current band, the Radio Bemba Sound System, and with Mano Negra, this is his first fully fledged tour of the US as a solo artist. 'You cannot fight terrorism with terrorism,' he pronounces from the stage, a massive banner flag draped over his shoulders. 'You should fight violence with education not more violence.' The flag bears the slogan 'Immigrants are not criminals'.

With the skill of a sorcerer, Manu sings as if this huge audience were sitting in his front room, sharing a moment of intimacy. His records are full of loping, lazy rhythms, but live, his band regularly breaks down into a double-time hard-core thrash assault, led by the front-line trio of Manu himself, sinewy and elfin-like centre stage. He's flanked by Madjid, resembling the Brazilian footballer Ronaldo, on electric or battered Spanish guitars, and the gentle-giant Gambeat on bass – both 'loveable, shirtless brutes', according to *Village Voice*. Behind them are Philippe 'Garbancito' Teboul on percussion and drummer David Bourgnignon, adding an essential Latin edge to the assault, together with Angelo Mancini on Mexican style trumpet and Javier Galiana, with his intellectual features, pumping out synth chords.

It is one of the tightest, fiercest bands I've ever seen and they whip the crowd into fist-punching frenzy from midway through the first number. The mix of Hispanic, world and rock music fans sing along in Spanish and English to "Clandestino", that hymn to the lonely and dispossessed, and "Mr Bobby" ('Hey Bobby Marley, sing something good to me'), whose shadow seems to linger on in the bitter-sweet "Welcome To Tijuana" ('*tequila, sexo y marijuana*'), "Bongo Bong" and what has become his most famous song, "Me Gustas Tú". Snatches of *flamenco*, *rumba* and Mexican *banda* brass music drift in and out of focus. Sadness, celebration, *saudade* and fiesta are never far from each other. There are a couple of Latin-punk numbers from the Mano Negra days, including "Casa Babylon", where Manu takes the opportunity to remind us that we're actually in the 'House of Babylon', or at least its antechambers. He even reaches back to his beginnings and plays "Mala Vida", the first song he ever wrote, with its fears of servitude and dreams of escape.

From the splendid isolation of the backstage world I venture out into the middle of the crowd and stand next to a group of fans wearing Mexican wrestling masks. The Latin

American cult of Lucha Libre, or free wrestling, seems to be taking off in the States. Each wrestler has their own distinctive mask. Blue Demon's is a classic blue and white. Now, his son is carrying on the family tradition, sponsored by Coca-Cola, who launched a Blue Demon energy drink. El Santo was buried wearing his silver mask, and other fighters like Místico, El Rey Mysterioso and Mephisto all have their own masks and followers. Losers can be unmasked or humiliated by having their hair shorn. There's even a *mini estrellas* division of dwarves. I have my very own party with that masked crew, shadowboxing with a Mephisto fan. We sing. We drink. We dance.

Brooklyn's Anglo-Hispanic crowd are already sympathetic to Manu but other dates on the tour present a far steeper challenge. Backstage I meet Adam Shore, the boss of Vice Records. 'I saw them play the Coachella Festival, just before Rage Against the Machine,' he tells me. 'There were 90,000 Rage fans impatient to see their comeback gig, and it could have been a disaster. But Manu managed to totally win them over. If he makes it in the States, that will be a key moment.'

A couple of days earlier in Boston, on the Manu Chao tour bus, the nerve centre of the travelling music circus, with its sleek exterior and scruffy interior, I bumped into Manu's tour manager Paget Williams. He looked so relaxed and in his element that initially I thought he was a member of the band. Whilst I was waiting for Manu, I asked Paget about the nuts and bolts of tour logistics. He has worked with Nine Inch Nails. 'They have forty or so people on the road,' Paget said with mild disbelief. 'A stadium band like Muse has sixteen big trucks to tour their live show. On this tour, it's just me with an amazing sound man and the best band in the world!'

A good tour manager is both diplomat and gatekeeper. You have to treat him with a certain wary respect should you desire, for whatever reason, good or bad, to gain access to the backstage kingdom. Unlike most, Paget managed to perform his circus ringmaster duties and be highly personable at the same time. He had a tattoo on his arm, which read 'Stand Up For What You Believe In'.

Manu climbed on to the bus, unshaven but looking in great shape and, despite the 'No Smoking' sign, rolled a cigarette. Not for the first time, it struck me that success in many competitive fields such as music, literature or even journalism, is as much about physical fitness and stamina as it is about creative power.

I compliment Manu on the funkiness of the bus; he says he loves going to sleep in one city and waking up in another. The band is like 'a great family. I can imagine touring with these guys for years,' he adds. 'We stopped in the desert in Utah and made a fire. We stopped in parts of the far West, deep down America, not just the big cities. We were jamming with Russian guys in San Francisco. We did a crazy *batucada* with some Iranians. All of them were trying to get into this American way of life.'

The whole band had fallen in love with New Orleans, which reminded Manu of Rio, of Africa, with its 'malicious' sense of humour and its jazz, swamp blues and zydeco music. They saw some of the neighbourhoods that had been destroyed by Hurricane Katrina.

I asked an obvious question: 'Why come to the heart of the beast if you seem to hate America and all it stands for?' Manu was ready with his answer: 'I always criticise the government not the people. And if I am criticising, it's better to understand what it is you criticise. For people in South America and Africa, the United States is seen more and more like the devil. There's a heavy cost to the way of life here, and the rest of the world pays it. But everyone here applauds when I criticise their government so I just don't understand why there aren't thousands protesting outside the White House every day.'

Not that Manu was proud of his own governments in France or Spain. He has passports for both countries.

'From the days of Mano Negra, everyone always said you have to make it in the United States,' Manu continued. 'But I always thought the best way was to tackle South America first. Now we have a lot of our people at the shows in the States.' Once again, Manu's maverick, unconventional approach seemed to be delivering the goods in the end.

The only concert outside the States on this tour was over the border in Tijuana. Manu's song "Welcome To Tijuana'" from *Clandestino* has become a classic. Somehow Tijuana remains emblematic for Manu, the place where desperation, corrupt politics, drug violence and wild fiesta collide. Manu mentioned a music journalist he met there who had to have a bodyguard following the assassination of his editor. 'Actually, I really love the place,' he concluded with a wry, non-committal smile.

When we meet on the American tour, I haven't seen Manu for more than a year – not since that night at the Mariatchi bar in Barcelona. Back then a new album was supposed to be on the verge of release but it seemed to have disappeared into the cosmic wormhole of Planet Manu. But then it seems the album release is, once again, on the cards: the idea is to release it to coincide with the US tour, though Manu is still tinkering on his laptop, changing titles and shaving off a few seconds here and there. The album, *La Radiolina*, is eventually released in September 2007, by which time the tour is pretty much over.

My trip to see Manu's American dates is down to an invitation from Manu's manager, Emmanuel de Buretel, who with the album imminent, suggests I join a couple of legs of the US tour and write it up for the *Observer*. Meeting me at Heathrow airport, Emmanuel hands over a rough copy of the album, treating it as though it was microfilm in a spy movie. He gives me strict instructions to hand it back on arrival in Boston.

Record company execs are understandably paranoid about pre-release leaks, as an album can often turn up pirated on the internet before it is even released. But I couldn't help comparing his cloak-and-dagger attitude with the careless generosity of Manu, who had, with no concern, let me record him playing several songs from his as-yet-untitled 'Brazilian' album in the Mariatchi.

Emmanuel de Buretel had scaled the rarefied summit of the international record business when he became head of Virgin Europe, then EMI Europe, before setting up the Because label. After checking into the hotel in Boston, which was the stop before New York on the tour, we meet up at the bar for a drink. He is keen to emphasise that, despite the obvious caricature of being a capitalist who manages anarchists, his prime motivation for managing Manu is not the money, but the challenge ... and because of his personal fondness for the man himself.

'Manu is like a wild animal,' says Emmanuel, in answer to my question that he can't be the easiest guy to manage since he refuses to commit to anything far in advance. 'You can't put him in a cage.' The comment is a vivid illustration of the eternal tension between art and business. Music is very much a commodity on one level and, on another, as far from being a commodity as it's possible to be. But, like Jerry Wexler of

Atlantic Records or Nick Gold of World Circuit, Emmanuel is highly unusual in that he possesses both a sharp business sense and good ears. He was instrumental in the success of French acts like Air, Les Négresses Vertes and Daft Punk, and established the first French hip-hop label Delabel. He signed top African acts like Youssou N'Dour and Cheb Khaled to publishing deals and later helped establish the mainstream success of acts like Amadou & Mariam and Justice when he set-up his Because label.

In Boston, I get to see something of the Manu-manager relationship in action. Manu is pissed off. He is having stiff words with Emmanuel about the ticket prices the previous night, which, at $50, felt way too high. Emmanuel's explanation is that the show was part of some kind of festival and, because of that, no one can control prices.

It seems that, despite their apparently regular rows – and Manu's oft-muttered dictum 'Never trust a Frenchman' – Manu does trust Emmanuel and has said that he might well have given up without him. 'Without management, I get fucked,' he tells me. 'Every time! Well, not every single time, but when it happens, it's *desesperating*!' (one of those typical Manu non-words). 'The reason our relationship works', Emmanuel commented later, 'is that we don't need each other'.

Manu talks later about some of the difficulties inherent in holding down a reputation like his. 'I'm known for doing free concerts in aid of various causes,' he tells me, with a mix of resignation and frustration. 'So if I turn down a normal commercial concert, some businessman will pay someone, say from Chiapas, to say, "We need you to do a benefit concert for the indigenous people there". And when I get to the concert, I realise it's all been set-up by this businessman, and that it's commerce disguised as charity.'

The uncomfortable proximity of commerce and charity is an unavoidable reality of Manu's world. 'But in these things, the only way that works is instinct,' Manu says with a shrug. 'And sometimes I miss. Sometimes I give money and now the result is not there and sometimes it's good. But that's life. It's not because you had a bad experience that you have to stop.'

'I don't have to smash nobody or do tough business,' he asserts. 'Business is not dirt. When you do business with someone, you should both go out happy. The problem of business in the West is that if you try to do good for the one, it is gonna fuck the other. When you try to do good business, often they fuck you. But I don't care, I'm clean. But the band have all got families and need to be paid. So there has to be an equilibrium. Anyway, as soon as you get up to a certain level you need some infrastructure, which has a good part and a bad part.'

Then there's the whole minefield of sponsorship and advertising, with its multiple temptations for any artist of Manu's stature. Thomas Cookman, Manu's American record company representative, mentions in passing that another 'alternative music' act he looks after, Los Fabulosos Cadillacs, who were inspired by Mano Negra, had pulled in half a million dollars for sponsorship deals during a tour. Manu's comment on that story was: 'I don't need sponsorship and I don't want it, either.'

When it comes to Mano Negra's music, these issues get even more complicated. Although Manu was the main driving force and the chief songwriter in the band, La Mano still vote democratically on such matters – and, of course, the band often want to take the money. Manu always votes against the use of his music for TV ads. Emmanuel tells me that Manu turned down an offer of $100,000 to use one of his songs for an advertising campaign, and on another occasion the HSBC bank offered even more. They had inadvertently used some of Manu's music, which had been sampled by Fatboy Slim. The ad was ready to go, and they offered Manu a cheque which could be written to any charity he wanted. He still turned it down, though it was too late to stop the ad in some territories, and the bank's cash helped set-up Manu's foundation, which has helped finance causes such as the Zapatistas.

Of course, if *La Radiolina* sold big, all these problems were only going to get worse. Emmanuel would love Manu to be huge in the States, but what about Manu? Does he even want the album to be a colossal hit? 'If it's big, it's good for a lot of things,' he answered. 'But maybe bad, as well. I honestly don't care.'

I would have been suspicious of that answer if it came from most other rock stars, but my bullshit detector doesn't pick up any bleeps or buzzes.

Later, in the backstage warren at the Boston venue, I manage to corner Manu and ask him about *La Radiolina*. The first few tracks grab you by the throat, but the less obvious and more captivating ones are buried deeper into the album, like hidden treasure. They include "Otro Mundo", which imagines another, better planet, and "La Vida Tómbola", a song about the lottery of life, inspired, like "Santa Maradona" from Mano Negra's album *Casa Babylon* – by the bittersweet life of Diego Maradona. It was later to earn Manu a meeting with Maradona himself and end up in Emir Kusturica's film about the football legend. The record's stand out is "Me Llaman Calle", a gorgeous *flamenco*-flavoured tune which was originally commissioned for the soundtrack of a film entitled *Princesas* about two prostitutes in Madrid.

These songs may well be the ones that lodge in the heart and endure better than banging tracks like "Rainin' In Paradize", which is the first single release. This reels off a list of the world's main trouble spots from Angola to Baghdad and is rescued by the wonderful insanity of the chorus 'Go Masai, go!' It's also probably the only hit single in the history of rock'n'roll in which 'democracy' is rhymed with 'atrocity'.

Until *La Radiolina*, there had been a clear distinction between the studio albums and the live shows, which were always much rockier. According to Manu, *La Radiolina* is 'more of a combination of the two', partly because he had Madjid at his disposal, who was able to unleash heavy guitars at the flick of a plectrum. The result is slightly schizophrenic, less of an artistic whole than *Clandestino* or *Próxima Estación: Esperanza*.

Again, some of the backing tracks are reworkings of older tunes, like favourite places revisited, while the lyrics to

"Besoin De La Lune" (Need The Moon), perhaps the sweetest on the album, are recycled from Manu's French-language disc *Sibérie M'Était Contéee*, which had been released as part of a book collaboration with the French-Polish artist Wozniak in 2004. 'I need my father to tell 'em where I come from,' Manu sings in French. 'I need my mother to tell me when I am lost.' I told Manu, because it seemed to be the sort of thing I could tell him, that I'd lost my mother a few months earlier. 'I cannot imagine what that must be like,' he answered, suddenly grave and genuinely concerned. 'I suppose it will come to most of us, but I can't imagine it.'

Despite the fact that *La Radiolina* wasn't even released yet, and the promotional campaign had only just begun, Manu seemed a lot keener to talk about his next project: a collaboration between himself and the inmates of a mental asylum in Buenos Aires. Poetry and songs were to be provided by the patients, who put on a weekly radio show called La Colifata. 'They have so much lucidity,' Manu enthused excitedly. 'What they are saying is huge. It's gonna be a much more important album than mine, all in a very poetic Spanish which is impossible to translate, all about using God's name to make wars, about everything … '

Some of the La Colifata inmates, in fact, appear on one of *La Radiolina's* strongest opening tracks, "Tristeza Maleza", which echoes "Infinita Tristeza" from the *Próxima Estación* album, with lyrics about the pain that Washington's policies inflict on the world. The patients are sampled talking about the winds of Washington and the watching eagle. It's one of the new songs in the live set for the American tour.

There is more of a political edge to the songs on the new album. When Chris Blackwell, the founder of Island Records, heard *La Radiolina*, he picked out the track "Politik Kills" as a winner and did a remix of it. The song sounds a bit like Ennio Morricone in a Mexican *mariachi* style, but with an implacable force in its conviction that politics needs violence, drugs, ignorance and 'your mind' in order to thrive. "Mundo Revés" means 'The World Turned Upside Down', the slogan of a radical seventeenth-century group of

English proto-communists known as the Levellers. It's also an expression of Manu's personal sense of bafflement and incredulity with the state of the world. The title of the song also alludes to the Argentinian street slang known as *vesre*, where syllables are reversed. '*Reves*' becomes '*vesre*', '*tango*' becomes '*gotan*' and so on.

Every second on *La Radiolina* has weight and significance, to Manu at least. When I meet him in Boston, he's still agonising whether to shave a second off here, another there. "The Bleedin Clown" is a punkish workout that lodges surreptitiously in your head, 'an old-style song', according to Manu, about unrequited love: 'I wrote the song twenty years ago and every album my friends ask me why that one is not on it.'

The day after the Boston gig is a rest day for the band. I manage to scrounge a lift from Boston to New York with the photographer Jamie James Medina and his girlfriend. Jamie had flown in to do portraits of Manu for our feature. Manu gave him fifteen minutes. Nonetheless, those photos were then used for the entire tour and subsequent album campaign.

In New York, we hook up again with the band, who are staying at a rather unglamorous chain hotel in downtown Manhattan. On the recommendation of Adrian Dannatt, a local journalist friend, I entice Manu out for a drink in a funky, scruffy bar nearby in Chinatown; it has the resonant name of Double Happiness.

The bar plays old-school reggae and we spend a few beers discussing New York. We both miss the old Times Square, with its little bookshops, porno cinemas and its street chess tables where you could pass the time playing with old black guys. And you could smoke. Sleazy, perhaps, but with a scruffy freedom and individualism. Manhattan was the cultural centre of the world when Manu first came in the 1980s, a rough town that had revolutionised the music world several times over, from the underground punk explosion at CBGBs on the Lower East Side, through the disco warehouse parties and

Gambeat and Madjid – bass and guitar powerhouse.

Studio 54, the minimalism of Philip Glass and Steve Reich to the birth of hip hop in the South Bronx. It all happened here in the Big Apple, in the space of a few miles and a few years. Now it was a safer city, but it had also become a lot more boring.

Somehow the talk bifurcates back to spiritual matters. I mention *Shaman: Wounded Healers*, Joan Halifax's extraordinary book, and Manu admitted that he's fascinated by the subject. 'I met many shamans in my life,' he says. 'Some who say that's what they are. Others who don't, but who are.'

I suggest to Manu that he himself is a bit of a modern shaman, channelling bigger energies, travelling to other worlds and reporting back to the tribe.

'No,' he replies, 'but, in my own way, I try to be a medicine man. For the moment my passion is music, and I'm tied to it. But if this passion goes down a little bit, I would like to learn more. I want to cure with my hands. But that takes years and you have to live more on the inside. Now it's all on the outside. Everyday, I try to find a little place, maybe a tree or a river. I've learned how to auto-repair because there's a lot of stress in my job.'

Manu doesn't meditate exactly, but he does have his mantras 'because I'm a shy guy, getting onstage is something almost violent for me. But I repeat to myself that, "Shame don't kill. Shame don't kill. Shame don't kill." If it's a bad concert, it's not like someone's gonna kill me.'

Manu and fame make a strange couple; fame inevitably injects an element of unreality into his existence, if only in the way people treat and interact with him. And then there are the temptations of celebrity; for example. the bevies of Latinas who sweet-talk their way backstage after the shows ' I'm too romantic for all that. Maybe that's stupid, or maybe that's my salvation. I've got friends who love to be the centre of attention – but I'm a shy guy. Now I can handle it, more or less. Or I realise which bars not to go to. I used to be the guy observing in the corner at parties, more like a journalist, maybe writing a song about it – now that's not possible any more.'

Then there's the temptation to believe the hype, inflating the ego until you believe you can do anything. Be a political leader, for example. At the Genoa G8 summit the Italian government asked Manu to represent the anti-globalisation protestors, and he's been present at other forums since. 'That would be an error, the worst mistake,' Manu says in a tone verging on anger, as if riled by a much greater danger than being a rock star lothario. 'There's nothing so corrupt as being a leader.'

Nonetheless, politicians have tried to co-opt him. President Hugo Chavez of Venezuela among them. 'I'm not a Chavista,' Manu elucidates. 'But I would like to see some equilibrium in how things are reported. I used to go to the neighbourhoods in Venezuela and there was no hope. Now there's hope.' He tells me he was invited to meet Chavez, got in the car – and halfway there told the driver to turn back. Then he fixed me those intense unnerving eyes and told me that he'd met the Devil in person, twice. 'Once in Madrid, and once in Tokyo. He was like a man and I spoke to him, but I knew he was the Devil. One of those times he was an Englishman.'

Sometimes it all gets too much and Manu feels like he's losing himself, making too many compromises with the business world. He has a few potential ways out, like going to India, where nobody will know him, or studying healing with a shaman in the Amazon.

While he muses that he is sometimes tempted to give up life in the spotlight, quite often over the New Year's chill-out period he usually takes in Brazil he thought that his role for now was to help out with causes that seem to need him. Often, when he has come close to dropping out completely, he has found it impossible. 'I have a few weeks on the beach,' he tells me, 'writing songs, smoking, writing more songs. Then I start to think of all the people struggling out there, and I don't feel so comfortable doing nothing about it.' Manu has the microphone and can't just walk away.

When I ask what he is scared of, he says, 'I do have a terror of routine.'

There's nothing routine about the show in Brooklyn. Looking at Manu onstage, he reminds me of a Latin Charlie Chaplin, a little guy with a big heart. The word *corazón*, the Spanish for 'heart', is all over Manu's lyrics, and at the end of the set he bashes his own heart with his mic. An official gets onstage to warn the crowd that there will only be one encore because the storm is imminent and could be dangerous. A couple of minutes later, there's huge peal of thunder followed by blinding flashes of lightning and the heavens open. Rain chucks down in sheets. Undaunted, Manu races through the encore and the crowd sing "Próxima Estación: Esperanza" in unison as the rain and music conduct a mass baptism of hope for the future, for the belief that music can be more than a commodity.

In the tour bus afterwards, upfront with the driver, I re-
mark that Changó, the god of thunder, was in the house.
Manu smiles wearily, drenched and elated. Hanging in a
corner of the bus, there's a jacket with a pair of cow's eyes
painted it on it. Oh yes, the cow that saved Manu life. The
one that might lead him to tranquillity some day. I remember
something that Manu had told me before the storm broke:
'I'm glad I got lost, because now I'm better with people. I'm
stronger.'

CHAPTER 14:
BUENOS AIRES – TANGOS AND DELIRIUM

'Reality is not always probable, or likely.'

Jorge Luis Borges

O pulent, squalid, grand, decaying, European, Latin, contradictory – we must be in Buenos Aires. Manu is here working on an extraordinary project: an album with patients from South America's largest mental hospital. It's a radical idea, subverting the religion of celebrity culture and undermining received notions of the creative genius and the star singer. These performers were never going to make it into *Hello!* magazine. But, for all Manu's genuine empathy for the marginalised, the project is also deeply personal: 'Craziness – a lot of people are depressed in this world. I experienced it myself. It's not usually something dangerous, it can be positive. How you feel in yourself when you are crazy depends on how other people see you, and how people think of people who are crazy.'

The aim of the project is to benefit La Colifata (The Crazy One), a weekly radio show that's recorded at the Borda hospital, during which inmates can read a poem, sing a song, have a rant and more or less do whatever they want. An edited half-hour version of the show is broadcast and has been picking up listeners. It's reputedly having a therapeutic effect on the patients, as well, who seem to benefit from having their voices heard and enjoy the feedback they receive.

One night, later in the week, Manu tells me that there is another highly personal reason for his interest in madness. It's possible that insanity runs in the family: his maternal grandfather, the courageous Tomás, who fought against Franco, ended his days in an asylum.

In Buenos Aires, I'm staying with Manu at a guesthouse called the Tango House, a stylish if dilapidated mansion that was once the home of *tanguero* heartthrob Hugo del Carril. We'd travelled here by train from Córdoba, where Manu had done a spontaneous and incendiary benefit concert for the home-less charity La Luciérnaga with a pick-up band of buskers and friends called Roots Radio. It's a companionable journey, drinking *maté* tea through a metal straw called a *bombilla* and smoking joints while we chug across the rolling pampas.

The Hugo del Carril connection feels right. The actor and singer directed a pro-union film called *River of Blood* in 1952 and composed stirring Peronist marches. There was incidental synchronicity, too, in the title of his last film, *La Malavida*, the name of Manu's first hit song. The Tango House is a treasure trove of assorted del Carril memora-bilia, vinyl discs, a wind-up record player, his typewriter and numerous old photographs, del Carril looking distinctly Valentino-like with his slicked-back hair and melancholy, debonair playboy looks.

Manu gives me a guided tour of the house, mentioning a museum he went to dedicated to the greatest star of tango, Carlos Gardel, who died tragically in 1935 in a plane crash. According to Manu, there's an under-eighteen part of the museum that shows a handsome model of Gardel and then an 'adults only' section featuring a waxwork of what he looked like when they dug him out of the plane. Another waxwork shows the extent of Gardel's venereal diseases, no doubt another reason for the melancholic nature of some of the tango romantics.

There is a dusty *bandoneón*, the serpent-like squeezebox, in a corner of Del Carril's house. The instrument is a nineteenth-century German invention and became the key to tango, more suited than the accordion for 'reflecting the melancholy and nostalgia of the Italians who missed the mother country,' according to María Susana Azzi, biographer of Ástor Piazzolla, the great tango revolutionary.

We talk about Piazzolla. How the Argentinians took their tango seriously enough for Piazzolla's *nuevo tango* style to cause fist fights in TV studios – and how some taxi drivers would refuse to take him, and others would refuse payment. On a previous trip to Buenos Aires, I'd met Piazzolla's guitarist Horacio Malvicino, who told me he'd received death threats for ruining tango and that physical confrontations were fairly common. 'Fortunately, Ástor had been a boxer and knew how to take care of himself, and playing the *bandoneón* every day gives you strong arms.'

Manu retires to his room off the courtyard. As a guest at The Tango House, you get free entry to one or two local *milongas* or nightly tango sessions. The atmosphere in the local one is fairly gloomy, but as the novelist Ernesto Sabato once wrote, 'only gringos dance tango for fun'. Sabato also wrote that 'The Argentine is unhappy with everything, including himself.' I meet a Japanese girl in the *milonga* who is studying the dance. She points out the curious fact that, as well as the expected *machismo* of many tangos, there's also was a curious *mamismo*. Several of the tangos are mother songs.

It seems that discussions about the Oedipal and other psychological subtexts of tango are unavoidable in Buenos Aires. If anything, they are to be encouraged. Manu's project with the mental patients feels appropriate to the city. If Paris is known for its fashion, LA for its films, then Buenos Aires, apart from tango, is a mecca for psychotherapy. There are more psychoanalysts or therapists per head in Buenos Aires than anywhere else in the world. It's estimated that there's one for every fifteen citizens. The *barrio* of Palermo also boasts an area called 'Villa Freud', because of its high

Street view: Manu takes a break outside La Tribu, his Buenos Aires 'office'.

concentration of shrinks. But there's a flip side to the Argentine obsession with psychiatry: an interest in anti-psychiatry. This was a movement which came to fruition in the 1970s, led by such characters as R.D. Laing, David Cooper and Thomas Szasz. According to Laing, madness 'need not be all breakdown. It can also be breakthrough. It is potential liberation and renewal.' That's something Manu had experienced for himself.

The slogan of the La Colifata radio show is 'In a society where everyone is unbalanced, only the mad are really sane', an echo of Laing's statement that madness is 'a perfectly rational adjustment to an insane world'. Also relevant both to Manu and to Buenos Aires was Szasz's analysis that 'doubt is to certainty as neurosis is to psychosis. In short, the neurotic has problems, the psychotic has solutions.' Many of those in the mental hospitals – and, presumably, most of the 'regular' folk discussing phobias and complexes in downtown Buenos Aires – were neurotics.

The psychotics, meanwhile, had used their implacable conviction and insane certainties to get into positions of power. This was the country of the Disappeared, the roughly 10,000 to 30,000 so-called subversives (no one knows the exact figure) who were killed in the Dirty War that raged between 1975, when a military coup ousted an elected government, and 1983, when democracy was reinstated in the wake of Argentina's defeat in the Malvinas/Falklands War.

General Ibérico Saint-Jean, the junta's military governor of Buenos Aires, had a simple plan: 'First we will kill all the subversives; then we will kill their collaborators; then their sympathisers; then those who remain indifferent; and finally we will kill the timid.' There was brutal and systematic state-sponsored torture. Parents were tortured in front of their children and vice versa before being killed. A favourite method of disposing of the bodies was to dump them at sea. But, before the authorities got the hang of the currents, bodies were often washed back ashore. All this dark history was an important context of the Colifata project. Manu was simply asking, 'Remind me who, exactly, are the insane?'

I wake up the next morning with a strange rash over my body. Before Argentina, I had been in Belize – where I caught what turned out, tragically, to be the last concert of the great *Garifuna* singer, Andy Palacio – and, after a couple of weeks of intense travel, I am laid out. Manu calls a doctor, a Manu fan naturally, who confirms a diagnosis of exhaustion exacerbated by an allergy to the Tango House's cat and jams my rear with an injection of antihistamine. 'Aha! A Malvinas cat,' says Manu, highly amused.

With that sorted, we head off to a scruffy, friendly alternative radio station called La Tribu, where Manu has set-up a makeshift office for the week. There's a press conference for over a hundred assembled Argentine media. Manu fields the questions, including ones about La Luciérnaga, the homeless charity in Córdoba, and others about the La Colifata radio project.

Wherever Manu goes, especially in South America, the majority of questions are about politics. Someone wants to know his opinion of the *Piqueteros*. He says he's sympathetic. The *Piqueteros* (pickets) movement developed after the Argentine economic collapse of 2001, when two out of three residents fell below the poverty line and unemployment rose to around forty-five per cent. Their favoured means of protest was the roadblock. Banging on a drum and shouting *'Que se vayan todos!'* (They've all gotta go!) was one way of expressing frustration with the politicians and the establishment. The wave of protests and activities receded as the economy recovered in the 2000s, but have returned since the global economic tsunami of 2008.

Not everyone appreciates Manu here. The Argentine singer Fito Páez is a contemporary of Manu's who has re-leased politically charged albums like *Ciudad De Pobres Corazones* (City of Poor Hearts), dedicated to the memory of his aunt and grandmother, who were assassinated. He has also raised large sums at benefit concerts for the likes of UNICEF. 'Who is this guy posing as a French urchin, with sixteen credit cards, coming to lecture us?' he was quoted as saying. Manu is cool, as ever, when he is asked about this. 'There are at least twenty different Manu Chaos who are not like me at all,' he responds. 'If I start worrying about the stuff people think about me, I would be stupid.'

When the talk eventually gets back to his music, Manu is asked about the genesis of "Rainin' In Paradize", his new single, whose accompanying video, by the celebrated Serbian filmmaker Emir Kusturica, features several scenes shot during recordings of La Colifata ('Emir suggested we hire some actors to look crazy in the video,' Manu tells me later. 'I told him I knew some real crazy people who would be much better.') The song's lyrics reference the illegal Iraq War, sanctioned by our democratic leaders, and mentions other atrocities like the civil war in the Congo and the massacres of Liberian refugees fleeing to Monrovia, which have taken place below the radar of the Western media. The chorus has a manic urgency: 'This world go crazy. It's an atrocity.'

Manu says the song started life as a reggae number, and it was the musicians he was with, guitarist Madjid Farhem in particular, who transformed it into a guitar thrash. But then Manu's songs have the kind of strength and simplicity, built with sturdy structures, that can stand being sung in different styles and Manu himself often recycles them to suit the moment or the band he happens to be with.

After the conference, Manu picks up his guitar and sings a few songs, including "Desaparecido" (The Disappearing One), which has obvious dark resonances in Argentina, even if Manu claims it is merely autobiographical. He's then joined by Radio Roots, the pick-up busker-style band who had accompanied him to Córdoba, for a roughneck version of Camarón de la Isla's *nuevo flamenco* classic "Volando Voy" (I Fly Out). The assembled journalists start dancing, something you don't generally see at press conferences.

We go back to the Tango House before setting off for the Cantina Cervantes. The name seems apt for this trip, for there are times when I feel distinctly Sancho Panza to Manu's Don Quixote, a deluded sidekick following him on his madcap adventures.

Cervantes is a simple cantina that inspires confidence because it's so packed with locals. There's a twenty-minute queue to get a table. I chide Manu that if he was proper rock star, he'd make a fuss. After all, what's the point of fame if you can't get a table at a restaurant? He just shrugs. 'I'm too shy.' With us are Paulo and Mark, who are staying at the Tango House and making a TV film about La Colifata, and when we everntually get seated the wine and conversation flows.

I ask Manu about the local pop hero La Mona Jiménez, who he had mentioned when we were in Córdoba. There was a glammed-up picture of him in that day's local paper, looking like a cross between Gary Glitter and James Brown. Manu tells me that he plays to several thousand people each weekend in Córdoba, where the gangs stop fighting while he plays, but only rarely does gigs in Buenos Aires and never further afield. He never tours, apparently because he doesn't want to and doesn't need to. La Mona Jiménez has made 72 albums and, according to Manu, is obsessed getting past the 100 album mark before he dies. He's also supposed to have so many children that he's lost count. He's quite possibly on track to exceed the 100 children as well 100 album mark. 'It's a great thing for a girl from the neighbourhoods to have his baby,' Manu says, rolling another cigarette. 'She knows they will be looked after.'

The subject of "Rainin In Paradize" comes up and I suggest that what saves it from becoming a political rant is the insane chorus 'Go Masai, go! Be mellow, go Masai go, be sharp ... ' I said that an English writer would never have written that and pass on Charlie Gillett's observation that Manu's English is for people to whom English is a second language – which is the majority of English speakers. 'My father used to say that about my Spanish lyrics,' Manu responds, as he takes a swig of wine. 'He'd tell me, "You can't say that, it's not correct!".'

I tell Manu I've been reading the Italian philosopher Giambattista Vico and cogitating on his belief that progress comes from misunderstanding. In other words, if you understand something completely, you will never innovate. Manu nods his head and crooks his neck. 'That's maybe what happened with us,' he reflected. 'Mano Negra never really understood English punk, so we did something new.'

I realise, having dropped the names of Cervantes and Vico, that Manu hardly talks about books, although he sometimes mentions Chester Himes, the black thriller writer he read in order to learn English, and Eduardo Galeano, whose *Open Veins of Latin America* is one of the most incisive critiques of North American imperialism in the continent, or his family friend Márquez's *One Hundred Years Of Solitude*. But he says his university is the road and his teachers those who he meets on his voyages. Manu prefers to eat the meal rather than read the menu.

After going via the local *supermercado* to pick up a bottle of Scotch whisky we arrive back at the Tango House, where Manu asks if I want to listen to some of his new music on his computer. I do of course, although it's always nerve-wracking when a musician plays their new music to you. Faking enthusiasm is not my strong point and I haven't loved every single one of Manu's productions.

In Manu's room the laptop is open on his bed. He lights a joint, plugs in a lead to a small beat-up boom box, and plays me demos that he's been working on with Amadou & Mariam's son Sam and the band SMOD, which Sam formed with his friends Ousco and Donsky. The mix of guitars and beats recorded mainly on Amadou & Mariam's roof in downtown Bamako, the capital of Mali, are richly layered. Sam raps in Bambara, the local language, and in French. The dynamics are impressive, from disco tunes to ballads. It's very African, but totally modern. I tell him I think it's a winner.

Then he plays me some roughs from his *La Colifata* album, recorded at La Tribu and at a studio outside Buenos Aires owned by one of one of Argentina's top bands, Los Piojos. The tracks are mainly spoken word numbers using Manu's music as backing track. He translates some lines for me: 'This is a broadcast from Mars / We're alone / We're hungry / Green cars helicopters / Too much wars in helicopter'. Another track went like this: 'The loneliness at the hospital / We feel it / There is a sun, above / So far from the other stars / I love the sun / I love the stars / The sun kills nobody / Women drive me crazy'. There's quite a lot of stuff about mothers, too.

I've got my notebook out but can't keep up with the speed of the texts Manu is reciting. The music adds to the strangeness. Manu tells me how he first heard about La Colifata from a neighbour of his in Barcelona, Carlos Larrondo, whose TV film about the project had just won a prize. Manu became fascinated by the poems of the inmates, and started using them for a compilation he was making of busker bands in

Barcelona, which was eventually sold on the street to raise money for his street musician friends. He then met some of the people connected to La Colifata when he went to the World Social Forum in Porto Alegre in Brazil.

I pour Manu a whisky, thank him for letting me hear the new music – I don't think even his record company people have heard it – and crash out. It's difficult to sleep under the whirring fan of my room but I shoo the Malvinas cat out, and eventually drift off with the sounds of West Africa, killer bass lines and snatches of mad poetry floating in my head.

The following day, Manu emerges at midday and we head off to the Borda hospital, or the *Neuropsiquiatrico Dr José T. Borda* to give it its precise name. According to the journalist Santiago Roncagliolo of the Spanish daily *El País*, the complex of buildings – the largest mental asylum in Argentina – was, during the so-called Dirty War, the site of absolute horror, as scores of *desaparecidos* were burned in its ovens.

Every Saturday the radio programme La Colifata 100.1 MHz is recorded in the open air, close to the wards where the patients sleep. This is by far the most pleasant area of the complex, an airy courtyard overlooked by flowering trees. I'm introduced here to some of the Colifatas, as they call themselves. Hugo, running around manically, I recognise from the "Rainin' In Paradize" video.

Later, I meet Beatnik, the voice from "Tristeza Maleza" on *La Radiolina*, a song about Señor George Bush and how the American Eagle sees everything he does. He seems pretty sane, but obsessive. When I invite him for a chat the next day at the Tango House, he spends at least an hour talking in minute detail about bands from 1968, particularly about the betrayal, as he sees it, of Brian Jones of the Rolling Stones, before recalling how he had a job as a customs officer when Mano Negra first visited Buenos Aires on the Cargo Tour in 1992. 'I'd never seen anything like it,' Beatnik tells me with a distraught expression. 'They came from another universe. They were like Cortez arriving on horseback to meet the Incas!'

It was Beatnik who persuaded Alfredo Olivera, the psychologist who runs La Colifata, to let him vent his obsession on a 'classic rock' hour for the patients, while 'in a state of euphoria'. He wrote and read his poems on his show and a few of these made their way on to Manu's *La Colifata* album (this was released in 2009, as a free download, as clearing the rights to the poems and songs, some of them mangled versions of classic songs of the past, became a nightmare).

Beatnik told me that he realised he wasn't crazy. 'Madness is a prison you feel can't escape from,' he said. 'But I was exploring the depths of my mind.'

The format of La Colifata's radio show is explained to me by Alfredo Olivera. Patients who want to say something, read a poem, sing a song or play some music, can do just that. The names of all those who want a turn are written up on a blackboard. About four hours of 'rushes' are taped each Saturday and the most interesting material is edited down into a forty-five-minute radio show, or 'microprogramme,' which is broadcast on several Argentinian radio stations as well as on the Colifata website. Usually there's a score of people or so who attend the recording in the hospital's garden, but when word leaks that Manu is coming several hundred turn up, including a posse of dreadlocked fans.

One after the other, various patients go up to the mic. One guy in a dishevelled suit sings a romantic old tango called "El Reloj" by Luis Miguel, completely out of tune but with emphasis on the heart-rending line 'don't tell me the time, because she's gone forever,' which he delivers with true feeling. Some contributions are little more than a shriek of pain. Others are untranslatable nonsense. One patient says 'I went everywhere in the world, now I'm just having a rest,' slowly, in a deep voice. Another just says, 'with the help of God I will recover' and 'a hug and love is worth a thousand pills'.

A couple come to the microphone and relate how God has spoken to them both and brought them together. It makes me think of Thomas Szasz's comment that 'If you talk to God, you are praying. If God talks to you, you're schizophrenic.' There are surreal moments of poetry, too, such as the line 'I look forward to a country where there is no food and people eat songs'. A woman in a threadbare dress says, 'I'm bad, I am selfish and everything is for me. I want everything that's bad in the world.'

Then there's the sports news. Football results are read by a gent with slicked-back hair and manically overwrought sportscaster tones. He criticises the behaviour of the fans at the Boca Juniors match and expresses indignation at the performance of striker Leonel Núñez, who plays for Independiente at the time. It's all very convincing, until someone points out that the results he is reading are from tomorrow's matches – our commentator knows the future.

Music drifts on between these contributions and sometimes underneath them, often with startling incongruity. The disco standard "Last Night A DJ Saved My Life" is played while a man wails about how Palestine should be liberated and the world free from mental terrorism.

Manu accompanying members of La Colifata, recording their album.

When Manu comes on, he plays guitar under some of the poems, then takes the mic himself. He dedicates a Galician bar song called "Carreteiro" to 'all the mothers in the world', and performs a song based on the *repentista* troubadour style of northeast Brazil, but with his own words, before continuing with several hits including "Welcome To Tijuana". Roots Radio join him, after hanging about for hours. 'We'd only do it for Manu,' says Markos from the band. When they come on, the crowd go crazy, perhaps as a kind of release from the tension of the afternoon, dancing with each other and with the mental patients. A strange afternoon of poetry and pain turns into a wild, surreal, Felliniesque fiesta.

Afterwards I speak to Alfredo Olivera. 'One approach to the definition of insanity or psychosis indicates that those stricken have lost language. They do not utilise language as we do or they speak nonsense,' he says. 'Radio permits the patients to begin to reconstruct this aspect. And by people hearing the patients, we are able to change the idea that all people in psychiatric facilities are dangerous.' Alfredo calls this 'media therapy'. The hospital sends the programmes out for free and only asks that the patients are given whatever feedback comes from the outside. It's a way of increasing communication both ways.

I ask if there's a relation between the Colifata project and the anti-psychiatry movement or the ideas of people like Laing and Szasz. The anti-psychiatrists were suspicious of the very notion of asylums, which they saw as places for parking uncomfortable social elements, more to insulate the outside world against the mentally ill rather than perform any healing function. Alfredo concurs that one of the functions of the project is to debate the uses of the very institution we are in.

A criticism of the anti-psychiatrists, which could perhaps be also levelled at Manu when he talks of the poetry of the patients who 'are close to God and super-lucid', is that they are over-romanticising the insane. 'I think that is a danger,' Alfredo says but thinks Manu understands the situation here well enough. 'Madness is an illness to be cured,' Alfredo declares, but adds that some insane people can access intensely poetic and creative states of mind. He doesn't think Manu is exploiting them. 'He's become a friend and the royalties from the record will bring us much-needed money. Without Manu, we may well close.' We agree that it's probably better, anyway, to romanticise the patients than ignore or criminalise them, as happens all too often.

That evening, walking near the Tango House, three girl fans start chatting to Manu in the street and he invites them for a drink. Paulo films this exchange on his video, and we find a cantina with outdoor seating so we can smoke. Paulo has put the video camera by his chair, but somehow it gets stolen. Manu thinks someone may have seen us filming in the street and followed us. Paulo is completely distraught, but Manu is philosophical. 'There's nothing you can do, it's gone. Don't let it ruin your evening.'

The girls are gorgeous and flirty. They're amazingly self-assured, although they can't be more than seventeen. I remember that when I met David Bowie in my twenties I was almost speechless. I dub them Sporty, Posh and Baby. Sporty says she watches everything Manu does on YouTube. 'These days, even if he sleeps, it's on YouTube.' Manu is perfectly friendly, but doesn't flirt back.

Back on the terrace at the Tango House, I ask Manu about his radio obsession. It's curious that his father and brother both work in radio, his band is called Radio Bemba and his last album was called *La Radiolina*. He loves radio for the space it gives to the listeners' imaginations. 'For the real reason, you would have to ask my therapist,' he says, not for the first time in our conversations.

I ask Manu if he's had many friends with mental illnesses. He responds by saying it's possible some kind of madness runs in the family. His only contact with mental patients before La Colifata was his grandfather Tomás, who ended his days in a mad house. 'The first time I went to visit was with my mother. It was hard to see him there, but it wasn't a bad place,' he reminisces. 'We were all in a garden and it wasn't the horror that an asylum can be. When I saw he was more or less well, it was a minor domestic tragedy, but everybody was with their madness and accepting the folly of the other. It was there that I said, "What grace!" That boundary between who is and who is not crazy is not clear to me. If madness causes terrible pain, then it should be treated. But if not, what is the problem? What's wrong if someone is not formatted as required by the Judeo-Christian society?' Manu rolls up a joint and we retreat into silence.

CHAPTER 15:
SAHARA LIBRE!
DAKHLA, ALGERIA

I am not the lord of the desert
But the slave of naked horizons

From the poem 'Pas de nom' by Issa Rhose

T he in-flight entertainment on the Air Algeria flight from Algiers to Madrid is first class. Even before take off, Manu Chao and Madjid are strumming their guitars and, as the plane zooms off with the lights of Algiers twinkling below, they simply carry on playing, despite the panicky looks on the faces of the cabin crew. Johnny McLeod magics a megaphone from under his seat and announces that everyone can smoke. No one does. Half-Scottish, half-Algerian, Johnny is a musician, philosopher and genial host of the Babel bar in Ménilmont-ant, one of Manu's favourite neighbourhoods.

Johnny is court jester to King Manu, always ready with a string of obscene jokes and puns; a couple of stewardesses re-ceived matrimonial proposals, as so do I. Johnny's behaviour seems an anarchic shadow of the thoughts and impulses that Manu, being shy, would never express himself. By the time the plane is soaring half way across the crystal blue water of the Mediterranean, people are dancing in the aisles.

An hour later, we're flying over Andalucia, which apparently channels its flamenco spirit up to us from 20,000 feet below. The guitars and chanting just get rowdier, bottles of brandy appear (we had been in an Islamic, officially non-drinking zone for the past few days), and the party really takes off. We feel relief, tinged with guilt, to be escaping the unforgiving desert, mindful that hundreds of thousands of refugees are still stuck there.

Joining in at the back of the plane are the Oscar-winning actor Javier Bardem, his brother and fellow thespian Carlos, and other celebrities, charity workers and organisers, all fresh from the Sahara Film Festival which takes place in one of the most remote parts of the Algerian desert. 'The backyard of hell' was how Bardem describes the place to me. Running into Bardem's instantly recognisable face, like the fleshy incarnation of an Easter Island statue, was alarming. I'd just seen the film *No Country for Old Men*, where he plays a terrifying and convincing psychopathic killer and I half-expected him to produce that compressed-air cattle-gun which he uses to murder his way through the badlands of Arizona and New Mexico.

A week before, we had all flown to Tindouf in the far west corner of the Algerian desert, jumped into a convoy of mini-vans and travelled through shifting dunes and sandstorms for three hours to a refugee camp in Dakhla, where the festival was taking place. Our intention was to highlight the plight of the Sahrawis, who have lived for more than thirty years in exile in the Algerian Sahara. An estimated 200,000 of them languish in a number of dust-blown refugee camps near the border with their homeland.

According to the United Nations, the area referred to today as the Western Sahara is one of the world's last major non-self-governing territories. Since the 1970s, an Algerian-backed rebel movement called the Polisario Front has demanded independence from Morocco, who occupied the territory in 1975. Conflict between Morocco and the Polisario ended with a ceasefire in 1991, but a promised referendum on a future Sahrawi state has never been held. In the meantime, the status quo remains immovable and the refugees are trapped in their melancholy exile. An entire generation of Sahrawi have been brought up in those refugee camps, with their Polisario-run schools and hospitals, almost entirely off the media radar.

How do you get the outside world to pay attention to your cause if you are a marginalised people that has been largely ignored for more than three decades, living in one of the loneliest and most isolated places on earth? Violence and suicide bombing would be a speedy route to the headlines. There were disturbing rumours that the camps, with their despairing young men, were beginning to be infiltrated by al-Qaida in the Magreb (AQIM); indeed, in 2011 three aid workers at the camp were kidnapped.

A more civilised route, which the Sahrawi government in exile opted for, was to host an arts festival and invite some celebrities along. Both Bardem and Manu held Spain (the ex-colonial master of Western Sahara) largely responsible for the situation. The presence of both men in Dakhla would glean significant coverage in the Spanish media.

My desert adventure begins when I receive a call from Manu's management company inviting me along to the film festival. Could I meet Manu in Madrid in a week's time? I am given a time, 2pm, and a place, the Plaza Tirso de Molina. Further details are not forthcoming. The phone goes dead. Like some old-school espionage outfit, Manu's team seem to operate on a need-to-know basis.

When I get to the square, there sitting outside a café are the familiar figures of Madjid, the French-Algerian singer Akli D (whose album Manu had just produced), and the genial Johnny McLeod. Johnny's nickname for me is Sheik Spear, ever since I'd told him in his Parisian bar that some Muslims believed the immortal bard of Avon was actually an Arab called Sheik Spear. 'Sheik Spear has arrived!' he announces ceremoniously. Manu arrives soon afterwards, clad in desert boots, and we go off to a local TV station for a show called *Don't Shoot the Piano Player*, where Manu is booked to

Madjid and Manu playing in the Madrid Bar, El Palentino, in the video for 'Me Llaman Calle", drawing attention to the rights of Spanish prostitutes.

sing "Me Llaman Calle" from *La Radiolina*. He had composed the song originally for the soundtrack of a gritty feature film, *Princesas*, about two prositutes in Madrid, and had later dedicated it to a prositutes' collective in the city, filming a beautiful, life-affirming video for the song, featuring the prostitutes of the Malasaña district, to publicise their campaign.

Carolina, a working girl from Ecuador and member of the Hetaira Collective (or, to give it its full title, the Hetaira Collective for the Defence of the Rights of Prostitutes), who had appeared on the video, was on the show as well. She explains that the *hetaira* were ancient Greek courtesans who had a wide access to culture and managed to achieve respect and recognition in society, and talks about the collective itself, which fights for the rights and welfare of street women by providing information and support about health, psychology and legal issues. When Manu was awarded a major Spanish song prize for "Me Llaman Calle", he suggested some of the women accept the award in his absence. Cue massive publicity.

We reunite with the rest of Manu's posse at the airport. As we walk through the crowds, several people stop him. There is a nice example of Manu's organic information-gathering technique when a Mexican journalist called Francina Islas asks him whether he knows about the current teachers' strike in Oaxaca in the south of the country. Manu proceeds to suss her out: she is a serious journalist who has made a documentary on Nobel-winning author Octavio Paz. The authorities in Oaxaca had treated the strikers brutally and there were allegations that a couple of teachers had been raped. Manu knows about it, but wants Francina to email him up-to-date information. One of the posters onstage for his Mexican tour later in the year proclaims support for the Oaxaca strikers.

The flight to Algeria is delayed a couple of hours but Manu, Madjid, Johnny and Akli D entertain the waiting crowd at the gate with an impromptu jam session. I'd asked Aitzi from Manu's management company whether there was anything specific I should bring to the camps, and she told me that they had received requests for particular medicines and various other useful items which they would bring and I was not to worry. Based on my experience of previous visits to Muslim countries, from Morocco to Pakistan, I guess that some people in Dakhla are likely to appreciate a few less practical gifts, so I stock up on whisky and cigarettes.

After a fitful few hours of attempted sleep on the plane, which are continually interrupted by Johnny's ribald jokes from the seat behind, we touch down in Tindouf. We dump our suitcases on a lorry and jump into four-by-four vehicles for the three-hour ride across the scrubby desert to Dakhla. After half an hour, we are out of mobile phone signal range. I sense a slight panic from the journalists as we leave the wired world behind. Manu doesn't have a mobile, so he is serenely unconcerned.

When we arrive at the refugee camp, a couple of figures wrapped in brilliant white *djellabas* and cool shades seem to stand out among the small gaggle of people waiting for us in the sharp dawn light. 'I wonder if they run the place?' I say to Manu. 'The boss here is the sun,' he replies. I don't have any answer to that. When it's at its midday peak, the desert sun is implacable and vicious, draining all colour from the landscape.

Manu and the VIPs are escorted to a rather gorgeous tent, furnished with cushions and rugs and with a four-by-four vehicle with driver on standby. The journalists' accommodation is a bit less salubrious. Francina and I are billeted in a one-storey sandstone dwelling as the guests of a Sahrawi family. We are introduced to Nuena, the matriarch, and her teenage sons, Sidi, Nagem and Basir. They tell us that they work only occasionally, looking after visitors, helping out on building sites or doing any other odd jobs. Francine begins unpacking her heavy bags, stuffed full of presents which she has carried from Madrid: torches, pens, drawing books, pasta, rice. I don't know the family well enough to know if whisky is forbidden, though my sleeve of cigarettes, sheepishly proffered, is received with a show of gratitude.

Johnny McLeod and Manu en route to the Western Sahara.

We are given a dinner of couscous topped with a small lump of gristly camel meat. Francina, despite being a vegetarian for ten years, tells them that it was delicious. I had thought she was about to retch. In the family room opposite where we are staying, there is a solar-powered satellite TV with a hundred channels. The reception isn't great and most of the channels are only in black and white, but it is enough to keep the family highly informed about the outside world. They are all experts on the latest Egyptian and even Brazilian soap operas.

Our sandstone dwelling is identical to a thousand others, and the multitude of white tents in the camp are also seemingly indistinguishable from one another. With no mobile to summon help, it is going to be very easy to get lost, especially at night. Sidi tells us that we are in Barrio 4 of what I write down phonetically as 'Wilaya Daira Ben Faran'. According to him, we are going to have to 'trust the desert. Its people will look after us.'

We manage to find Manu's tent before night falls, only getting lost about three times. As we walk up, Johnny is talking to their personal driver on the walkie-talkie. He asks us if we need anything and I suggest a pizza takeout. Johnny launches into one his manic fantasies, offering to get his favourite pizzeria in Rome to deliver a twelve-incher in a private jet in return for 5,000 euros.

Whilst Madjid strums on his guitar in a corner of the tent, Francina starts filming the opulent carpets and drapings with her little video camera. Aitzi orders her to stop, telling her in no uncertain terms that she should have asked before starting to film. She is then banned from the tent altogether. Later, Aitzi takes me aside and said, 'I need your help creating some distance between Manu and all the journalists here who want interviews.'

She is enlisting my support for her role as Manu's gatekeeper and I don't feel comfortable about it. Manu had said that everyone was welcome in the tent, but this episode heralds what is to become a problem, not just here in Dakhla, but in other trips I make with Manu later in the year. The tour

Manu with Javier Bardem (right) and Sahara Film Festival director Javier Corcuera in the camp.

manager's job is to keep people, especially journalists, away from Manu. Manu can be the nice guy, welcoming everyone into the tent, while Aitzi has to be the bad cop keeping them out. What is the problem here, anyway? Francina is a serious journalist and Manu is here to publicise the plight of the refugees. His presence will get her TV film more coverage in Mexico.

To Manu's credit, he apologises to Francina the next morning at an elaborate ceremony to mark the opening of the Film Festival. He explains that he wants to experience the camp before making any pronouncements. At the event, Manu, Javier Bardem and his brother Carlos and other Spanish TV stars, are seated in the front row. Festival director Javier Corcuera welcomes the assembled delegates and assorted bigwigs from the Polisario. Pepe Toboada, from a Spanish NGO called Los Amigos del Sáhara, talks about the way that Spain has 'betrayed the promise they had made to the Sahrawi people when they turned over the country to Morocco'.

Pepe helps to organise summer holidays in Spain for hundreds of children from the camps and organises monthly protest demonstrations in Madrid. Afterwards, he tells me that he had been a member of the Spanish army at the time of Spain's withdrawal from the colony and that he 'felt remorse for what had happened', before adding, 'I felt I should try to right a wrong.'

Then there are camel races followed by an extraordinary procession of teenage kids in khaki uniform, synchronised female basketball players wearing the hijab and teachers carrying placards in the local Hassani language. The display has been organised by the Polisario's government in exile. Despite the seriousness of the Sahrawi cause, it all seems strangely but charmingly Ruritanian.

The Festival, then in its fifth year, features numerous political films, including Ken Loach's *It's a Free World*, which focused on the exploitation of immigrant workers in Britain. There are documentaries on the Sahara amongst other more straightforwardly entertaining movies from around the world. The screen is set-up in the dunes and the audience sit on rugs in the open air. There is no admission fee. A Mongolian film with the intense hallucinogenic greenness of the central Asian grasslands is a treat for local eyes, tired with the monotonous colour of their surroundings. Sidi, Nuena's son, also reckons that the most controversial or erotic films are shown in the one indoor venue, which had Polisario guards on the door. 'Some films are for everyone, some only for the foreigners,' Manu adds.

Most locals seem to dress up for the movies. Two girls called Fatimatou and Lala, who sit next to me, are friendly and flirtatious in their full evening regalia and make-up. They are in their late teens and as well as Hassani and Arabic, they also speak excellent French and Spanish and some faltering English, which confirms what others had said about the high level of education in the camps. Sidi tells me that local girls consider a film screening to be a good place to find a husband.

Back in Manu's tent, similar conclusions about the quality of local education are being reached. Johnny is doing subtractions, additions and some writing with an eight-year-old girl from the camp. 'She's at a very high level,' he says, clearly impressed. 'Much better than a similar girl from Algeria or Morocco, or even Paris.' Manu is also astounded. 'In the middle of the desert, that's incredible,' he says, explaining that many of the teachers and doctors spent eight years or so studying in Cuba before returning to the camps. 'It's not easy for these people. A couple of guys I met had experienced the beaches, music, girls, maybe rum, in Cuba. And then they have to come back to this. But they do return, because they know why they're doing it there. That's *perseverancia*.'

When I tell Manu about the girls at the film, he says he is also impressed by the dignified bearing of the women and relatively easygoing relation between the sexes. 'It's very modern, compared to other Muslim countries,' he says. 'I have a problem with the position of women in Islam. But here there seems to be a kind of Islam of the future, an educated, tolerant Islam. The politicians are always going on about the problem of radical Islam, but here there's a positive, modern version. Maybe the solution is right here in the desert and no one in Europe and none of the politicians are paying any attention to it. In fact, they are forgetting and ignoring the people here.' He suggests that the next Olympics should be staged in the Sahara.

That night, I hitch a lift with Manu and the gang to a concert in the dunes. A stage has been set-up with a generator, and a local band – a cheesy synthesiser and guitar combo – performs. But the star of the night turns out to be a Venezuelan singer called Luzmira.

The sand dunes are shaped like a concert bowl and we sit at the top looking down. There is a magic hour in the desert, just before the night drops, and it falls fast, when colour comes out, the roses, soft pinks and ochres, and there are shadows thrown by the thorn trees. As anyone who has slept in the desert will tell you, the stars suddenly appear,

Libertad para Sahara! Manu performing at the stage in the dunes.

like myriad glinting daggers that have rent holes in the fabric of the sky, brighter and more infinite than in Europe. The camp conveys a curious and contradictory impression, mixing the claustrophobic atmosphere of a prison with the endless space of desert and sky.

I tell Manu that when I was last in the Sahara, staying with the Touareg band Tinariwen, they'd explained that songs can help travellers navigate through the desert and that each town or oasis has its guiding star. The Touareg have stories attached to many of the stars: the Pleiades are the sisters of the night and nearby Orion is a Touareg warrior, doomed to watch the beautiful women from a distance, for eternity. 'It's their TV', is Manu's deadpan reaction.

The camp has its own local radio station in a fly-blown studio, where Manu gives his only official interview. On the way there he tells me about the time he was in Macedonia and gave his one interview to a gypsy radio station: 'They had an exclusive and they broadcast it every day.' At the station here he tells the listeners that 'music goes back millennia but film is only a hundred years old, so it's a baby. No one yet knows what it's capable of.'

Later, we catch Gillo Pontecorvo's *The Battle of Algiers*, a classic 1966 black and white film based on events during the 1954–62 Algerian War against French rule, which portrays atrocities committed on both sides. 'I guess it's the perfect place to see such a film,' Manu says. When a fighter talks about the day the Sahrawi would get their country back in a documentary about the Polisario, the crowd start cheering. Manu tells me he hates films that are too intellectual. He's a fan of *The Blues Brothers*.

Coming back from Manu's tent in the dark that night, I get totally lost before following some music in the distance. A figure appears and beckons me into a tent, where I find Javier Bardem playing bongos with the Venezuelan singer Luzmira, who had sung beautifully in the dunes the previous night, with Madjid on top form on guitar. I even do a spot of percussion myself. It is a surreally glamorous event in the circumstances. 'Better than the *Vanity Fair* party at the Oscars?' I ask Bardem, as we trade bongo licks.

Next night, it is Manu's turn to perform at the stage in the dunes. The gig is superb, Bardem playing bongos with Manu, Luzmira, Madjid and Johnny McLeod. Akli D sings his song "Good Morning Chechnya", adapting it for desert conditions. The banner behind the stage reads, 'FISAHARA 08 – LIBERTAD PARA SAHARA' and Manu wraps himself in a Sahara Libre flag, which makes the local audience go wild as he pumps out "La Vida Tómbola", "Me Llaman Calle" and "Mr Bobby".

CHAPTER 16:
MEXICO – MACHETES, MARIACHI, METHS

Libertad! Libertad! Libertad!

Lake Chapalá begins just south of Guadalajara in the state of Jalisco. In case there's any doubt we're in Mexico, a *mariachi* band are propositioning the families who stroll along the waterfront and doing good business in their silver tunics and red cummerbunds. A shoeshine boy with his box and brush is pointing hopefully at dusty footwear, and another boy is selling hammocks. Couples are sweetly holding hands on their Sunday-morning *paseo*. It's a tranquil scene.

Glittering dark birds skim the surface of the water and waterfowl wallow in the reeds. Swallows swoop and elegant white egrets perch among the water hyacinths. I'm told there are ten kinds of fish in the lake. But it's drying up. The jetty and the lighthouse are further from the water's edge than they used to be.

We've come here to have lunch before the sound check for tonight's concert. The view prompts Manu to mention his mother's prediction that the wars of the twenty-first century will be about water. He talks about an article on the Amazon which he saw in the French international affairs periodical

Le Monde Diplomatique that suggests the multinationals are already positioning themselves for the Water Wars. We talk, too, about Lehman Brothers, the banks and the vertiginous collapse of the stock markets and about the abstract nature of money, its zeros and ones zipping across continents. We talk about the fact that only a handful of clever nerds understand the financial vehicles dreamed up in the fantasy world of a profit machine in perpetual motion. The dream, at least, is over. Not that Manu's surprised. 'Now the party's finished and everyone has a hangover,' he says, and goes on to quote the famous Uruguayan writer Eduardo Galeano: 'The yachts and ocean liners are rising in response to new opportunities, but many rafts and lifeboats are taking to the water – and some are sinking.'

I'm observing the watery scene and tuning out. Lake Chapalá was the place where that other nomadic artist D.H. Lawrence lived for a while at the end of a 'savage pilgrimage' that took him to Australia, Sicily and New Mexico. Like Manu, Lawrence had an aversion to the coldness of the mechanised world and, also like Manu, he was a prophet of the instinct, claiming that Europeans thought too much, though in Lawrence's case his 'thinking with the blood' strayed into proto-fascism. He wrote most of his strange late-period book *The Plumed Serpent* in a villa in Calle Zaragoza, just by the lake. The book's two Mexican protagonists are revolutionary leaders, but they're also resurrected incarnations of the Aztec deities Quetzalcoatl and Huitzilopochtli, who revive the ancient tradition of human sacrifice.

In my head, Aztecs blood sacrifice mixes with narco gangs. La Familia, one of the main drug cartels, are based in the neighbouring city of Michoacán. They're the fastest-growing drug gang, founded by Nazario Moreno González, whose nickname was El Más Loco (The Craziest). Twenty men had recently burst into a low-rent disco called the Sol y Sombre in Uruapan and bowled five decapitated heads across the disco floor. They left a message behind that read. 'Know that this is divine justice.' For a modern drug boss, a reputation for being the craziest is a distinct advantage.

Contemplating water wars and financial meltdowns – Manu at Lake Chapalá.

The gang has set-up super-labs that manufacture metham-phetamine, an operation familiar to fans of the TV series *Breaking Bad*, and they function like a parallel state, extorting 'taxes' and paying for community projects. They've also branched out into pirate DVDs, people-smuggling and a debt-collecting service which involves the kidnapping of defaulters. Meanwhile, in Guadalajara, there have been regular outrages, like the murder of twenty-six young men who were found stuffed inside three vehicles with the words 'Millennia Zetas' and 'Millennium' painted in oil on their bodies. Both are references to allied drug cartels. All the men had been asphyxiated.

This is enough to make anyone feel nervous, and the fact that several tourists had also been kidnapped recently didn't help. The brother of Francina Islas, the journalist we had met in the Sahara, was one kidnap victim. The drug godfathers were asking a quarter of a million dollars ransom for his freedom. It was all a bit too close to home.

I decide to ask Manu whether I can travel in the tour bus to Querétaro for the next gig and then on to Mexico City. The alternative is to catch a public bus in Tlaquepaque, which is a forty-minute taxi ride from Guadalajara. The journey would take many hours longer, cost 400 pesos and have at least an element of danger. The tourists had been kidnapped on just such a bus. There's also the fact that I'm experiencing a credit crunch of my own. I'm flat broke.

Being allowed on a tour bus is a rock'n'roll privilege granted only to those who are part of the inner circle. Journalists, along with groupies, are considered to belong to a category of person liable to cramp the star's style. But when I put the question to Manu, he says he doesn't have a problem. Nonetheless he suggests I should check with Paget Williams, the affable tour manager I'd met in Boston, just in case. Paget says he doesn't have a problem, but that, as it's Manu's tour, it's up to him to decide. I can see this one going round and round in annoying circles.

In the taxi back to Guadalajara we talk about *lucha libre*, the Mexican wrestling tradition that has become hugely popular, even in Europe, without necessarily losing its popular roots. In Barcelona free wrestling is 'trendy', a word Manu hates because it reminds him of the chic, expensive bars in Barcelona that he thinks are killing the spirit of his local *barrio*. The taxi driver has tuned into a local radio station that is playing Manu tunes. He becomes visibly embarrassed. A girl calls in to ask what kind of footwear she should wear for the concert – heels or sandals. The DJ recommends *zapatos sevillanos*, which are more sensible shoes with only a small heel.

Manu remains uncomfortable; it's as though he doesn't know how to react. To be pleased would be arrogant, perhaps, but to ignore the attention might also be construed in the same way. I try to break the mood when "Bongo Bong" comes on, saying I prefer the Robbie Williams version, which, in truth, was terrible. Silence from Manu. He only brightens when we go past the plastic statue of a cow. Perhaps the night will go well, after all.

Later that evening, we're at a venue just outside Guadalajara, the Arena VFG, named after the singer Vicente Fernández (Gómez) who lives nearby. He's a huge star in Mexico who sings *ranchero* music with its torrid tales of the old Mexico: revolution, rural ranches and philandering *caballeros*. Arena VFG is a 15,000-seater indoor arena that has played host to bands like Judas Priest and Iron Maiden as well as top boxing matches. When the Mexican boxer Sal 'El Canelo' Álvarez beat a top Argentine, Vicente Fernández offered him a horse.

The venue is almost sold out, which is exactly how Manu likes it. If it's completely full, the scalpers and touts out front make a fortune and the fans get ripped off. If it's only half full, the atmosphere isn't great. Most big bands announce their shows months in advance, but this gig was only scheduled a couple of weeks ago, which Manu sees as yet another example of his strategy of organising everything at the last minute paying dividends (though it means huge inconvenience for the people who work around him).

The band is due on at 9pm. Around 5pm, Manu throws a minor tantrum backstage. He ordered a steak about an hour ago and it hasn't turned up yet. A Manu show is like a sporting event involving an intense workout onstage that last up to three hours. In order to do that, he needs fuel. Too near show time and there's no chance of digesting the food, especially as the adrenaline starts flowing as the minutes tick down to liftoff. In a way, I'm relieved: Manu is normally totally cool and I had been wondering when I'd see him lose his equilibrium.

As ever, before the show, he becomes introverted and thoughtful. He might have a whisky or a beer to take off the edge, but a certain terror seems to be a necessary part of the ritual. Like some actors before they go onstage, or some journalists sitting in front of a blank screen, the dreaded thought is always there: maybe this time it really will be a total screwup. People who turn up to pay Manu a visit in the hour or two before one of his shows, like Damon Albarn did in London, sometimes come away with the impression that Manu is aloof, even arrogant. But it's only nerves. He's using all his available energy to compose and prepare himself.

Roxanne Haynes, a photographer friend of the band, is backstage. She had bought a bead necklace in Greece and it had travelled with her back to LA, where she lives. She had then given the necklace to Manu in Austin, Texas, and now he's wearing it in Guadalajara. They are globalised beads. Also backstage is Tania Ramírez of *La Jornada*, a liberal left-leaning newspaper based in Mexico City. It's the only paper in the country that Manu talks to. And there's Ana, a vivacious, eccentric woman who must be in her seventies. She saw the band in Austin and has become a camp follower.

Even before the band go onstage, the noise in the auditorium is intense and frightening. They haven't played a note yet, but the audience is already in their grasp. You realise that this really is Manu's audience, his tribe, much more so than when I've seen him play in Europe or the States.

They walk onstage, one by one. Angelo Mancini, the trumpet player strolls on jauntily. Bassist Gambeat lopes on. Madjid Farhem runs to his amp with his arms wheeling like a demented aircraft. Drummer David Bourguignon, keyboard player Julio García Lobos and Philippe 'Garbancito' Teboul on percussion follow. Finally, Manu runs to the lip of the stage and the crowd erupt.

The atmosphere is transformed. I get the feeling that, if Manu were to ask the audience to take up arms, overrun the local radio, trash the police station, occupy the army barracks and government buildings right after the gig, he would conscript an instant army. The show is more intense that those in Europe on every level. It's more playful, as Madjid mimcs catching the waves of energy coming and throwing them back to the audience, grinning. Gambeat drops the bassline in a couple of numbers, just for the sheer pleasure of joining the music again after a theatrical pause, like a child who deliberately loses a toy for the joy of finding it again. Everything is hotter – not just the humid Mexican night, but also the music, and somehow, when a couple of girls throw their bras onstage, I'm not in the least surprised.

We are all dissolving into one energy field, a group monster, each of us – Indian, Aztec, Spanish, African, European – all mongrels, delirious in the mix of our blood, tonight, right now, in this moment, at least. The rhythm section is locked in and earthy, the bass below the ground. Madjid's guitar shimmers electrically through the seven different realms of mythology. Angelo's trumpet could have brought down the walls of Jericho. And, at the centre of it all, there's Manu, the little magus of this mayhem, the ringmaster of this circus.

Numbers flow into each other: "Mr Bobby" segues into "Primavera" into "Me Gustas Tú" into "Politik Kills". "Welcome To Tijuana" is dedicated to all those migrants killed on the border. For "Clandestino", the band exits the stage, leaving just Madjid and Manu behind. Then they're back and the line *'Mexicano illegal!'* from "Desaparecido" is greeted with a roar, before the band ramp the heat up even further with old Mano Negra numbers "King Kong Five" and "Sidi H'Bibi". A rare cover – José Jiménez's classic Mexican tune "Volver, Volver" – gets an inflammatory punk-*ranchero* treatment and goes down a storm.

Then it's all over. The band are wiped out but exhilarated. 'It was like a *temazcal* out there,' Manu says, referring to a pre-Hispanic sweat lodge that, he explains, was used as a kind of healing sauna. Not many fans have managed to get into the backstage area, but Manu, of course, chats to them for at least an hour, posing for shots taken on their camera phones. There's a Mexican journalist who has seen Manu and Radio Bemba perform many times. He thinks this was the best, the most intense, Manu show he has ever experienced. And I agree.

The audience empties out of an arena strewn with the detritus of an apocalyptic party, the aftermath of a pleasure storm. The banners in the auditorium, fierce and beautiful after the battle, are still standing. And they're part of the story. The biggest celebrates the struggle of the striking teachers in Oaxaca, that most atmospheric of Mexican towns. The strikers had been camping out in the main square, demanding better salaries and more investment to build decent buildings and ensure students don't have to find work to support their studies. They had eventually met with violent repression, when 3,000 police charged in and cleared the square. At least a hundred strikers were injured. The demonstrations expanded to include a wider coalition of unions, churches and universities, united to try and depose the hated governor, Ulises Ruiz, who the opposition believed had rigged the election that brought him to power.

We drive back to the hotel in Guadalajara to get some sleep, as we have an early start the next morning. I nip over the road to a cheap restaurant and order a chicken *quesadilla*. With drinks and dessert, the bill comes to 130 pesos, about five euros. When I tell Manu, he reminds me that for many people living around here that's a very expensive meal.

Are you on the bus or off the bus? That was the question posed by Ken Kesey and his Merry Pranksters during his epic road trip around the States with his fellow freaks in 1964. I'm still not sure of my status with Manu and his own pranksters, but I decide just to walk on the bus anyway. Paget Williams grins as I get on. I seem to have passed some obscure test.

The tour was originally going to visit the colonial city of Morelia, but there has been a drug gang outrage there. The week before, on Independence Day, grenades were thrown into a crowd of civilians who were innocently celebrating the holiday. Seven people died and over a hundred were injured. Now, everyone is feeling unsafe.

Once on the bus, I decide I had better lie doggo for a while at least, and avoid asking too many questions. There are times, around cool people, when you have to act as if you have been given a shot of elephant tranquilliser, as a friend once observed. I notice Ana, the seventy-something tour mascot who had become a kind of guru, halfway down the bus, as well as Roxanne the photographer.

The landscape is repetitious, like a minimalist piece of music. The bare scrub and grasslands are alleviated only by these giant pink ferns that I keep seeing, even though I haven't taken any drugs. After an hour or two, Manu comes by and we get involved in a discussion about football. Manu says he found Zidane's headbutt at the 2006 World Cup Final disgusting, but that Maradona's Hand of God goal was justified. Pelé was 'an asshole but a good businessman.' Rather than Pelé, the real Brazilian deal, according to Manu, was Garrincha, a drunk, womanising, footballing genius. He was also known as Mané (short for Manuel) by his friends, and his other nicknames were 'Alegria do Povo' (Joy of the People) and 'Anjo de Pernas Tortas' (Angel with Bent Legs). The truth is that Brazil never lost when both Garrincha and Pelé were in the team. In the Estádio do Maracanã in Rio, the home changing room is known as 'Garrincha', whereas the away changing room is known as 'Pelé'. Who was the 'greatest' of the two remains an eternal dispute among Brazilian lovers of the beautiful game.

Ana launches into a tale about how she ended up spending a month in jail in Mexico for some minor misdemeanour. Her passport was stolen but the police chief fell in love with her. You have to be charmed by the fact that Manu's tour bus idea of a good-time girl is the septuagenarian Ana.

Gambeat shows me a few pictures of his child on his phone, with a massive grin on his face. He's missing his family. He goes on to say that possibly the most incredible concert of his life was when Radio Bemba played that celebrated open-air show in the Zócalo, Mexico City's main downtown square, in front of over 100,000 people. Then he goes off into a discussion of a book he and Manu have been reading on chiropractic medicine, a treatment that believes in the body's innate intelligence and in healing with energy. Madjid, Philippe and the others seem less interested in alternative medicine.

Madjid, strumming a Bob Marley tune, declines an interview, claiming he has nothing to say. When I ask Philippe, who's been with Manu since those busking days in the Paris metro, for some anecdotes, he says he'll have to ask Manu if that was OK. Much later, Philippe does agree. Although the atmosphere is perfectly friendly, Manu the shy guy at the back of the bus, is most definitely boss here.

Good-time gal Ana on the tour bus with Manu, Mexico. PHOTO © ROXANNE HAYNES

Soon we're in Querétaro, and driving straight to the theatre for the soundcheck. This concert, only announced a couple of days earlier, is smaller and less intense than the gig in Guadalajara, with a capacity of perhaps 5,000. But still the audience jump on their plastic chairs and trash them in the process.

Next day, I end up chatting to Manu about Mexican music, specifically the *narcocorridos* – the drug troubadours – after a Valentin Elizalde song wafts over the sound system in the courtyard of our hotel, where Manu is strumming his guitar.

'It's the Mexican equivalent of gangsta rap,' Manu explains. It's played polka-style by ageing gents on guitar, bass, accordion and drums. The songs are often paeans to drug lords and tell approvingly of murder, torture, extortion and drug smuggling. The style was developed in the 1930s but has spread in the last couple of decades. The life of a *narcocorrido* singer is a dangerous one. Valentin Elizalde was shot dead, one of literally dozens of *narcocorrido* stars that have met the same fate.

Our conversation digresses on to the subject of South American leaders. Manu is more in favour of the pragmatic President Lula than I thought he might be, reasoning that Lula has lifted so many Brazilians out of poverty. He likes Evo Morales, too, the left-wing hero of the indigenous people in Bolivia, and a more obvious candidate for Manu's approval. Moreover, he was apparently a rather fine trumpet player in his youth.

I ask Manu about the other banner that I've seen onstage, the one for the FPDT, the People's Front for the Defence of the Land. It mentions something about a place called Atenco. It's a story that Manu has been getting increasingly involved in. The FPDT was formed in response to plans to develop an airport at San Salvador Atenco, on the edge of Mexico City. The project was peacefully and successfully resisted in 2002 by 500 farmers and their supporters, who included Subcomandante Marcos and the Zapatistas. A grand scheme for the airport to become part of an 'industrial corridor' through Mexico was dropped. It was a significant victory, which embarrassed the government.

Then another dispute kicked off in 2006, when police tried to stop sixty flower vendors from selling their wares at the local market in Texcoco near Atenco. Things rapidly escalated. The flower sellers called on the FPDT and Subcomandante Marcos came to the town and talked about how all these anti-state movements should come together in what he called 'The Other Campaign'. The protest began to have a powerful symbolic value.

Around 300 protestors blocked the highway and a policeman was injured, an incident which was caught on camera and replayed endlessly on national TV. The next day, up to 3,500 policemen responded with extraordinary violence and crushed the protests. Armed with sketchy intelligence about the ringleaders, they knocked down the doors of suspected homes, trashed them and brutalised their inhabitants A fourteen-year-old boy, Javier Cortés, was killed by a police bullet. A university student called Alexis Benhumera died from head wounds. Women were raped. A report by the National Human Rights Commission claimed that 207 people had been injured and 26 women suffered sexual assault. Several protestors, but none of the perpetrators of the violence, were jailed and a dozen of them received ridiculously long sentences. Ignacio del Valle, the 'intellectual author', who was considered the troublemaker-in-chief, was handed a 100-year jail sentence. We're due to meet his wife, Trini, in Mexico City.

For Manu, what happened in Atenco was simply 'state terrorism', a phrase he went on to use with maximum impact the next year, when he returned to Guadalajara for the International Film Festival and programmed an evening of films that included a documentary on La Colifata.

At the Film Festival, Manu also spoke out in favour of Ignacio del Valle and the other prisoners. He was supposed to give a concert the next night. The state authorities started quizzing the Film Festival organiser Jorge Sánchez about whether Manu was in possession of the required working visa or whether he had entered Mexico with only a tourist visa. They also invoked Article 33 of the Mexican Constitution, which states that foreigners may not in any way interfere in the political affairs of the country, and gives the government the right to evict an offender without trial. Manu cancelled the next day's concert, fearing that his arrest would end in violence and, in the end, the authorities didn't use Article 33 against him. But Manu's speech did create a media firestorm which kept the plight of the prisoners in the public eye.

When we get to our hotel in Mexico City, Manu throws another wobbly. The advertised wi-fi isn't working and he needs to

Manu speaks out against state terrorism at the Guadalajara International Film Festival, 2009.

make some connections. When I ask him out for the evening, he says, slightly conspiratorially, that he has things to do.

Instead, I do a quick tour of some Manu landmarks including the giant Zócalo square where Radio Bemba played to the biggest crowd of their career and the market in Tepito, full of pirated goods, which Manu namechecks in the song "El Hoyo". Then I ask the cab driver to drop me off at Foro Alicia, named after the Lewis Carroll book, which has been ground central to Mexico's alternative bands for the past decade or so. It's like New York's CBGBs with a social conscience. The Alicios offer space to alternative groups like the Zapatistas and put out scores of ska, garage, reggae, new metal and other albums. A selection of names from their artist roster gives a flavour: La Divina Pistola, AK-47, Los Auténticos Decadentes, Zero Child, as well as the peerless Kinky Beat. Manu has played here several times, and a superior semi-bootleg entitled *Próxima Estación: Mexico* can be found on the web.

I track down a Cuban friend, Juan de Marcos González, from the Afro-Cuban All Stars (and musical director of the *Buena Vista Social Club* album) and finish the evening at Plaza Garibaldi, the Mecca for mariachi bands. A wizened guy who looks old enough to have fought with Zapata shuffles up and offers me a cigar. He also has a contraption for giving people an electric shock. Naturally, I'm buying. You have to choose a dose between one and ten. I choose seven and, yes, it's a hell of a jolt, all for five pesos.

Manu doesn't usually surface till midday, so I spend the next morning doing essential tourist stuff including the Frida Kahlo Museum and the Museum of Anthropology. Manu still isn't back at the hotel at lunchtime. I head to the venue, the Foro Sol, a sports arena which is home to the Red Devils, the *Diablos Rojos del México*, a Mexican Baseball League team. We're assured that the place will be nearly full to its 55,000 capacity, which is about the same size as the Shea Stadium where the Beatles played in 1965 – the biggest gig ever at the time. The rain starts coming down in sheets, monsoon-style.

Manu's absence is explained – he's been on a cloak-and-dagger mission to visit Ignacio del Valle and the other prisoners in Atenco prison. Several of the activists from the FPDT are there at the Foro Sol, along with Ignacio's wife, Trinidad Ramírez, or 'Trini' for short. Backstage there's a solemn ceremony. Manu and Gambeat are each given a bandana, a straw hat and a machete. 'The machete doesn't mean violence,' Trini says. 'It is a symbol of the defence of the land and the heart of Atenco.' Hortensia Ramos, also from the FPDT, explains that the bandana is 'a symbol of the sweat of labour and marches, the tears of the mothers of political prisoners, to wipe the tears and sweat of Atenco, as well as the Chiapas and Guerrero'.

What might, in other circumstances, at least to an English sensibility warped by Monty Python, have a certain comic potential, is actually quite moving. The ceremony is given extra

Not your usual backstage action: Trinidad Ramírez initiates Manu into the ranks of the *macheteros*. PHOTO © ROXANNE HAYNES

weight by the apocalyptic rain, the 50,000 strong crowd outside and the complete sincerity of Manu, Gambeat and the *macheteros* from the FPDT.

I've never seen Manu quite so fired up and passionate before a gig, and this translates into a powerful performance by the band. The rain has eased off, but such a vast crowd needs warming up and, to begin with at least, the intensity is at a lower wattage than in Guadalajara. But the set starts to soar about halfway through, powered by the rhythm section of David, Philippe and Gambeat, with Julio's keyboards adding bedrock to the Madjid and Manu show up front. Angelo's trumpet is perfectly 'Mexican'.

The crowd really kick off when the band play "El Hoyo", the song about their city, and "Volver, Volver". Then Trini is brought onstage. 'Here we are,' she shouts. 'We want you to remain free and enjoy. Be happy!' The audience as one shout 'Libertad! Libertad! Libertad!' in return. The universal cry for freedom echoes through the centuries.

CHAPTER 17:
PARIS–SIBERIA

'And since he seeks, he seeks, and he looks ... '

From Manwoz biography

Pig's Alley is the servicemen's nickname for Pigalle, the seedy Parisian neighbourhood where Manu has a tiny bedsit above his management company, Corida. I go to meet him there. Round the corner, a man with aetiolated skin, pale as a baby polar bear due to lack of sunlight, abuses me for not taking his business card, which advertises the name of a nearby lap-dancing club.

Pigalle is full of blinking lights designed to hypnotise the unwary visitor and switch off his brain. Korean massage parlours alternate with shops selling the most banal tourist tat. It's the kind of place where, after midnight, the ATM machines should flash the warning message: 'ARE YOU REALLY SURE ABOUT THIS?' Within a few blocks there are joints that aspire to more sophisticated and artistic manifestations of the erotic craft, with their quaintly seductive burlesque shows and historical pedigree, places like the Moulin Rouge or the Musée de l'Érotisme. Toulouse-Lautrec and Picasso lived hereabouts. Slightly further east, towards the North African neighbourhood of Barbès, there's a funky concert hall called La Cigalle, which is run by Manu's management company. Pigalle, of course, was also the place where Mano Negra did their riotous tour, playing the strip clubs.

Manu's bedsit, also owned by his management, where he stays when visiting Paris, is like a student garret: mattress on the floor, basic sound system, computer, a few clothes on a rail. A half-eaten box of Valentine's chocolates lies forlornly on a shelf. He reminds me that when he was young and living in suburban Sèvres – he had always wanted to escape Paris as soon as he could. 'There wasn't that much to do there as a teenager,' he remembers. 'You'd hang about by the petrol station in a little gang. Maybe the police would move you on. Then you'd go home.' Of course, Paris was never a centre for his beloved rock'n'roll, which only fuelled dreams of other horizons. 'When I go back to Sèvres, it hasn't changed that much. I was the only one to escape. I was the lucky one. Now the kids of my gang are hanging around the same places.'

Several of his friends didn't make it out alive. 'We used to deal a bit in marijuana, some speed,' Manu tells me. 'Then I recall one of the big guys coming round one week with some powder … it was heroin … saying we should sell that. I was lucky. Never touched it.' But several of his gang got hooked and at least a couple of them OD'd. How much of his escape was just dumb luck, another spin of the wheel of *la vida tómbola*? Unlike many in his Sèvres gang, Manu had a loving family living in a house full of books to give him a moral core, confidence and a global outlook. As a teen dreamer, he was driven not only by a deep-rooted desire to break out of the suburbs, but fierce ambition and an aptitude for hard work. He had been endowed with a strong constitution and intelligence by the genetic lottery. Mano Negra were in the right place at the right time, but Manu was ready and set before the space opened up.

'Sometimes when something lucky happens,' he thinks, 'your hand is burned, because you are not ready for it.' But when fortune did smile on him, Manu seized every opportunity with both hands.

It was only when he came back to Paris, as a 'foreigner', after avoiding it for years, that he was able to appreciate the beauty of his native metropolis. It was in this Pigalle garret that he made his own kind of peace with the city he describes as 'cold-hearted', by recording and putting together a book and CD called *Sibérie M'Était Contéee*, in collaboration with the Polish illustrator Jacek Wozniak. Wozniak was introduced to Manu by his father Ramón, who had met him in Paris magazine circles, and liked his work so much he had several images tattooed on his body (one for each book, remember).

Manu's relationship with Wozniak, since their initial collaboration, has become almost symbiotic, with Wozniak almost a visual equivalent to Manu's music. He created Manu's distinctive logo, the artwork of *Radiolina* and other albums, a myriad of features on his website and videos, and a 2012 book (*Manu & Chao*). Manu and Wozniak have also collaborated – under the name 'Manwoz' – on art exhibitions in Perpignan, Barcelona, Guadalajara and Mallorca. They gave their Manwoz character the following, oddly familiar, biography:

> Born in the distant plains of Ukraine in 1959, near the sinister Chernobyl, Manwoz was an only boy in a large family. His father was Galician, his mother ran a tavern. At a young age, Manwoz became bored of school and family and at fifteen decided to travel the globe in search of ... Disappeared. And since he seeks, he seeks, and he looks ...

The *Sibérie M'Était Contéee* book and album effectively marks Manwoz's first appearance. But, for Manu as a musician, the most striking innovation is that the album's lyrics are in French and the subject matter is Paris. Like so many of Manu's projects, it evolved as he (and Wozniak) continued to work on it. It was originally issued as a 48-page book with a CD of 6 songs – but it grew to 148 pages and 23 songs in a second edition.

In the corner of Manu's studio flat, there's a brown box full of tattered sheets scrawled with lyrics and a black box full of technological toys. These are the raw materials and

The *Sibérie* book – dedicated to all the fishers in the river of love. It has become a collectors' item. You need to imagine the grey as yellow, of course.

tools that he used to create the *Sibérie* songs, recording and mixing by himself for the first time, overdubbing trumpet and accordion on sometimes very basic electronic sequences. The music – a low-key, dreamy delight – is influenced by *musette*, the popular Parisian dance music of the 1930s, and by the switchblade cabaret and 'dirty waltzes' of earlier Parisian generations.

Manu recalled how much he had hated French language songs in his youth: 'French music to me was bullshit. It was the music of my grandfather, and I never wrote songs in French. French was the worst, it was old school.' Only much later did he appreciate the treasures of French *chanson*, discovering singers like Jacques Brel and Edith Piaf, who, he slowly realised, were rock'n'roll in their own way, of a totally French stripe.

On *Sibérie* there's a delving back into fertile former eras of Parisian cultural history. One influence is the colourful, one-armed (the other was blown off in the First World War) literary figure of Blaise Cendrars, who knew and influenced poets like Breton and Apollinaire. In the 1920s he lived in a room in Biarritz with murals by Picasso and drove around in an Alfa Romeo with customised paintwork by Braque. Much later, in 1954, he collaborated with the painter Fernand Léger on *Paris, Ma Ville*, a love letter to the capital, full of disillusion and nostalgia. His poem of a Trans-Siberian journey with his lover Jeanne has her repeating: 'Say, are we really a long way from Montmartre?'

Another figure hovering behind the album-book is Jacques Prévert, the surrealist poet and political activist, who was also an accomplished collagist and screenwriter. His most celebrated film, *Les Enfants Du Paradis*, is referenced in *Sibérie*. His playful poetry is loved by children and is often read in schools in France.

Manu had gone mining for inspiration in the Dada and Surrealist movements of the 1920s, which were, in large part, a reaction to the mindless slaughter of the First World War. The wayward anger, nihilism and anti-authoritarianism of those movements shared some sensibilities with punk and the New York scene of the 1970s. In the 1920s, Paris was the stage for wildly original performances like *Parade*, a surrealist ballet with jazzy music by Erik Satie, designs by Jean Cocteau and costumes by Pablo Picasso which included people dressed as skyscrapers. Or George Antheil and Fernand Léger's *Ballet Mécanique,* with its music for pianolas and aeroplane propellers.

In the 1970s, as Manu had discussed with me in New York, Manhattan could boast a similar blurring between the avant-garde and popular music. Rock bands such as Television and Talking Heads had high-art credentials, while composers like Steve Reich and Philip Glass were reaching a rock audience. Within a few years and within a few square miles, punk, hip hop, disco and salsa were developed before exploding worldwide.

Unlike in the era of punk, so inspirational to Manu, whose energy came almost entirely from elsewhere, the French capital was the global centre of the cultural action during the 1920s. That time of Paris' cultural apotheosis began to fascinate and inspire Manu. The alternative heyday of 1980s Paris, with its music, street theatre and anarchic circus, had possessed a similar potential, perhaps, but it imploded before lift-off. Manu missed the camaraderie that had existed back in those times, as well as individual friends like Helno, of Les Négresses Vertes, who died of a heroin overdose in 1993.

Helno's memory inspired the album's most original and haunting track, "Helno Est Mort", which mixes the tunes and some of the words of the nursery rhyme "Au Claire de la Lune". Midway through the lament, a counterpoint tune comes through, with the celebratory flavour of a New Orleans funeral blues while Manu repeatedly chants 'Don't wanna lose nobody close to me'.

After the noisy breakup of Bérurier Noir, Les Négresses Vertes (The Green Negresses) were the other potential world

Quintessential Manu: Wozniak's cover for the *Sibérie* CD.

beaters, besides Mano Negra, to come out of the alternative cauldron of the Paris 1980s underground. They mixed punk, mambo, *flamenco*, Algerian *raï* and riotous choruses, and their first single was called "200 Ans d'Hypocrisie" (200 Years of Hypocrisy). They were signed to Virgin in the same week as Mano Negra. Helno, their charismatic lead singer, and songwriter, was not just a friend; he was perhaps the closest parallel to Manu in the Paris music scene, a shadow and mirror.

The title *Sibérie M'Était Contéee* (Siberia was told to me) is multi-layered. 'Sibérie', for example, can be read as 'If Paris' (*si* means 'if', while *bérie* is a slang pronunciation of 'Paris'), and may have a resonance of Jean Tiberi, mayor of Paris in the 1990s. The subtitle '*A tous les pêcheurs du fleuve amour*' (To all those fishing in the river of love) plays with the words *pêcheurs*, which means both 'sinners' and 'fishermen', and *amour*, which means 'love' but also refers more obliquely to Amur, the river in Siberia which winds its black, serpentine way along the Manchurian border and was regarded as sacred by the Qing Dynasty.

With its unholy bleakness and frozen winters, Siberia seemed to Manu to be a reasonable if unlikely metaphor for Paris, which he evokes with poetic images like the 'small golden neon sun' setting bleakly over the Gare du Nord. 'I spent my first twenty-six winters in Paris,' he tells me. 'I felt that so many of the human relationships were grey. These days I come as a foreigner – my Paris is really Ménilmontant and the bars in that area.'

The first track, "P'tit Jardin" (Small Garden), describes Manu's magical garden, which contains garbage, cockroaches, his dog and factories, but also includes pretty girls who cry, the bike of his brother, great pine forests and a single wild flower. "Il Faut Manger" (One Must Eat), with its Afro-blues guitar loop courtesy of Amadou Bagayoko from Amadou & Mariam, is about the struggle of immigrants for food and money. There are also echoes of Manu's childhood in Sèvres. In "J'ai Besoin De La Lune" (I Need The Moon), which was recycled later on *La Radiolina*, he sings that touching phrase of how he needs

Manu with Wozniak – and Woz-customised guitar – by the sea in Barcelona.

'my father to know where I come from, and my mother to show me the way'.

Sibérie M'Était Contéee was a first in several ways: it was Manu's first French language album, accompanied by the vibrantly coloured book illustrated by both Wozniak and Manu, and the first time Manu had mixed and produced an album alone on his laptop. Another major step towards autonomy was the fact that the album was released independently, through his management company Corida, who distributed the limited run of 150,000 through bookshops.

After the death of his manager Jacques Renault, Manu had signed a deal with Emmanuel de Buretel, previously head of Virgin Europe, whom he had known for years. 'It was a syndicalist decision,' Manu said of his reason for leaving Virgin. 'I worked with them for a lot of the time and many of the people working for Virgin, are my friends. They are workers and when EMI Virgin tried to say, "Next September thirty per cent of the people here are gonna be fired," I immediately said "You can include me in the first thirty per cent. I'm in solidarity with my people." They were not losing money, so there was no excuse to fire people.'

But Manu also concedes that the split was actually more complicated than that. The contradiction of being a leading advocate of anti-globalisation whilst also being signed to Virgin – by now part of the multinational EMI – was becoming a strain. Most importantly, Manu was ready to go it alone. When de Buretel left Virgin shortly afterwards, it seemed logical enough for them to team up. De Buretel started his own label and named it Because (for the pun – 'Be Cause' – and after the Beatles song). Its early releases included both Amadou & Mariam's *Dimanche À Bamako* and Manu's *La Radiolina* albums, and it now handles all Manu's solo work, as well as launching bands like Metronomy and Django Django.

But if *Sibérie* signified a *rapprochement* with the city Manu had escaped from all those years before, it was still a wary one. He didn't perform in Paris at all between 2001 and 2008. And this wariness was reciprocal. Many of the French capital's arbiters of taste and music business trendsetters profess indifference or outright hostility to their most globally successful native son. 'I'm not fussed', one journalist said to me. Others I spoke to dismissed Manu as, variously, a rich poseur, a plagiarist, a dictator to his band, and – the most damning accusation in Paris – unfashionable.

It's a biblical truth that a prophet is without honour in his own land. You might expect taste-makers and those concerned with being of the moment to be more interested in the next big thing than in an artist who has already achieved success and is therefore beyond of the thrill of discovery.

Perhaps, too, Manu's scruffy sense of non-fashion (seven-year-old sneakers, come on Manu!) was an affront to Paris's dearly held ideas of style and chic.

De Buretel's theory was this was a case of jealousy, pure and simple. Perhaps it was also that the Parisian rock elite never quite forgave him for being their bestselling export, and thus upsetting their long-cherished feelings of victim-hood. And Manu had never been comfortable in the hip, snobbish, high fashion bars and clubs of Paris, anyway, saying they made him 'feel like a peasant'. According to Kieron Tyler, an English journalist who writes about French music, 'his fans are mostly working-class and also largely in the south of the country (where rap outsells everything else) – the combination of working-class and a rap-type territory make Manu beyond the taste barrier for the urban cognoscenti'.

On a previous trip to Paris in 2008, on Manu's birthday, I saw Radio Bemba play a free gig in Bondy, one of the *banlieues* or suburbs beyond the *périphérique* ring road. The burgers of Bondy still had positive feelings towards Mano Negra, ever since their Caravane des Quartiers tour and its fondly remembered mayhem. Manu was sharing a bill with Idir, the Berber Algerian singer whose hit "Denia" had been covered by Manu on *Próxima Estación: Esperanza*. The crowd were a mix of North African youth or *beurs*, as well as white working-class fans and a sprinkling of intrepid bohemians who had hazarded the trip to the suburbs. The reaction was fiercely partisan.

On that trip I had lunch with Malcolm McLaren, who lived much of his later life in Paris. Malcolm, who had been a global catalyst not just for punk but also hip-hop, world music and even French *chanson*, was fascinated by Manu, and was contemplating doing a remix of one of his songs. 'What do you think, Peter?' he mused. 'Is he a genius? I mean, he's not Bob Dylan, is he?'

I said something about how both Manu and Dylan had carved out a distinct artistic territory – though in truth Malcolm himself was rather more like Manu. Both were anti-

Manu and Radio Bemba play Bondy, out in the Parisian suburbs.

authoritarian, against the music business corporations, but strong-minded enough to have got good deals from them that preserved their autonomy. Both were fascinated by Parisian cultural movements, whether Dada, surrealism or the *événements* of 1968. In contrast to Manu, though, Malcolm enjoyed elements of fashion and the great restaurants of Paris.

When I was backstage at Bondy, just as Manu was tucking into his birthday cake, Malcolm called and I suggested a meeting to Manu. However, there seemed to be caginess on both sides, like big beasts unexpectedly confronting each other in a primeval forest. Then, in 2010, Malcolm died, and an introduction I would loved to have made was never to happen.

That other accusation by some Parisian hipsters of Manu being a 'dictator' is probably best answered by the earlier chapters of this book: Manu tried collective decision making

in Mano Negra and it ended up a disaster – and an egalitarian approach to artistic creation only very rarely works.
'But he forces his musicians to stay in cheap hotels', was a
further complaint that I heard in Paris. Which is half true.
Manu hates expensive, bland chain hotels and uniform five-
star glitz makes him uncomfortable. So he and his band tend
to stay in quirkier, cheaper places. Is he non-materialistic,
drawn to more characterful places or merely careful with his
money? Probably a mixture of all three. He's not so strict
about this, anyway – it happened to be practical to stay at the
Holiday Inn in New York, as banal as any top hotel, when I
saw him there. Certainly, he's not like some stars who stay in
the good places and force the band into a local fleapit.

No doubt the band moan about Manu sometimes, and he
can be demanding, but the *esprit de corps* and the good-
humoured atmosphere on the bus, as well as the energy and
cohesion onstage can't be faked for long. In contrast, there
are several big bands who don't actually speak to one another,
and arrive at their gigs in separate limos. And, impressively,
according to de Buretel, if Manu wants to play a benefit, the
band still get paid the normal rate.

Talking in Paris, I ask Manu bluntly about what happens to all
the money he earns. 'A lot gets raked off by lawyers and bankers, that's for sure,' he tells me. He has set-up a trust because,
so he claims, 'they make it difficult to give money'. A trust also
saves tax. Manu has said in public that he has donated to such
causes as La Colifata and the Zapatistas. After drinks in the
Bar Mariatchi in Barcelona, he mentioned a few projects in
Africa. He prefers to know who he is giving money to personally, as he doesn't trust that money given to charities ends up
where it is supposed to. I pictured Manu, like a backpacking
Santa Claus, arriving somewhere in the Congo or high up in
the Andes and distributing largesse for a school roof, a water-
collecting unit, or whatever else might be needed.

Manu feels that announcing what he does with his money
would make him more of a target. 'If I made publicity
with all my support and donations, I would be labelled an

opportunist,' he says. 'It would be said that I was profiting from it to sell my discs. It's the snake that eats its tail.' Then he shakes his head and adds, 'The only thing I can say is that I have earned a lot of money and don't have a bad conscience. I didn't steal from anyone and I've earned my living from the sweat of my brow. What I do with it is my private life and it only concerns me and the people I'm together with.'

What does seem to get to people, even those quite close to Manu, is – according to Fabrice Brovelli, the manager of SMOD – his 'schizophrenic attitude to money'. There's some truth in that. Manu always says that 'money is the devil'. But it also buys freedom. To Manu money is necessary because with it he can keep his treasured independence and feed his addiction to travel.

Both Brovelli and Marc Antoine Moreau, the manager of Amadou & Mariam, commented on the fact that when Manu was working in Mali with them on *Dimanche À Bamako*, he never had any of his own money on him. You could argue that this was compensated by the fact that the album sold in the hundreds of thousands and established Amadou & Mariam's international careers. But, for Bovelli and Moreau, it felt as if Manu was posing as a gypsy who didn't need money. Nevertheless, it's true that Manu can and has survived with no cash in many cities by jamming in bars and crashing with friends or fans.

One of the reasons I initially got on with Manu wasn't just our common love of pre-punk bands like Dr Feelgood or obscure salsa, a mania for travel or a common fascination for metaphysical and spiritual matters. It was also that some friends and I had once conducted an experiment in living without money whilst squatting in the then shabby-chic Bloomsbury neighbourhood of London. We found our heating fuel in skips and our food among the crates of vegetables that were thrown out by the street markets at the end of the day. Travel was by bicycle. For a few months at least, we had the liberating illusion of defeating the demon of money.

But that was just a good jape. I wouldn't like to live now in a house where the roof leaked and there was no central heating.

Manu undoubtedly admires Zen monks who have no desire for material possessions, or even his mad homeless friend Aldi, who blew any cash he ever had. In reality, both of us are property owners (Manu never sold the flat in Barcelona, and bought the Mariatchi Bar – one way of making sure your local pub stays open – as well as more recently a flat in Paris where one of his cousins lives). The escape strategies of adolescence may be no longer appropriate in maturity.

But Manu is certainly an accidental millionaire. He couldn't and didn't predict the huge success of *Clandestino* nor *Dimanche À Bamako*. 'The times when I have thought of the audience or having a hit have all been failures,' he says. 'When I do music for myself, by instinct, as a kind of therapy, that is when it seems to reach an audience.'

Although it's not a problem he will get much sympathy for, what to do with his riches is a problem. There are endless possible projects: an online network of local political and cultural websites and new water retention technology for dry countries, for example, have been discussed. But charitable projects are time-consuming as well as in need of good managers and, when he gets involved, Manu wants to know the people and see the results for himself. And, unlike many celebrities in the arts, he remains a French citizen, paying his seventy-five percent taxes, rather than opting for a change of domicile to Spain or elsewhere.

At what point does a pose, if kept up every day, become real? One of the great things about pop music is the artificial but sometimes heroic personal reinvention of its stars, usually into something more deviant and glamorous. With stars that have certain prophetic qualities, they get to become close to sainthood with their fans. John Mellor, a diplomat's son, becomes Joe Strummer, David Jones of Bromley becomes a space alien, Robert Zimmerman dons shades and visits Woody Guthrie and becomes Dylan, José-Manuel Chao dreams in the suburbs of Paris and gets to become Manu Chao, some kind of cross between Bob Marley and Che Guevara. All these figures become inspiring and powerful symbols, harbingers of potential new worlds, walking archetypes.

The danger and potential for self-destruction lies when the star gets confused between public and private personas. That way madness lies. Manu himself seems to have a relatively sane attitude to his fame and both the brickbats and the adoration, recognising that an unreal attitude to oneself is part of the deal when you get famous. As he had told me in Córdoba, the thing about fame is that 'People treat you as a god, or as a fucking asshole.' What is difficult for the people around any star, including Manu, is the disconnect between the icon and the man. 'I bet Che Guevara was a bastard to his friends sometimes,' was Marc Antoine Moreau's rueful comment.

Manu's need for spontaneity and aversion to planning ahead can unhinge those around him. One small example is Manu's refusal to carry a mobile phone or a watch. 'I look at screen all day doing mixes. Looking at a small screen the rest of the time would be too much', is how he excuses himself. But as rock star foibles go, Manu's are hardly mortal sins. If Manu wants to spend his money on staying free, giving himself time to daydream and escape the leash, rather than on sports cars and houses in the country, that's his choice. Likewise, the people around him, his band, managers, labels, agents or the journalists, have a choice whether to work with him or walk the other way. No one twisted our arms. The inconvenience and his elusiveness is more than outweighed by the amazing energy you're exposed to when you're part of the Manu circus.

It's not always easy to be Manu. As Fabrice Brovelli said, Manu is a 'loner' and fame only increases that sense of loneliness, of separation from others. One Spanish woman who had met Manu numerous times once made a curious observation to me. 'I like Manu, but each time I see him it's as if we're meeting for the first time.'

Being a *loco mosquito* means it's problematic to really nurture close friendships and a difficulty is that many friends could be seen to have a vested interest. Madjid, Gambeat,

Philippe and the other musicians are close, but Manu is also their boss. Emmanuel is a good friend but he is also the manager. Jacek Wozniak has done a picture book and designs album covers. Manu is kind enough to call me his friend but he knows that I'm writing a book and anything he says could end up here. Johnny McLeod benefits from Manu's endorsement of his bar in Ménilmontant and is launching a music career. Even his girlfriend makes tour videos.

People expect Manu to be this indefatigable champion of the underclass. They continually ask him for help with some project or another. But, while he may sometimes get angry with his band or his management, I've never seen him be less than civil with the myriad of people he runs into in the street or backstage at his show, even if it takes hours to say hello to everyone.

When I met Ramón, Manu's father for a coffee at the Café Ondes near the RFI radio station where he works in Paris, he tells me an instructive anecdote. When Manu was touring Peru, an old friend of Ramón's called him – a man who was once an imprisoned activist but is now an ambassador. 'I rang Manu to tell him he was going to be in the gig and that he would like to meet him.' The day of the concert Manu didn't pay much attention to him. 'Days later, I told him off. He is a respectful man and a friend of mine, and Manu replied "Yes Dad, but he is an ambassador." Manu doesn't want to become friends with the powerful.'

Ramón also said he was worried that Manu was actually more fragile than he seemed. He'd seen him at rock bottom, in Galicia, depressed and vulnerable. Does he think Manu is happy? 'No,' was Ramón's answer, 'but then that is the fate of all true artists, to be continually dissatisfied.'

That evening, after our chat in his garret, Manu tells me he's doing a favour for some friends who are in a band called Les Ogres de Barback. He cycles to the gig, plays his old faithful acoustic guitar on a few numbers, says hi to a few friends backstage including Johnny McLeod, puts his arm round some fans who want their photo with him, then bikes back to his monk-like cell for a night of work on his computer, editing films, mixing music. Andres Garrido points out that any other star of even a fraction of his magnitude might easily have caused a fuss about his guitar and had his own special guitar roadie or two.

It's all rather impressive. But it is also what keeps Manu going, what defines him. For Manu, playing music is all about 'the exchange of energy'. The live experience is the heart of it for him, when on a good night the audience and, for Manu too, can be lifted out of despair into hope into a collective ecstasy. 'One good thing about music,' as Marley sang. 'When it hits, you feel no pain.'

Before leaving Paris, I meet a Brazilian photographer for lunch in Le Marais. She's a bit of a hippy chick, and a huge fan of Manu's. She wants to know what I have learned from him. I say I knew a lot more about the refugees in the Sahara Desert, the mental patients in Buenos Aires and the *macheteros* in Mexico. I think Manu is right about the importance of neighbourhood action and the lack of power of politicians – I had, perhaps naively, expected Obama, for example, to take on the banks and support things like the rights of Palestinians, whereas Manu was more realistic. 'Yes,' she replies with intensity, 'but what about more *spiritual* matters?' I answer that perhaps I trust my instinct more and am more aware of things like coincidences, that maybe they are signs of an unknowable force trying to create order out of chaos. That maybe there really is some bigger universal energy we should all trust, which may take us in directions our ego hasn't planned.

The day after returning to London, I watch a YouTube video of Manu sweetly teaching some kids how to play the guitar in the *favelas* of Fortaleza. It had been watched by about ten people. I also received an email from the scriptwriter and film director Menno Meyers. 'I love Manu,' he wrote. 'He's a really positive force in the world.' And I thought – that's true.

CHAPTER 18:
BRIXTON BABYLON

'A river needs banks for the water to flow.'
___
From the I-Ching – Manu's favourite book

The sleek vixen was bold as brass, slinking across Acre Lane, to the manor born, as dusk fell on the Saturday of the Jubilee weekend to celebrate the Queen's sixty years on the throne. I was with Maria Santos, Manu's girlfriend. Manu had told me the last time we met, over a year ago, that he had written a song about the urban foxes you see all over London. 'It's a love song as well,' says Maria, humming a couplet. That makes sense – Maria is an elegant beauty, funky, luxuriant unkempt hair, bright eyes. 'So *you're* the Brixton Fox?'

We had caught a glimpse of the flotilla of boats sailing up the river at Vauxhall Bridge, then decided to sidestep the collective swoon for the monarchy by going to see Kevin Macdonald's epic documentary on Bob Marley at the Brixton Ritzy. Afterwards, we go to a cheap but good Mexican restaurant in Brixton's market. The waitress, Maritza, a friend of Maria's, supports the Zapatistas. The owner of the place, another Mexican, thinks they're very good at getting money from Europeans. For him, they're like the IRA, Irish Catholic fighters who maybe once were on the side of the good guys but who had long since become corrupt. He thinks they're just using Manu.

Naturally, we discuss the movie, too: the clash between the symbolic visionary with a white father and black mother, who preached unity, the Marley who belonged to the world, and Bob Marley the man, who was frankly a pain to his wife, Rita, and most of his children

Manu has been compared often enough with Marley, a revolutionary agent for a change of consciousness, a champion of the underclass and man of the people. I tell Maria that when I had been doing some reports for Oxfam in the Philippines, we went to visit an island with most remote tribal people I had ever come across – several of them wore Bob Marley T-shirts. At the start of the Arab Spring, there was graffiti on Tunisian walls scrawled with Marley quotes like 'Get Up, Stand Up'.

Manu could quite possibly have capitalised on the dizzying success of *Clandestino* and *Próxima Estación: Esperanza* to have the same kind of global reach, to be the picture on radical students' walls next to Che Guevara and Marley. Millions do revere him, but, with only one major CD release in the last ten years, I suggest to Maria that it was maybe because he actively, and understandably, didn't want the next level into premier league fame. Marley was shot, Lennon killed and list of stars who self-destructed is a long one. The crazy, pressured life of Santa Maradona that he had sung about in "La Vida Tómbola". She doesn't think that was it, but with a laugh says it was 'stubbornness'. Having had his instincts proved reliable often enough, he thought he was always right.

It's not that Manu hasn't got a treasure trove of unreleased material. There's an album's worth of *rumba* recordings done in Barcelona that at one time were going to go out under the enjoyable title *The Worst Of The Rumba Volume 1*. I'd heard most of his 'Brazilian' album which he played most of me in the Café Glaciar, including his song to his son, "Kira", and the singalong "Ta De Bobeira" which has already become a delirious live staple. Some fierce remixes emerged of "Politik Kills" and "A Cosa" by Mike 'Prince Fatty' Pelanconi, the Brighton-based DJ, but there are other delicious vintage-style reggae-ish originals from the same sessions which haven't been released. Not to mention the odd mythical song like "Salaryman" or, indeed, the "Brixton Fox". Manu claims to have hundreds of songs in various forms on his hard drive and he could release several albums in one go if he chose to.

A valid question in an industry where the business model changes so fast, and all that is solid turns into air, is how to release this material. Maria thinks Manu would be probably perfectly happy to put them out for free, his management predictably less so. Another issue, both technological and creative, is that, while working on a laptop is liberating, it also gives you too many options. When exactly is a track finished anyway, if ever? When I had last met Manu, I suggested the old-fashioned studio constraints had some advantages – for his 'Brazilian' album why not just book three weeks in a studio with a top Brazilian producer like Jaques Morelenbaum and see what comes out? I even quoted a line from Manu's favourite book, the *I Ching*: 'A river needs banks for the water to flow'. It's also true that, just as most writers need editors, for a musician an empathetic producer can have a valuable, more objective, perspective. After all, Manu's biggest successes, both artistically and commercially, came from the two albums that had Renauld Letang as co-pilot.

Although in Mano Negra, Manu was accused by the band of being a *bosseur*, a hard-driving Jesuit with his unrelenting work rate, now he's more likely to be criticised for slacking, with a dearth of major albums. In fact, generally Manu is doing all kinds of things, but if he's seen as flying the flag for slackers, maybe it's admirable. What Thoreau wrote, in 1863, applies even more now: 'If a man walks in the woods for love of them half of each day, he is in danger of being regarded as a loafer; but if he spends his whole day as a speculator, shearing off those woods and making earth bald before her time, he is esteemed an industrious and enterprising citizen. This world is a place of business. What an infinite bustle! I think there is nothing, not even crime, more opposed to poetry, to philosophy, ay, to life itself, than this incessant business.'

A charitable view would be that one of the reasons Manu feels at home in Africa or South America is because he doesn't quite believe in the European notion of time. Not an excuse that would wash with your own boss in New York or London, perhaps, but then most of us haven't been described as 'the last free man'. And a considerable part of this powerful symbolic appeal of Manu is as a free man, a 'post-European trickster' beyond borders, whether musical, ancestral or geographic.

Back at Maria's Brixton basement flat, I ask how she copes with Manu's elusiveness and *loco mosquito* tendencies. She replies that some people's dream may be to live in a cottage in the country and raise kids, but not her's, nor Manu's. She then turns the tables and it seems that she may have another motive for meeting me when she fixes me with her dark eyes and says: 'I hope you are not mythologising Manu.'

The observation is so astute, and direct, that it startles me. I'm focusing on the more exciting events in Manu's life and to do that there's a necessary selection process. In that respect, this book is like any novel. Conversations that took place on different days end up concertinaed together. And who was it who said that facts are stranger than fiction, but fiction is truer? I tell her I'm trying to make my book as honest as possible and won't merely portray Manu as some kind of warrior-saint that some of his fans seem to think he is. This possibility concerns Maria. She tells me of a weird incident on the previous summer's US tour when a very pregnant woman came up to Manu and asked for her unborn child to be blessed.

Manu's no saint, for sure. But people expect things of him, even on a mundane level. Maria mentions that when he has a hangover he reckons the best cure is Coca Cola. One time in Miami, she went to the local shop to buy some Coke because there had been some heavy partying the night before, and this couple came up to her and said, 'but you're Manu's girlfriend'. The couple had been to the concert the night before and had seen them together (Maria is quite a striking-looking woman). The couple were shocked and actually rather horrified. Surely Manu didn't consume Coca-Cola?

Maria asks if I want to see some footage she had shot of the last US Tour in the summer of 2011. It's good stuff. She had picked up a quality video camera in New York and was excited about putting it to proper use for the first time. She did have, as they say, access to all areas and expertly shot some charmingly frank but professional-quality material starring Manu, Madjid, Gambeat and Philippe as they toured North America as La Ventura. The tour achieved what was possibly Manu's greatest success in the States yet: playing to wildly enthusiastic crowds in sold-out arenas, like the 12,000-seater Klipsch Amphitheater in Miami. Having avoided North America for most of his career, was Manu, in his middle age, finally seducing the Great Satan?

The tour finished with a free concert in Phoenix, Arizona, and some high-profile agitprop sponsored by the National Day Laborer's Organizing Network. Maria includes footage of Manu and Madjid performing right outside Sheriff Joe Arpaio's infamous tent-city, which houses over 10,000 undocumented immigrants in very basic conditions. 'The duo sang "Clandestino" of course. *'Me dicen "el clandestino" por no llevar papel'* (They call me 'clandestine' because I have no papers) rings the chorus,' remembered one blogger, 'and while the song alludes to unauthorised immigration from Africa to Europe, as well as Chao's own family's fleeing from Spain, the message hits powerfully in Arizona in 2011.'

'It may sound stupid, but Arizona, for me, from my childhood, was the centre of the world because I used to spend so much time watching films of cowboys with my grandfather,' Manu told the *Arizona Republic*. A commentator on the newspaper's website was not impressed: 'Yeah? And I've formulated my political stance on foreign countries like China by watching Jackie Chan movies.' When the paper asked Manu why he was getting himself involved in politics, he answered: 'Because everywhere you go, there are social problems. You can't close your heart and say nothing is happening. Politics is all around you. So my way of writing songs is a little kind of journalistic way. I've never found

Madjid and Manu in Arizona.

a place where people told me, "Manu, here, everything is going good".'

Maria's video captures a festive, gang atmosphere on the tour bus. Gambeat dabbles with chiropractic medicine, which Manu turned him on to. Madjid sings Bob Marley songs; it turns out he has a useful, soulful voice. Philip bashes away on a tambourine. Manu loiters, his old-faithful acoustic guitar in his hands, rolling joints, meeting the fans. There's another scene showing them all cracking up at some images on a phone. Maria smiles. 'Probably porn,' she says.

Her video ends on a high note of the band playing "Ta De Bobeira" with the lights swooping over an insanely pogo-ing crowd. The title is Brazilian slang, from Bahia where Maria was born, meaning 'Messing Around' or 'Fucked Up'. A rough translation of the lyrics: 'You walked up to the shantytown, and danced the whole night / You were high, and put rum into the baby bottle / You used drugs, and rolled over the bed, the whole night / You slept and someone stole your wallet ...' After the heavy politics, it's back to fiesta.

Later, Maria sends me this text: 'Why do they say – never meet your hero?'

My last interview with Manu had been a year earlier, also in a café in Brixton before the US Tour. We had talked about the curse of fame – 'a dangerous drug', as Manu put it. 'Though I was lucky, because it happened little by little. It wasn't something massive that happened when I was twenty-five, which can burn you. I had a little bit of neighbourhood fame with Los Carayos, more with Mano Negra and even more with *Clandestino*. I had to learn to protect myself, because it can send you crazy. I know that. The relationship with people can be false. I experience that very often. People can talk to me for half an hour before recognising me – then they change, so I know perfectly well it's different before and after. I used to be the guy observing in the corner at parties, maybe writing a song about it. Now that's not possible any more.'

Since then, Manu's gone off the radar. No response to emails. Maybe it's because of the last session, when he had finally opened up to me about the Mano Negra split. It's a wound that clearly hasn't healed and Manu had been obviously upset remembering the events. By coincidence, the writer and musician Marcus O'Dair had just shown me a chapter in progress from the book he is writing on the British singer Robert Wyatt. Wyatt told him something striking: in comparison to falling out of a window, becoming a paraplegic and being confined to a wheelchair for life, he felt his ejection from Soft Machine, his first successful band, was far more painful. These bands can be closer than family.

After our last meeting, though, I'd seen Manu playing with a stripped-down trio with Madjid and Philippe Teboul, during a benefit appearance for Colombiage, a festival of Colombian culture that took place at an antique theatre, the Coronet, near the Old Kent Road. For the first time since before Mano Negra, Philippe was back behind the drumkit rather than in his usual percussive role, and was clearly relishing every moment.

Manu and Madjid in their flat caps, playing the Brixton community festival.

Then I saw Manu again at Hop Farm Festival in Kent in the summer of 2011. For me, it was the most uplifting and intense performance I'd seen since Mexico. His old cohort Gambeat joined the trio to provide the bass bedrock of a four-piece band Manu was now calling La Ventura; the fourth wheel was back on a turbo-charged car. It was notable how, during the set, people drifted away from another stage on which Morrissey was playing to come and watch Manu. By the end of the show, the audience was sweat-drenched and euphoric, singing along with choruses in English, Spanish or just a kind of improvised Esperanto.

The following year, in August 2012, Manu played just one gig in Britain – at a small under-the-radar community Festival called Brixton Come Together, organised by Maria. Playing on a ramshackle stage on the green outside St Matthew's Church, he seemed entirely at home; much more so than at some of the more conventional rockstar places I'd seen him in, like Glastonbury, where he said all the fences and passes made him think of Palestine.

At Brixton, there were a few food and charity and environmentalist stalls and a sympathetic crowd of a few hundred. The spendidly named La Troba Kung-Fú, a band of Catalan rebels from Barcelona, played a *mestizaje* of infernal *cumbia*, reggae and *rumba* which warmed up the audience nicely. Then Manu's band, wearing the kind of flat caps that were last briefly fashionable worn by Gilbert O'Sullivan forty years ago, had Madjid on guitar and Philippe on drums, the accordionist from La Troba Kung-Fú, and on percussion a kid from the local Hill Mead School, which Manu had visited earlier. They rattled through acoustic versions of some of Manu's classics before ending with a scorching singalong tune by 1980s Spanish bad boys Los Chunguitos.

On the way back from that Brixton gig, I thought of some other times I've seen Manu in London. One night back in the autumn of 2007, I swung down to Peckham in deepest south London, where I saw Manu DJ-ing at a squat fundraiser. He'd promised a Latin American political/music organisation called Movimientos to spin some tunes and had turned up with discs in his rucksack to play records till the small hours. To get in you had to bang on some iron gates, which creaked open a crack to reveal Manu, wearing long shorts and a white jacket, standing around a large open fire with drummers jamming. Nearby, a squatter wearing a large housecoat was holding a pet snake. A couple of bands, including the exuberant Colombian outfit Malalma, played to a crowd of a little over a hundred. Then Manu took to the decks and spun a mix of reggae, *cumbia* and *reggaeton*. Emmanuel de Buretel, the only guy in the whole place wearing a suit, said it was typical of Manu to do this kind of benefit, while refusing, for example, to speak to the French press to promote his latest album *La Radiolina*.

Then there was the time in the spring of 2008 when we spent a morning at the London offices of Al Jazeera, where Manu faced one of Britain's most renowned interviewers, David Frost, famous for his historic interviews with the disgraced US President Richard Nixon in 1977, which spawned the hit film *Frost/Nixon*. Manu felt Al Jazeera had been a little more balanced than the others in its coverage of the Iraq war and politics of the Middle East, so he had agreed to talk to Frost who had a chat show on the channel. Neither man said anything unexpected, but the ability to talk directly about the lyrics of "Rainin' In Paradize", about Iraq and the Congo, was a refreshing rarity on TV.

Afterwards we had played table football in a bar – Manu won and, oddly, apologised sincerely. Then he started telling me what he said was the 'genesis myth' behind the creation of *Clandestino*. The key to the record. It was, he warned, a long story, about Cancodrillo – a mix of crocodile and dog – and a god called Superchango:

'There's this little dog called Pepiño who comes from Galicia in Spain and at that time there's no food, only

Superchango and Cancodrillo by Wozniak and Manu.

misery. The cure is emigration. So the dog emigrates to Venezuela and the only thing he takes with him are these seeds of *pimientos*, like peppers. This dog is so awful that everyone laughs at him. He's like a cross between a mongrel dog and Charlie Chaplin. Anyway, he gets to Venezuela and everybody laughs and laughs and laughs. Everybody except this one girl, a crocodile black woman. She can't talk, she's mute, she doesn't laugh. They fall in love, get married and go to the countryside. They plant the little *pimiento* seeds from Galicia and one of the seeds grows into their son, a mixture of European dog and crocodile ... a *mestizo* Cancodrillo!

'When he comes out of the belly of his mother, the first thing Cancodrillo sees is the face of his father and, like everybody else, he starts laughing, laughing, laughing and crying, crying, crying. But the cry is a good cry, and the more he sees his father, the more he cries, and the more he cries, the more he gets rich. He becomes an asshole. He builds factory after factory selling *pimientos*. He becomes a big businessman. Very quickly he understands that it is better to do your business during the night, and he becomes like a Mafia man. The more money he makes, the more he cries, and the more he laughs, the more he makes money. He turns all the people from the countryside who belong to his mother race into slaves working for him. That's the song "Lagrimas De Oro" (Tears Of Gold).

'Cancodrillo lacks new challenges and he always wants more. First he buys the army, then he buys all the politicians. He has everything and he wants more and more. Then one day he goes into a bar in the middle of the night, a bar for Mafia, and he meets this guy. Now everybody is scared of this guy because when he laughs, he opens his mouth and you can see his crocodile teeth. He is the first person ever to stand up to Cancodrillo. This guy is Superchango and he is a god from Nigeria, born as a slave. He laughs at Cancodrillo. He's not scared of him. They fight, they get drunk, fight again, get drunk. Nobody wins.

'Cancodrillo is a businessman, Superchango is a god. At six in the morning, they're still in the bar and Cancodrillo says,

"Now there's going to be a real battle, a real challenge! You see this little table football … We're going to play this game. And if I win, you are going to give me your powers of a god. And if you win, I'll give you all my business." Superchango says, "OK."

'They play table football for ten centuries and nobody wins, or, rather, nobody knows who won and who lost, but after the battle, Cancodrillo isn't a businessman anymore and has become a god, and Superchango isn't a god any more and has become a businessman. Their roles have changed and both of them become really sad. They don't laugh any more. They get lost. They lose the treasure. And the only good thing about this sadness is that they become friends. They decide to travel all around the world to find love and laughter. They experience drugs and go to Patagonia. They go to France, New York. They go everywhere, everywhere … '

At that moment Manu was distracted by something and had to go. 'If you don't know this story,' he said, 'you cannot really understand *Clandestino*. It isn't really a record. It's part of a story. Next time maybe, I'll tell you how it ends.'

CHAPTER 19:
BRAZIL – AN ENCOUNTER WITH THE GODDESS

'If you don't accept your darkness, you have to project it somewhere else.'

Gilberto Gil

I thought that meeting up with Manu in Brazil would be easy. For the last few years he's spent a couple of months or so there every winter, mainly in the north-east, around Fortaleza and the neighbouring beaches in the state of Ceará. His management told me that he'd be there, but by the time I arrive he's gone ... *desaparecido*. Maybe he's gone off with the *repentistas*, the medieval troubadours of the *sertão*, skilled in creating ballads on any subject to order, whom he invited to his Feira de Las Mentiras in Spain. He once told me that he sometimes goes on the road with them, surviving on the lethal sugarcane liquor known as *cachaça* and little else.

Once upon a time, Ceará was one of the most fertile regions in Brazil. The humid coastal fringe had a soil rich in mineral salts and humus. It was a region of savannahs, blessed with frequent rain. Then human hands came along and turned all that green to mud and dust as a sugarcane monoculture took over. There were riches for the mill owners, but Ceará is today one of the most underdeveloped parts of the Western hemisphere. In the Mariatchi bar in Barcelona, Manu told me, 'The first thing you need to know about Ceará is Luiz Gonzaga, he's the Bob Marley of Brazil,' and launched into "Asi Branca", a beautiful song in which Gonzaga says he will return to the backlands when the rain comes, when the land is as green as his beloved's eyes. It is a Brazilian classic and has been covered by, among others, Tom Zé, Gilberto Gil and David Byrne.

Ceará is the place where Manu recharges batteries, smokes a few joints and writes some songs. It's a perfect environment in which to kick back or even retire. Many Europeans have done exactly that. I met the British consul and she told me that numerous Brits had hooked up with local Brazilians during a holiday in the Ceará, then married and stayed. She was surprised how successful and long-lasting these relationships seemed to be.

For Manu, the most important fact about Ceará is that his son Kira was born there. His name means 'the bird that takes flight' in the local Indian language *Guaraní*. It also means 'sun' in Persian. Manu's mother has met the child more than once, and Ramón hoped to do the same, but was taken ill when he was due to travel to Fortaleza. Kira's mother and Manu had a short-lived relationship when they were on a trip together in the Amazon and, despite his crazy global schedule, Manu sees as much of both of them as he can. In 2009, he took the ten-year-old Kira on tour from Salvador to Recife, further down the coast from Fortaleza.

In 2011, Manu also investigated the idea of setting up a project to harvest rainwater and irrigate the *sertão* during the dry months. With his girlfriend Maria Santos, they looked into solar-powered pumps and new, portable, filtering techniques. He also talked about setting up a factory to make the T-shirts and other items sold as merchandising at his shows, using organic material, naturally.

I had already spent the last of my advance for this book, but when a bucket-shop charter flight to Fortaleza turned up for less than £400, I couldn't resist it. I had this fantasy that Manu and I would hang out on the beach for a few says, shooting the breeze, puffing on some superior weed, downing some *cachaça* and maybe writing a song or two. Who knows? But the fact is that I'm here uninvited and whether Manu is away on the road or simply avoiding me, I have no way of knowing.

He's told me often enough that his favourite city is Rio de Janeiro. He takes pride in being accepted as the 'house' guitar player in some of its neighbourhood bars. 'The old guys don't know I'm Manu Chao,' he told me, 'and five minutes after I walk in, a guitar comes along and I have to sing for them for hours and hours.' I love Manu's line about Rio: 'It's the only city in the world where you can turn up to a bar at midnight banging a drum and they complain when you stop playing at 3am.'

Of course, the *favelas* or shantytowns up on the hills around the city are dangerous. 'Some people criticised the film *City of God* because it was so violent,' Manu says, 'but the reality is like that. There are the problems of alcohol, coke, ganja. I talked to the boss of a gang. He's twenty-four but he said he was scared of his little brother and complained to me the youth have no morals any more. You have to be invited into the *favelas*, and I know people there.'

Although Manu is attracted to and even in love with such places, the misery provokes his anger and he channels it into his music. 'I've seen women thrown out of hospitals when they were about to give birth, guys being tortured in the *favelas*. And there's nothing I can do about it.' There are *favelas* in Fortaleza too, if slightly less dangerous ones, where Manu made that touching video of him playing guitar with the *favela* kids.

Almost as soon as I land in Fortaleza, I check out the current trends in *Forró*, the dance rhythm of Brazil's northeast. Today's *Forró*, however, turns out to have little in common with the now antique poetic world of Luiz Gonzaga, who died in 1989. In fact, it has all the kitsch appeal of an endless Eurovision Song Contest, which might be quite amusing

The beach of the future – Praia do Futuro – celebrates the goddess Yemaya.

after several *caipirinhas* but sounds less good if you happen to be sober. I go and see Montage, a camp duo who sing an ode to Benflogin, a painkiller that teenagers use to get off their heads, and a song about prostitutes called "I Trust My Dealer". Charter planes, mainly full of Italians, fly regularly into Fortaleza for cheap, good times with the local girls. Another curious song of theirs features lyrics about the Afro-Catholic religion Candomblé, whose variously coloured beads denote devotion to different deities. For example, blue and white are the colours of Yemaya, the ocean goddess. Daniel, the singer of Montage, tells me that he ran the lyrics of his Candomblé song past a local priestess in order to check they were OK.

Candomblé fascinates Manu, partly because the different deities each have their own distinct rhythm, but also because each deity has his or her own very human qualities. Candomblé gods and goddesses are more human than holy. A

Candomblé priestess once told Manu that he was the son of Changó, the fearsome Yoruban god of thunder, and she then initiated him into the religion.

I once met Gilberto Gil, superstar of Brazilian *tropicalismo*, the radical music style of the 1960s and 1970s, who later became Brazil's Minister of Culture. He was also a priest of Changó. Candomblé theology runs counter to the black and white worldview prevalent in Christianity and Islam. 'It's like the Greek pantheon, in that figures like Changó are both good and bad,' Gil told me. 'If there's one thing I've learned, it's that I'm both good and bad. If you don't accept your darkness, you have to project it somewhere else.' It was hard to disagree with him when he added: 'The world could do with a bit less fundamentalism and a bit more Brazilian tolerance.'

When Candomblé gets mixed up with other African traditions, or even the reading of Tarot cards and other divination or witchcraft techniques, they call it Macumba, especially in and around Fortaleza. I'm told that any black man wearing a fedora hat will definitely be a practitioner. There are Macumba myths about animals like the Boto porpoise who can shape-shift into the form of an attractive man and seduce young women. Shops or market stalls will sell potions and herbs that are part of the Macumba pharmacopeia. Herbal Viagra is a top seller. If someone needs money, a Macumba herbalist will give them a potion to bathe in, and cash should then flow into his coffers. I recall a story Manu told me about feeling he was under a bad spell and being told to cover his body in salt, once a day, for several days.

All this has a very poetic, curious and charming aspect, but I get glimpses of the real power of Macumba in Fortaleza. Whereas Manu's views on things like politics or music are relatively rational and understandable, his more esoteric ideas on chance and energy, which underpin his philosophy of life, are opaque. He certainly takes coincidence and portents very seriously. Certain colours mean certain things to him, but he doesn't want to elaborate too much. 'If we get really stoned one night, maybe I'll explain,' he told me. 'You shouldn't get too hung up on this stuff.'

By pure coincidence, or *cow-incidence*, as Manu has started calling it, during my stay in Fortaleza an important festival dedicated to the sea goddess Yemaya is due to be held on a beach called Praia do Futuro – the beach of the future. I have this strong intuition that Manu knows I'll be looking for other consolations and will be tempted to attend the festival. I'm fairly sure that he knew I was coming to Brazil to find him.

This quest for Manu is beginning to unhinge me. What the hell am I doing flying to a strange city halfway round the world on the off chance that I'll run into this elusive rock star? Does Manu really want me to delve into the most private recesses of his life in pursuit of my journalistic quest? Does he really want me to trample all over the hallowed ground that he jealously reserves for spiritual recuperation and downtime with his son? Does he even want to see me at all? Or does he want me to try and understand something deeper about myself and my life, about the goddess of the sea and ultimately about him? Or perhaps I'm just a useful idiot in some guerrilla marketing campaign set-up by Manu and his manager. Or is the dope round here just too strong?

At the Yemaya Festival there are hundreds of people garbed in blue and white, the colours of the ocean goddess. Several women are dressed up as mermaids, and drummers beat the rhythms of the *orixas* or 'deities'. There are also a few politicians touting around for votes in the forthcoming elections. After asking a few people if they know what's happening, I end up talking to a woman who looks like an ordinary housewife. She turns out to be a priestess of Yemaya. As we're on the *Praia do Futuro*, I ask her if she makes predictions. 'Often,' is her reply.

She tells me that Yemaya is a rather chic and vain goddess, who loves perfume and flowers. People are pouring perfume into the sea and the shore is strewn with roses and other blooms. It's a ritual that expresses gratitude for the goddess and the ocean. Fishermen take it especially seriously, although many people from the parched interior are also here paying their respects to the goddess. How can it be that people with so little, and certainly so much less in material terms than most Westerners, are able to express such boundless gratitude?

The atmosphere is full of joy and I think of Manu's comment about the luxury of depression. 'If you are struggling to feed your family in South America, you don't have time or energy to be depressed.' Almost as if it were a throwaway line, the priestess casually tells me that I should leave the beach at five.

A few minutes after five, my translator from the tourist board reminds me of the priestesses' words and says that we should leave. But I just need a few more minutes while I photograph a wonderful-looking character in a white suit, who's up to his knees in the blue and white surf, distributing roses. Then, as I'm taking a flower from the beach and placing it in the ocean, to bid my own respectful farewell to the goddess before going, a couple of youths knock me over and steal my camera and MiniDisc recorder.

I struggle to my feet, severely winded by the blow, and after recovering my breath I think of the priestess. Had she foreseen this? Or had she set the whole snatch up, just to impress the gringo writer?

She's given me her address and, with help from an understanding taxi driver, I find her house in the backstreets of a Fortalezan suburb. Her entire unassuming home is a shrine to Yemaya, with paintings, candles, beads and statues of the chic goddess everywhere. Fortuitously, possibly even fatefully – although I realise I'm beginning to see pre-ordained fate in everything that's happening to me – the local English teacher happens to knock on the door just as I arrive and helps to translate.

The priestess mutters some incantations, throws water on herself, then throws some shells and deals the Tarot cards. In a semi-trance, she begins to speak. She is fairly accurate about my past, even though she talks in generalities. There are, nonetheless, a few impressive hits, such as the legal action that I'm considering bringing against someone. For the future, she predicts success and a 'powerful' house in Brazil, protected by Yemaya and Changó, amongst other things. She also says that I'm hanging on to the past and that this is holding me back, that I need more forgiveness and more gratitude in my life.

Before I leave Brazil, I go to another beach associated with Yemaya. I feel I haven't taken the goddess seriously enough. I buy a bunch of roses and a bottle of decent perfume and I wade in, asking the goddess for forgiveness. I feel a great healing force going through my body and find myself crying salt tears into the ocean. All the muck and detritus blocking me up feels like it's being dislodged, leaving my emotional arteries purged and clean. It's the first time, for example, that I genuinely wish my ex-girlfriend happiness and am thankful for the time we'd spent together. All resentment is washed away by the caressing ocean.

I ring up Manu's management in Paris to try and find out where Manu might be. No word. So I hole up on the beach for a few days, in a fishing village called Preá, a really tranquil place. It's so beautiful that I feel the urge to express my gratitude to someone and, since I'm alone, then who better than the deities? Signs and portents seem to be every everywhere. The door to my *pousada* requires a certain knack before it can be opened. It can't be forced. Sheer willpower isn't going to work. Under a multitude of stars I listen to a wonderful symphony of noise: the different sounds of the wind through the trees, the rush of the ocean, the occasional bird and every few minutes an electronic beep from somewhere, like the slowest dance music in the world, like the music of the future.

In the end, I do meet up with Manu in Brazil. I hear about a concert he's booked to play in Recife. Through a Brazilian journalist friend, I manage to get a backstage pass. Before the concert, Manu is nervous and isn't talking to anyone. Afterwards, expansive as always, he wants to talk to all his fans and to the locals backstage. At last, I grab my chance and walk up to him through the crowd. Manu looks at me, with a big smile on his face and, before turning to talk to the other people waiting in line, he hugs me and says, 'What the fuck are you doing here?'

OUTRO: FINISTERRE

I'm at Finisterre, the end of the earth. It's the furthest west you can go. Galician fishermen, Manu's ancestors, would hoist sail here and strike out, braving the dark waves towards unknown horizons. It was also the final destination for many pilgrims who made the long journey on foot to Santiago. Further back in time, there was a pre-Christian pagan temple called Ara Solis here, erected to worship the sun. It seems as good a place as any to say farewell to the man who was born on the longest day of the year and who, perhaps as a consequence, honours and loves the sun.

I heard Manu was rehearsing with his band in Galicia, the country where his father and grandfather were born. So I followed. But now I'm here, I realise I have to let go. I've spent enough time and money chasing the disappearing one. I'm in debt, my journalistic career is on the brink, I've become obsessive. Time to move on.

Somewhere near the beach, a musician is strumming a guitar. The music creeps by me on the waters. For a second, absurdly, I think of Prospero before he drowns his book and gives up magic. I take off my Manu Chao bracelet, which I bought at a merchandise stall in Mexico City, and throw it in the water. It bounces a couple of times and sinks deep into the bosom of the ocean. The end of the line. Even when, on my last day, I see a blog announcing an impromptu Manu concert in La Coruña, I don't go.

A few days earlier, I had swung by Vilalba, the Galician town where Manu's grandfather José used to own the Gran Hotel Chao. Ramón was born there. A long time ago, in the downstairs bar, José cold-shouldered the wayward Ramón, who had forsaken his father's dream of musical greatness to become a writer and a journalist. After several years of not communicating, Ramón returned to present his four-year-old son José-Manuel, nicknamed 'Manu', José's namesake, to his grandfather. The story goes that José was playing cards when his son and grandson came through the hotel door. He refused even to look Ramón in the eye. How blind you were, José. Your dream of 'Chopin' Chao, a musician of global renown who would conquer not only your beloved Cuba but the whole of Latin America, was standing right there in front of you, diminutive, shy, innocent.

In Finisterre, I recall my last conversation with Manu, back in Brixton, talking about the ubiquitous use of the word *'mentira'* (liar) on *Clandestino*, notably in the song of the same name, with its refrain of *'todo es mentira en este mundo'* (everything in this world is a lie). I said that Latin songs seem to use the word *'mentira'* almost as much as *'corazón'* (heart). Lovers are always suspecting their loved ones of lying to them. 'Well, lovers lie,' Manu said. Then, after a pause, he added, 'but absolute love is not a lie'.

This provoked Manu into a reminiscence about the moment he realised *Clandestino* might succeed. It was in Malpica, the next port around the coast from Finisterre, not long after the album's release. 'It's a fisherman town and there is a club by the sea. They play heavy metal – all the fishermen love Judas Priest and AC/DC. I had a friend who wanted to listen to *Clandestino* and I kept saying no. I thought these fishermen would hate it. But my friend put it on anyway and they let it play till the end. They accepted it, which was incredible to me. Except one guy, an old fisherman, who got angry at the line *"todo es mentiras en este mundo"* and started shouting at me – 'I don't agree with you! Come outside!' And so I went outside with him and there was a storm, and he pointed at the sea and said: "The sea is not a lie! The sea is not a lie!"'

Discography

Bibliography

Photo credits

Acknowledgements

Index

Discography

The Manu Chao discography is quite a complex affair, with many guest appearances, in addition to work with his earlier bands. For updates and intricacies, the French wiki site on Manu is worth checking out (*fr.wikipedia.org/wiki/Manu_Chao*).

In addition to the CDs and DVDs listed below, Manu and his bands and collaborators feature extensively on YouTube, including footage going back to Hot Pants and even Joint de Culasse. You'll find links to some of the best material on my website: *www.peterculshaw.com*

JOINT DE CULASSE (1982–84)

Manu Chao (guitar); Antoine Chao (trumpet); Santiago Casariego (drums); Jean-Marc Despeignes (bass).

1982: **SUPER BOUM ROCK'N'ROLL** (Force Records)

1. Blue Suede Shoes (Carl Perkins); 2. Have You Seen My Baby; 3. My Girl Joséphine (Fats Domino); 4. Great Balls of Fire (Jerry Lee Lewis); 5. My Dear My Dear; 6. Lonesome Train; 7. Memphis Tennessee (Chuck Berry); 8. Tutti Frutti (Little Richard); 9. Roll Over Beethoven (Chuck Berry); 10. Let's Have a Party (Elvis Presley); 11. Keep On Knocking; 12. Wait; 13. Louie Louie (Richard Berry); 14. Oh! Carol.

HOT PANTS (1984–86)

Manu Chao (guitar/voclas); Pascal Borne (guitar); Jean-Marc Despeignes (bass); Santiago Casariego(drums).

1984: **DEMO** [Cassette]

1. Mala Vida; 2. Readyé; 3. Give It Up.

1985: **SO MANY NITES** [45]

So Many Nites / Lover Alone.

1985: **HOT CHICAS (HOT PANTS, LOS CARAYOS, CHIHUAHUA)**

Hot Pants tracks: 1. Rosamaria; 2. Blue Jeans Talk; 3. I'm Ready.

1986: **LOCO MOSQUITO** (All Or Nothing)

1. African Witch; 2. Chicken Chat; 3. Ay Que Dolor; 4. Ball And Chain;
5. Rosamaria; 6. Gipsy; 7. Come On; 8. Ya Llego; 9. Craw-Daddy; 10. Lazy Pal;
11. Junky Beat; 12. Ma Dear; 13. Can't Let It Down (on 2000 re-release).

MANO NEGRA (1984–86)

Manu Chao aka Oscar Tramor (vocals, guitar); Antoine Chao aka Tonio del Borño (trumpet); Santiago Casariego aka Santi (drums); Joséph Dahan aka Jo (bass); Pierre Gauthé aka Krøpöl (trombone); Thomas Darnal aka Helmut Krumar (keyboards); Daniel Jamet aka Roger Cageot (lead guitar); Philippe Teboul aka Garbancito (percussion).

1988: **PATCHANKA** (Boucherie Productions)

1.Mano Negra; 2. Ronde De Nuit; 3. Baby You're Mine; 4. Indios de Barcelona; 5. Rock Island Line; 6. Noche De Acción; 7. Darling Darling (with Les Casse Pieds); 8. Killin' Rats; 9. Mala Vida; 10.Takin' It Up; 11.La Ventura; 12. Lonesome Bop; 13. Bragg Jack; 14. Salga La Luna.

1989: **PUTA'S FEVER** (Virgin France)

1. Mano Negra; 2. Rock'n'roll Band; 3. King Kong Five; 4. Soledad; 5. Sidi H'bibi; 6. The Rebel Spell; 7. Peligro; 8. Pas Assez De Toi; 9. Magic Dice; 10. Mad House; 11. Guayaquil City; 12. Voodoo; 13. Patchanka; 14. La Rançon Du Succès; 15. The Devil's Call; 16. Roger Cageot; 17. El Sur; 18. Patchuko Hop

1991: **KING OF BONGO** (Virgin France)

1. Bring The Fire; 2. King Of Bongo; 3. Don't Want You No More; 4. Le Bruit Du Frigo; 5. Letter To The Censors; 6. El Jako; 7. It's My Heart; 8. Mad Man's Dead; 9. Out Of Time Man; 10. Madame Oscar; 11. Welcome In Occident; 12. Furious Fiesta; 13. The Fool; 14. Paris La Nuit.

1992: **IN THE HELL OF PATCHINKO – LIVE IN JAPAN** (Virgin France)

1. Mano Negra 1; 2. Magic Dice; 3. County Line; 4. Don't Want You No More; 5. Lonesome Bop; 6. Mano Negra 2; 7. Rock Island Line; 8. King Kong Five; 9. Mad Man's Dead; 10. Bring The Fire; 11. Indios De Barcelona; 12. El Sur; 13. Killing Rats; 14. Mano Negra; 15. Sidi H'bibi; 16. The Rebel Spell; 17. I Fought The Law; 18. Mano Negra 4; 19. Darling Darling; 20. Patchuko Hop; 21. Mala Vida; 22. Junky Beat; 23. Madeline.

1994: **CASA BABYLON** (Virgin France)

1. Viva Zapata; 2. Casa Babylon; 3. The Monkey; 4. Señor Matanza; 5. Santa Maradona; 6. Super Changó; 7. Bala Perdida; 8. Machine Gun; 9. El Alakran; 10. Mama Perfect; 11. Love And Hate; 12. Drives Me Crazy; 13. Hamburger Fields; 14. La Vida; 15. Sueño De Solentiname.

2005: **MANO NEGRA: OUT OF TIME** (Virgin France, 2005) DVD.

As well as superb on the road footage, this documentary put together by Mano Negra (without Manu) has fabulous archive material including the Pigalle, Cargo and Colombian tours, mostly shot by François Bergeron.

MANU CHAO SOLO (1988–)

1998: **CLANDESTINO** (Virgin France).

Manu Chao (guitar/vocals); Antoine Chao (trumpet); Angelo Mancini (trumpet); Anouk Khelifa, Subcomandante Marcos (guest vocals). Produced by Renaud Letang and Manu Chao.

1. Clandestino; 2. Desaparecido; 3.Bongo Bong; 4. Je Ne T'Aime Plus; 5. Mentira; 6. Lágrimas De Oro; 7. Mama Call; 8. Luna Y Sol; 9. Por El Suelo; 10. Welcome To Tijuana; 11. Día Luna … Día Pena; 12. Malegría; 13.La Vie à 2; 14. Minha Galera; 15. La Despedida; 16. El Viento.

2001: **PRÓXIMA ESTACIÓN: ESPERANZA** (Virgin France).

Manu Chao (guitar/vocals); Roy Paci (trumpet); Antoine Chao (trumpet); Valeria (guest vocal). Produced by Renaud Letang and Manu Chao.

1. Merry Blues; 2. Bixo; 3. El Dorado 1997; 4. Promiscuity; 5. La Primavera; 6. Me Gustas Tú; 7. Denia; 8. Mi Vida; 9. Trapped By Love; 10. Le Rendez Vous; 11. Mr Bobby; 12. Papito; 13. La Chinita; 14. La Marea; 15. Homens; 16. La Vacaloca; 17. Infinita Tristeza.

2002: **RADIO BEMBA SOUND SYSTEM** (Virgin France). Also released as a DVD **BABYLONIA EN GUAGUA**.

Manu Chao (guitar/vocals); Madjid Farhem (lead guitar); Gambeat (bass); David Bourguignon (drums); Julio Lobo (keyboards); Bidji aka Lyricson (vocals); Roy Paci (trumpet); Gerard Casajús Gnaita, Philippe Teboul (percussion); B-Roy (accordion).

1. Intro; 2. Bienvenida A Tijuana; 3. Machine Gun; 4. Por Donde Saldra El Sol?; 5. Peligro; 6. Welcome To Tijuana; 7. El Viento; 8. Casa Babylon; 9. Por El Suelo; 10. Blood And Fire; 11. EZLN… Para Tod@s Todo…; 12. Mr Bobby; 13. Bongo Bong; 14. Radio Bemba; 15. Que Paso Que Paso; 16. Pinocchio; 17. Cahi En La Trampa; 18. Clandestino; 19. Rumba De Barcelona; 20. La Despedida; 21. Mala Vida; 22. Radio Bemba; 23. Que Paso Que Paso; 24. Pinocchio 2; 25. La Primavera; 26. The Monkey; 27. King Kong Five; 28. Minha Galera; 29. Promiscuity.

2004: **SIBÉRIE M'ÉTAIT CONTÉEE [WITH JACEK WOŹNIAK]** (Corida, France; Released as a book and CD in various editions – the tracks multiplying with each release).

Manu Chao (guitar/vocals); Roy Paci (trumpet); Madjid Farhem (guitar); Cheick Tidiane (keyboards).

1. Le P'tit Jardin; 2. Petite Blonde Du Boulevard Brune; 3. La Valse À Sale Temps; 4. Les Mille Paillettes; 5. Il Faut Manger; 6. Helno Est Mort; 7. J'Ai Besoin De La Lune; 8. L'Automne Est Làs; 9. Si Loin De Toi... Je Te Joue...; 10. 100.00 Remords; 11. Trop Tot, Trop Tard; 12. Te Tromper; 13. Madame Banquise; 14. Les Rues De L'Hiver; 15. Sibérie Fleuve Amour; 16. Les Petites Planètes; 17. Te Souviens Tu; 18. J'ai Besoin De La Lune (Remix); 19. Dans Mon Jardin; 20. Merci Bonsoir; 21 Fou De Toi; 22. Les Yeux Turquoise; 23. Sibérie.

2007: **LA RADIOLINA** (Because, France).

Manu Chao (guitar/vocals); Madjid Farhem (guitar and bass); Gambeat (bass, vocals); David Bourguignon (guitar); Roy Paci (trumpet); Antonio Mancini (trumpet); Beatnik, Flor, Tonino Carotone (guest vocals). Produced by Manu Chao.

1. 13 Días; 2. Tristeza Maleza; 3. Politik Kills; 4. Rainin In Paradize; 5. J'Ai Besoin De La Lune; 6. El Kitapena; 7. Me Llaman Calle; 8. A Cosa; 9. The Bleedin Clown; 10. Mundorévès; 11. El Hoyo; 12. La Vida Tómbola; 13. Mala Fama; 14. Panik Panik; 15. Otro Mundo; 16. Piccola Radiolina; 17. ¿Y Ahora Que?; 18. Mama Cuchara; 19. Siberia; 20. Soñe Otro Mundo; 21. Amalucada Vida.

2008: **ESTACIÓN MÉXICO** (Alicia Multiforo, 2008; 2 CD semi-bootleg, recorded live in Forum Alicia, Mexico City).

Manu Chao (guitar/vocals); Madjid Farhem (guitar); Gambeat (bass); Philippe Teboul (percussion); David Bourguignon (drums); Julio Lobos (keyboards); Angelo Mancini (trumpet).

CD1: 1.Clandestino; 2.Por Ti (Libertad); 3.Giramundo; 4. Cabra Da Peste; 5. Para De Beber; 6.El Contragolpe; 7. Carreteiro; 8.Mala Fama; 9.Desaparecido; 10..Cuándo Llegaré?; 11. Zapato Viejo; 12. Bienvenida A Tijuana; 13. La Vida Tómbola; 14. 5 Minutos.
CD2: 1.El Hoyo; 2.Peligro; 3.Casa Babylon; 4. Mamá Perfecta; 5. Sueño De Solentiname; 6. Tadibobeira; 7.Por El Suelo; 8. Mr Bobby; 9.La Primavera; 10. Radio Bemba.

2009: **BAIONARENA** (Because, France; Live album recorded at the Bayonne Arena 30 July 2008; 2 CD + DVD).

Manu Chao (guitar/vocals); Madjid Farhem (guitar); Gambeat (bass); Philippe Teboul (percussion); David Bourguignon (drums); Julio Lobos (keyboards); Angelo Mancini (trumpet).

CD 1: 1. Panik, Panik; 2. El Hoyo; 3. Peligro; 4. Casa Dabylon; 5. Tumba, 6. Mr. Bobby; 7. La Primavera; 8. Radio Bemba; 9. Bienvenida a Tijuana; 10. El Viento; 11. The Monkey; 12. Clandestino; 13. Desaparecido; 14. Rumba De Barcelona; 15. La Despedida/Mentira.

CD 2: 1. Rainin' In Paradize; 2. A Cosa; 3. La Vacaloca; 4. Hamburger Fields/ Merry Blues; 5. Tristeza Maleza; 6. Dia Luna ... Dia Pena; 7. Machine Gun; 8. Volver, Volver; 9. Radio Bemba/Eldorado 1997; 10. Mala Vida; 11. Sidi H'Bibi; 12. Radio Bemba; 13. Forzando Maquina/Mr Bobby; 14. Me Quedo Contigo (Si Me Das A Elegir); 15. La Vida Tómbola; 16. L'Hiver Est Là; 17. Crèv' La Vie; 18. Pinocchio (Viaggio In Groppa Al Tonno).

DVD Disc 3: 1. Full Concert Live At Bayonne Arena; 2. 30 Minute Tour Documentary; 3. Six Music Videos; 4. Exclusive Photos.

SINGLES AND REMIXES

1998–99: **CLANDESTINO**; Je Ne T'Aime Plus; Bongo Bong; Desaparecido.

2001: **ME GUSTAS TÚ.**

2004-2005: **PETITE BLONDE DU BOULEVARD BRUNE; IL FAUT MANGER.**

2007–08: **RAININ IN PARADIZE; ME LLAMAN CALLE; BESOIN DE LA LUNE; POLITIK KILLS; LA VIDA TÓMBOLA; A COSA** (Prince Fatty remix).

SONGS ON COMPILATIONS

2000: **TOUS LES JOURS ON EMMAÜS MOUVEMENT** (Virgin).

2002: **PUT IT ON** (version of the Bob Marley song) on *La Colifata* album; also on 2003 album Per Palestina (Xarxa).

2006: **MAMBO ESCUDELLERS** on *Mariatchi Boogie* (CD Baby). Benefit for Barcelona squatters movement.

2007: **ALLONS ENFANTS DE L'OVALIE** Version of the Mano Negra song "Ronde De Nuit" for the Rugby World Cup in France (broadcast only on Inter radio – but now on YouTube).

DVDs

2002: **BABYLONIA EN GUAGUA** Live concert recorded at Grande Halle de Villette, Paris, 4/5 September 2001. Plus backstage documentary **BABYLON'S FEVER** including footage of Manu at Genoa.

2009: **BAIONARENA** Live concert recorded at Bayonne Arena, 2008. See above for track listings.

MAJOR COLLABORATIONS/PRODUCTIONS

1997: **ANOUK** *Automatik Kalamity* (1997 Virgin). Produced and played guitar throughout the album. Anouk was Manu's long-term partner during the Mano Negra years.

2002: **LA COLIFATA** *La Colifata* (download only). Manu produced the album with La Colifata, the Buenos Aires mental asylum. He plays and sings along with the patients and created a backing track.

2004: **AMADOU & MARIAM** *Dimanche À Bamako* (Because). Producer, musician, singer, arranger. Also co-composer of several tracks.

2006: **AKLI D's** *Ma Yela* (Because). Produced album and contributed vocals and guitar for French-Algerian troubadour.

2010: **SMOD** *SMOD* (Because). Produced album for Malian hip hop group featuring Amadou and Mariam's son, Sam.

OTHER GUEST APPEARANCES

1991: **NEGU GORRIAK** *Gora Herria* (Esan Ozenki). Guests on album.

1992: **TODOS TUS MUERTOS** *Dale Aborigen* (Todos Tus Muertos Discos). Guests on album.

1994: **NEGU GORRIAK** *Hipokrisiari Stop! Bilbo* 93-*X*-30 (Esan Ozenki). Vocals on live version of "Gora Herria".

1995: **TIJUANA NO!** *Transgresores De La Ley* (BMG). Wrote and contributes vocals/guitar on "Borregos Kamikazes".

1996: **SKANK** *O Samba Poconé* (Sony). Guitar/vocals on "Sem Terra".

1996: **JOAQUIN SABINA** *Yo, Mi, Me, Contigo* (BMG/Ariola). Guitar/vocals on "No Sopor... No Sopor... ".

1997: **AMPARANOIA** *El Poder De Machin* (Edel). Guitar/vocals on "Sidi Beach" and "Que Te Den".

1998: **FERMIN MUGURUZA** *Brigadistak Sound System* (Esan Ozenki).
Guitar/bass on "Maputxe".

1999: **TONINO CAROTONE** *Mondo Difficile* (EMI).
Guitar/vocals on "Me Cago En El Amor" and "Pecatore".

1999: **AMPARANOIA** *Fiesta Furiosa* (Edel). Guests on tracks
"Desperado" and "Caravane".

1999: **IDIR** *Identités* (Sony). Plays on "A Tulawin (Une Algérienne
Debout)", which was reprised as "Denia" on *Próxima Estación:
Esperanza*.

2001: **WAGNER PA** *Brazuca Matraca*. Guests on tracks "Folía",
"Cold" and "Circo Místico".

2001: **NOIR DÉSIR** *Des Visages Des Figures* (Barclay).
Guitar on "Le Vent Nous Portera".

2001: **LUMBALÚ** *Me Voy Con El Gusto* (Ventilador).
Backing vocals on "Maria Angola".

2001: **KARAMELO SANTO** *Los Guachos* (Benditas).
Production and vocals.

2002: "People Dance" with **MIKI-LEZ** on *Barcelona Zona Bastarda*
(Double Compilation, Organic Records).

2003: **MOUSS & HAKIM** "La Gnake" on compilation
True Colours – The World In Union (Virgin, France).
Composed and produced the track, and plays guitar.

2003: **GO LEM SYSTEM** *Viaje* (Go Lem System).
Guitar on "See Me Dubbing" and "Salvavidas".

2004: **JANE BIRKIN** *Rendez-Vous* (Capitol).
Duets on "Te Souviens-Tu?"

2004: **SMOD** *Ta I Tola* (Mali release).
Plays on several tracks, with Amadou & Mariam.

2005: **GO LEM SYSTEM** *Cacería* (K Industria).
Vocals/guitar on "Calle Go Lem", a version of "Me Llaman Calle".

2005: **OS PARALAMAS DO SUCESSO** *Hoje* (EMI).
Guests on "Soledad Cidadão".

2005: **F.UR.T.O.** *Sangue Audiência* (Sony/BMG).
Vocals on "Todos Debaixo Do Mesmo Sombrero".

2006: **TOOTS & THE MAYTALS** *True Love* (V2).
Duets on a version of "Merry Blues" with Toots.

2006: **EL GAFLA** *Pa/Ris-Casbah* (La Veille/Sequenza).
Duets on version of "Clandestino".

2007: **LA PEGATINA** *Al Carrer!* (Kasba Music).
Guitar on "O Camareiro".

2007: **ROY PACI & ARETUSKA** *Suonoglobal* (Etnagigante).
Vocals on "Toda Joia Toda Beleza".

2007: **FERMIN MUGURUZA** Asthmatic Lion Sound Systems (Talka).
Vocals/guitar on "Milaka Bilaka".

2008: **MOKOBÉ DU 113** *Mon Afrique* (Sony/BMG).
Vocals/guitar on "Politique" (version of "Politik Kills".

2008: **TONINO CAROTONE** *Ciao Mortali!* (Nacional).
Vocals/guitar on "Me Cago En El Amor" and "Pecatore".

2008: **PLAYING FOR CHANGE** *Live* (online video).
Vocals/guitar on "One Love".

2012: **TOKYO SKA PARADISE ORCHESTRA** *Walkin* (Avex/Sony).
Vocals/guitar on "Let Me Come The River Flow".

Bibliography

In English

MANO NEGRA by *Cathy Lamri, Olivier Aubry, Tom Dard and La Mano* (Patchanka/Syros, 1994). A wonderful LP-sized scrapbook of Mano Negra photos and ephemera.

MANU & CHAO by *Wozniak* (Because Music, 2012). Another winning large-format illustrated book, created by Manu's regular collaborator, the Polish-born illustrator Jacek Wozniak. A playful, meditative collection of photos and images centred around Manu's life and causes.

THE TRAIN OF FIRE AND ICE: MANO NEGRA IN COLOMBIA by *Ramón Chao* (Route Publishing, 2010). Manu's father goes on the Colombian train trip and lives to tell the (evocatively written) tale.

ROCKIN' LAS AMERICAS: THE GLOBAL POLITICS OF LATIN/O AMERICA edited by *Deborah Pacini Hernandez, Hector Fernández L'Hoeste and Eric Zolov* (University of Pittsburgh Press, 2004). Fascinating collection of essays on the often criminal history of rock in Latin America, including a chapter on Manu by Josh Kun.

ROCK EN ESPAÑOL: THE LATIN ALTERNATIVE ROCK EXPLOSION by *Saúl Hernández and Ernesto Lechner* (Chicago Review Press, 2006). Excellent , if slightly dated introduction to alternative Latin music from Café Tacuba to Orishas.

THE SPEED OF DREAMS: SELECTED WRITINGS 2001–2007 by *Subcomandante Insurgente Marcos* (City Lights, 2007). Selection of lyrical and polemical writings from the Zapatista leader and Manu associate.

THE OPEN VEINS OF LATIN AMERICA: FIVE CENTURIES OF THE PILLAGE OF A CONTINENT by *Eduardo Galeano* (Serpent's Tail, 2009). Classic political work, much admired by Manu – and the book Hugo Chavez chose to present to President Obama when they met.

DANCING WITH DYNAMITE by *Benjamin Dangl* (AK Press, 2010). Good analysis of grassroots movements in South America.

SANTERIA by *Luis Manuel Núñez* (Spring Publications, 1992). A practical guide to Afro-Caribbean magic.

AMEXICA by *Ed Vulliamy* (Bodley Head, 2010). Top-notch investigative journalist on Mexican narco gangs.

PLEASE KILL ME by *Legs McNeil and Gillian McCain* (Abacus, 1997). Revealing and entertaining interviews with the major players of the Blank Generation. The best punk book, alongside *England's Dreaming* by Jon Savage.

A RAGE IN HARLEM by *Chester Himes* (Penguin Classics, 2011). Hard-boiled detective story set in the mean streets of New York. This was the book Manu used in order to learn English.

THE I CHING (Penguin, 2003). The ancient Chinese divination manual and book of wisdom and Manu's 'favourite book'

In French

MANU CHAO, LE CLANDESTINO by *Andy Verol* (Pylone, 2009). A fairly comprehensive account of Manu's life and times.

MANU CHAO, UN NOMADE CONTEMPORAIN by *Véronique Mortaigne* (Don Quichotte, 2012). A more expansive, literary book by *Le Monde* contributor Mortaigne.

MANU CHAO AND MANO NEGRA by *Souâd Belhaddad* (Librio, 2002). Short, sharp, amusing introduction.

MANU CHAO: DESTINATION ESPERANZA by *Philippe Manche* (Serpent à Plumes, 2007). Book of conversations with Manu.

Photo credits

We have attempted to contact all copyright holders of images used in this book, though some are lost in the depths of time (and the post-punk scene in Paris). We apologise to anyone who has not been properly credited and ask that they contact the publishers so that we can amend this in any future edition of this book.

Youri Lenquette: p.4; p.13; p.78; p.87; p.94; p.103; p.119; p.128; p.133; p.145; p.159; p.182; pp.188–189;

Manu Chao: p.16.

Ramón Chao: p.18; p.21; p.167.

El Mano (from Mano Negra book): p.83; p.99; p.109; p.112; p.116 (David Lorapido).

Renaud Letang: p.172.

Getty Images: p.201; p.211; p.282.

Because Music: p.239.

Peter Culshaw: p.215; p.246; p.272; p.295; p.309; p.320; p.323.

Wozniak (from the books *Manu & Chao* and *Sibérie M'Etait Contéee*): p.224; p.311.

JJ Medina: p.228.

Roxanne Haynes: p.279; p.284.

Maria Santos: p.292; p.307.

Marc Fernández: p.255.

Francina Islas: p.263.

Juan-Carlos Rincón: p.265.

Acknowledgements

A thousand thanks are due to Andy Morgan, who co-wrote the first three chapters. A couple of years into the project, I had a lot of material but was frankly confused whether it was a biography, a travelogue or some mutant hybrid. With ninja-like powers, Andy immediately saw the wood from the trees and, with unflagging enthusiasm and empathy, got the whole thing moving forward. A particular problem I had encountered was the early Paris years of Manu's various bands, and the alternative scene of the 1980s, about which there wasn't much available material. Andy had lived in the city in the 1980s, knew this background, and came with me to Paris and translated numerous interviews. His forthcoming book on the Sahara and its music (Andy managed Tinariwen for a decade) will be essential reading.

I'm hugely grateful, too, to my editor, publisher and fellow Manu enthusiast, Mark Ellingham at Serpent's Tail, who, using the (possibly apocryphal) Galician proverb 'One man's butcher is another man's surgeon', expertly fine-tuned the book to where it is now. He also had the vision to sign it in the first place. The team at Serpent's Tail and Profile have also been impressive in their dedication – notably Anne-Marie Fitzgerald, Pete Ayrton and Penny Daniel, while Nikky Twyman proofread beyond her wildest imaginings. My agent Kevin Conroy Scott and his team at Tibor Jones are due much gratitude as well – and Kevin was instrumental in the book happening, brokering a deal in the un-agent-like environs of a Peckham squat gig. Sophie Lambert at his office gave useful tips on the book. Marcus O'Dair read the book as it went along (I read his excellent Robert Wyatt biography in return) and sharpened up the text and encouraged me.

The book would not exist without the support of the team around Manu, especially his manager Emmanuel de Buretel, Jenny Adlington in London and Luc Sarrabezolles in Paris, all of whom were hugely helpful and generous with their time. Andres Garrido was particularly kind, hospitable and good-humoured and put me up more than once in Paris. Jenny was fabulously supportive throughout.

It would take too much space to credit all the people who helped in the many countries I visited in pursuit of Manu, but I would like to thank his road manager, Paget Williams, for letting me on the bus; and without Francina Islas, I would have been completely lost in the Western Sahara.

I'd like to thank all the scores of interviewees – notably François Bergeron, Bernard Batzen, Jackie Berroyer and Manu's father Ramón – who gave their time with amazing generosity. Tom Darnell should win some kind of prize for sitting through at least seven hours of interviews one day in Paris. Maria Santos was more than helpful and, as one of the first readers, her comments on the draft book were invaluable. The photographers, who contributed greatly to the book, are credited separately – but the images of Youri Lenquette, who took the cover shot and has photographed Manu since his early days in Mano Negra, are outstanding. The book's designer Henry Iles turned it into the handsome object you are holding. And thank you to Jacek Wozniak, Manu's artistic co-pilot, for the cover title lettering.

I would not have met Manu without being commissioned by Caspar Llewellyn Smith at the *Telegraph* and then at the late-lamented *Observer Music Monthly*, who sent me to Barcelona and the US. Other editors who let me write about Manu included Tom Horan at the *Telegraph* and Simon Broughton and Jo Frost at *Songlines*. Roger Short and James Parkin got me to do a BBC Radio 3 programme on Manu and sent me to Paris.

Closer to home, my father and his partner Pauline Law put me up several times, and I would like to thank them for their hospitality and my father for his love and support. Quayside in Wells-next-the-Sea in Norfolk was a beautiful bolthole.

The book probably wouldn't exist without Michelle Anslow, who tolerated writerly moodiness, came up with excellent suggestions and was unfailingly magnificent.

Finally, of course, I must thank Manu Chao, who put up with my intrusive questions and getting in the way on tour in several different countries. His positive energy remains an inspiration. Thank you, Manu. May all your travels be full of truth and beauty.

Index

Figures in *italics* refer to captions.

INDEX